Thomas L. Dynneson

City-State Civism in Ancient Athens

Its Real and Ideal Expressions

PETER LANG
New York • Washington, D.C./Baltimore • Bern
Frankfurt am Main • Berlin • Brussels • Vienna • Oxford

Library of Congress Cataloging-in-Publication Data

Dynneson, Thomas L.
City-state civism in ancient Athens: its real and ideal expressions /
Thomas L. Dynneson.
p. cm.
Includes bibliographical references and index.
1. Citizenship—Greece—Athens. 2. City-states—
Greece—Athens. I. Title.
JC75.C5D96   323.60938'5—dc22   2008014448
ISBN 978-1-4331-0311-7

Bibliographic information published by **Die Deutsche Bibliothek**.
Die Deutsche Bibliothek lists this publication in the "Deutsche
Nationalbibliografie"; detailed bibliographic data is available
on the Internet at http://dnb.ddb.de/.

Cover image: Baltimore Painter (Greek), active 4th century BC
Red-Figure Volute Krater (Wine Vessel), ca. 330–320 BC
Terracotta 42 5/8 x 23 x 17 3/4 in.
Fine Arts Museums of San Francisco, Museum purchase,
Dorothy Spreckels Munn Fund, 2005.24a-b

The paper in this book meets the guidelines for permanence and durability
of the Committee on Production Guidelines for Book Longevity
of the Council of Library Resources.

© 2008 Peter Lang Publishing, Inc., New York
29 Broadway, 18th floor, New York, NY 10006
www.peterlang.com

All rights reserved.
Reprint or reproduction, even partially, in all forms such as microfilm,
xerography, microfiche, microcard, and offset strictly prohibited.

Printed in the United States of America

In dedication to the memory of
Professor Richard E. Gross of Stanford University
and J. Huntley Dupre of Macalester College

Contents

List of Maps ix
Preface xi
Acknowledgments xv

Introduction 1

The Real Expressions of Civism

Part I: The Origins of Ancient Greek Civism
1. The Mycenaean Greeks 9
2. The Dawn of the City–State 15
3. The Spartan Constitution 21
4. The Athenian Constitution 29

Part II: The Athenian Democratic Constitution
5. The Democratic Reforms of Solon 39
6. The Democratic Reforms of Cleisthenes 43

Part III: The Golden Age of Athenian Democracy
7. Prelude to the Golden Age of Pericles 51
8. The Golden Age of Pericles 57

Part IV: The Declince of the Athenian Democracy
9. The Athenian Empire 67
10. The Tragedy of the Peloponnesian War 71
11. Athens in Decline 85

The Ideal Expressions of Civism

Part V: Political Art as Civism
12. Sophism and the New Political Art 97
13. Protagoras and Civism 107
14. Isocrates and Civism 117
15. Demosthenes and Civism 129

PART VI: PHILOSOPHY, IDEOLOGY, AND CIVISM
    16   Socratic Civism 139
    17   Platonic Civism 151
    18   Aristotelian Civism 169
    19   Xenophonic Civism 185

Conclusion 193

Appendix: Maps 199
Bibliography 205
Index 209

Maps

The Beginnings of Historical Greece 700 to 600 BCE 200

The Oriental Empires 201

The Persian Empire 500 BCE 202

Greece at the Time of the Persian War 203

The Athenian Empire in the Golden Age 204

Preface

Many years ago, Werner Jaeger issued a three–volume work on the education and culture of the ancient Greeks, which helped to suggest that the advancement of civilization relied on the advancement of a more sophisticated education. In this seminal work Jaeger wrote: "Through the increasing gloom of political disaster, there now appear, as if called into existence by the needs of the age, the great geniuses of education, with their classical systems of philosophy and political rhetoric" (Jaeger, 1971, vol. II, pp. ix-x). Jaeger's analysis of *paideia* (ancient Greek education) tended to focus on the influences of philosophy and rhetoric as the intellectual forces that gave shape and form to the later development of European humanism and citizenship.

In writing this volume, my intention was to focus on the development of *civism* as a contributor to ancient Greek culture and as a shaping force of the psychology of citizenship, in the Western world. This study was critical to my work because the ancient Greeks were the first to contemplate the idea of using cultural and educational means for shaping youth for citizenship and what was concretely accomplished often was accomplished outside the confines of the ancient schools. In his last known work, *The Laws*, Plato proposed a state–sponsored educational system for the purpose of developing citizens who would live in compliance with the state. *Civism*, in the eyes of Plato, came to represent an intellectual and educational compromise between the assertion of Protagoras, who claimed that he was teaching a political art, and Plato's demand for a philosophical education. Although Plato rejected the claims of Protagoras, he was willing to recognize that some form of universal education was needed for the sake of a unified society.

Athens was able to reach new heights of cultural achievement, but two centuries later, ended with a near abandonment of many important cultural values associated with its *civism*. Therefore, a re-examination of the rise and fall of democracy in Athens may provide new insights into the rise and fall of a state that lost its desire or its will to defend its political system, its laws, or its citizenship. The value of this lesson suggests that each state is vulnerable to decay and decline, and a meter of the degree of decadence is the extent to which the values and virtues of society are being effectively reinforced by its forms of *civism*. *Civism* is an instrument of state citizenship and when it fails to generate a body of worthy citizens, the state has entered onto the pathway leading to its demise.

The ancient Greeks did not develop courses of study aimed at promoting a formal course for citizenship education, nor did they use the term "civism." However, it long has been accepted that ancient Greek scholars were the first to realize that the state or civilization could not advance without the associated support of an effective form of moral training that was related to their ideas of the Good.

The purpose of this project was to explore ancient Athenian polis society in search of clues for the origins of western *civism*. I began this task by tracing ideas that influenced the development of the Greek city-state and by exploring the ideas that surfaced pertaining to the relationship between the ideal polis, its citizenship, and arguments about the role that education should play in the shaping of the ideal citizen in light of these political considerations. After years of study, I came to realize that the ancient Greeks faced many of the same problems that plague contemporary societies, and their mistakes, weaknesses, and strengths can be seen as useful resources for addressing contemporary social, economic, and political problems. While some have argued that Greek democracy was a failed system, the Greeks recognized and agonized over their mistakes and they used this knowledge to advance their political thinking, which is a measure of their success. In particular, the author is interested in tracing *civism* as a cultural phenomenon as it evolved in Athens following the transition from an aristocracy to a democracy, and the formation and decline of the Athenian democratic constitution.

This study attempts to address questions related to the advancement of educational means in support of political systems and constitutions, especially the changing role of *civism* in conjunction with the changing or evolving nature of the ancient constitution in Athens. In particular, this work focuses on the contributions of the sophists and the Philosophers as they came to realize that the state had a role in shaping the nature of its citizens, and that this role could be fulfilled through an alliance between education and politics as expressed in their realized and idealized conceptions.

In an earlier work entitled: *Civism: Cultivating Citizenship in European History*, I had stated that: "*Civism* is defined according to the same principles that define the citizen and the characteristics of citizenship. It is expressed in the virtues of what is considered an ideal or 'good citizen' within the realm of a particular society and culture" (Dynneson, 2001, p. 7). During the course of that earlier work I came to realize that *civism* is based on the following principle: *the power over a citizen's political perceptions is an important basis for the power to rule the state and this power can provide ruling agents with the means to create and maintain a specified political ideology.* I also realized that the maintenance of a political ideology was an important means to help determine the nature of social, economic, and political relationships, as well as the behaviors that are so essential to maintaining the dominant values that are built into the political system, or according to the nature of its constitution.

In addition, I recognized that *civism* was based on the interactions or the relationships between three important phenomena. These phenomena include: the development of an accepted citizen's perception of an ideal political reality; a leaders ability to persuade the citizen body to accept a prescribed view of worthwhile social, economic, and political goals; and the willingness of the citizenship body to accept the ways and the means needed to attain these goals. Therefore, in order to unify the citizenship body in the pursuit of a cause or certain identified political goals, political leaders often were willing to use persuasive techniques including educational means, to maintain the controlling aspects of their leadership. These techniques included the use of argumentation that often contains fallacies and techniques associated with rhetoric and propaganda.

As a consequence of the new insights gained in the 2001 study, I decided to attempt a more extensive re–examination of the role of *civism* as it related to the ancient polis of Athens in order to help gain more information on the origins and applications of *civism* in the ancient world, especially as it related to the rise and fall of the world's first democracy. The resources for this investigation would be limited to some standard historical and educational studies, and the periodic literature was limited to specific topics related to ancient citizenship; the timeframe of this investigation would be limited mainly to the fifth and fourth centuries BCE, with the exception of some historical materials leading up to the establishment of the polis.

Thomas L. Dynneson, Ph.D.
Professor Emeritus
The University of Texas
of the Permian Basin

Acknowledgments

A great debt of gratitude is owed to the following persons and organizations: Professor Richard E. Gross of Stanford University, who read most of the text prior to his death in May of 2004; the Librarians at The University of Texas of the Permian Basin, who provided assistance in procuring inter–library loan materials; Professor James A. Nickel, who gave me constant encouragement to persist; Professor Robert C. Rhodes who listened to my discussions on the ancient philosophers; the education department at The University of Texas of the Permian Basis, who helped to underwrite the cost of loaned library materials. I am indebted to Professor Jeremiah Reedy of Macalester College for his invitation and encouragement of my travel to Greece to attend the 18th and 19th International Conference of Philosophy meetings in Kavala (Macedonia) and Samos Greece, where I presented papers pertaining to *civism* in ancient Greece. I greatly benefited from the encouragement of Professors Edward Schiappa and Terry L. Papillion who shared with me their knowledge of the sophists, logos and rhetoric on several critical occasions during the drafting of the manuscript. I am indebted to Paul Rascoe of the Government Documents, Maps and Electronic Information Services Librarian, University of Texas, Austin, Texas, and The Legion of Honor Museum in San Francisco, California. A special thanks is due my wife, Barbara Dynneson, who read and edited the drafts of each chapter, as well as the final revisions.

INTRODUCTION

> *Who then shall I call educated? Those who manage well the daily circumstances of their lives, who possess accurate judgment and who rarely miss the proper course of action; those who are decent and honorable, good natured, slow to take offense, disciplined in their pleasures, brave under misfortune and unspoiled by success. Those who have a character which is in accord not with one of these qualities, but with all of them—these are the wise and complete men.*
>
> — Isocrates (translated from the *Panathenaicus*, 342 BCE)

Among almost all civic cultures there is an underlying belief that an ideal political system can be devised and perfected to bring about a better or a higher level of happiness through the implementation of an Ideal. Perhaps this underlying belief far outdates the ancient Athenians and was attempted over and again; and perhaps this belief helped to advance the development of western civilization. However old this belief, it was the ancient Athenians who attempted to realize this vision or myth in order to attain a higher state of political, social, and economic perfection through their democratic experiment. *Civism* is, in part, based on the assumption that by controlling perceptions about an Ideal Reality, the state can be transformed into a more perfect structure that is better suited to the needs of its citizens. The problem is that no perfect political system actually can be created, implemented, or perfected because no matter the nature of the system and its perfect design, human nature is <u>not</u> perfect. The imperfection of human nature will come into play to unwind, to undermine, and to destroy the political system once it has been established.

Human beings, in order to support the formation and advancement of a particular type of political system, must be *persuaded* that the political system is an advantage to them, so that they will be willing to submit to that system. In time, elements within the citizen body will come to realize that the Ideal political system is flawed and that they are not gaining the advantages that they sought. Consequently, some political leaders will begin to undermine the value underpinnings of the political system because they realize that it is not perfect or Ideal, nor did they gain the advantage that they had hoped for.

The problem is that political systems often are used to the advantages of one segment of the society over other segments of the society, but this is not known until the political system actually is established. The flaws of the political system remain hidden or unknown and *persuasion* is used to gain support for the political system. This flaw also is engrained in the illusions associated with the perfectibility of the Ideal State and is associated with what has been termed the definist fallacy. This fallacy, when applied by reformers, allowed them to make claims in favor of the Ideal System without paying attention to, or failing to recognize all of its weaknesses.

The reason for seeking an Ideal political system is the need to replace the existing system that has become unsatisfactory; consequently, the new system comes to be perceived as superior to the old system in almost every way. Once the citizen body has been convinced of the many advantages of the new political system and comes to accept that system, that political system must be maintained and supported for as long as possible. The work of *civism*, regardless of the nature of the state, is to prolong the existing political system; however the techniques of *civism* eventually will fail, as the political system no longer satisfies basic citizenship needs. The work of *civism* also is associated with the advancement of the new political system that is designed to replace the failing political system. The rise and the fall of the ancient Athenian democracy provides an important case study in the relationship between *civism* and the state.

Living within a group setting requires rules and values to help control and to regulate human behavior; therefore, group membership, including citizenship, is a product of social living that serves as a means of uniting, unifying, and controlling the members of the group. Families and tribes have, for millennium, lived according to unwritten kinship rules and values that were used to socialize or to assimilate infants, children and youth in a childrearing enculturation process. With the formation of cities and states, new forms of non–kinship means slowly evolved to produce new means, often associated with education, to socialize and assimilate children, and adults into the accepted rules, values, and behaviors of the civic culture in order to create the mind–set, or the *civism* of the citizen. *Civism* is a term that will be used to describe those cultural influences that have been employed in an attempt to shape, maintain, or reform the ancient political system of the ancient Athenian polis. It also reasonably can be suggested that differences in citizenship understanding are related to value factors that are transmitted in the culture through such activities as parenting, schooling, religious training, and various forms of community activities, and that some of these activities are the result of some form of *civism*. *Civism*, as a cultural phenomenon, can be used to explore the nature of citizenship, including its similarities and differences, with citizenship of other societies and states.

* * * *

The ancient Athenians have long occupied a unique place in the history of western civilization, as every aspect of Athenian culture was considered an expression of the whole idea of human nature and what it meant to be Athenian in the spiritual, as well as in the practical sense. They were the first people of the Mediterranean world to realize that cultural influences and various forms of learning could become deliberate means for shaping human character in accordance with the mandates and the accepted virtues of society, and as a result, political ideology became a driving cultural force that was used in shaping the individual to meet or to fit into a specific cultural mold. Josiah Ober (1989) credited differences in civic culture to underlying factors related to its political ideology or a commonly shared ideological framework that he described as *topoi*. He writes: "Political ideology is therefore an important part of the interior context that will help a subject to judge and to formulate an appropriate response on the political plane to changes in the exterior environment" (p. 39).

In ancient Athens politicians and orators used the accepted norms of society that were engrained in the culture to convince juries or audiences that their case or their interpretation of events was correct and should be accepted, and this gave rise to an ancient or early form of *civism*. The remains or the evidence of this mind–set could be found in the remains of public speech that was constructed in such a way as to embrace the ideology of the common citizens of ancient Athens. Ober, for example, found evidence of such *topoi* in the speeches used by orators in the Athenian courts or in it's Assembly. The evidence that does remain of the past consists of elements of literature, philosophy, fragments of histories, art and architecture or the skeletal remains of civilization, as well as some highly selective writings of scholars. Because common people usually did not write anything, the sources of ancient Athenian *civism* only can be found in a study of the events and cultural elements that have survived.

The Greeks used the word *areté* in reference to *excellence* (for example, the search or the seeking for perfection), such as virtuous excellence, and modern scholars have used changes in *areté* to detect differences in cultural understandings from the interval between the ninth century BCE and the fifth century BCE. Jaeger used changes in the meaning of *areté* to detect changes in cultural understandings. Its reference to a warrior in Homeric times was quite different from its reference to the development of Athenian polis citizenship. Regardless of the historical times, *civism*, as it related to *areté*, virtues, and values was not seen as an innate quality derived from a biological sense, but was considered a quality derived from pervasive cultural influences. Children, regardless of society, are immersed in cultural influences from the day of their birth, but no two children have the exact same experiences. At the same time, children do have many shared experiences related to culture. Cultural experiences include: language, diet, shelter, gender relationships, religious ritual, and technological levels related to occupations and to daily living.

Civism in ancient times also was used as a means to level out differences in cultural experiences by attempting to create a sense of unity in regard to acceptable behaviors and relationships; therefore it tends to be used as a means to establish a collective ethos that denies individuality to some extent. The goal of *civism* in ancient Athens was to create a shared identity that rewarded exemplary behavior as defined by the social norms of the polis. However, polis societies differ from one another in their degree of tolerance to deviations in social norms. These differences can be demonstrated clearly in the differences between Spartan and Athenian forms of *civism*. In ancient Athens these differences resulted in differences in instruction, courtrooms practices, assemblies oratory, temple worship, civic expressions in public works, and epithets in cemeteries. The media of *civism* also was different as it was expressed in celebrations, rituals, recognized ideal models, participatory group activities, legal and legislative procedures, the inculcation of acceptable habits, collective endeavors, historical narratives, literary forms containing moral lessons, and public patriotic displays.

Civism arose from social surroundings that included, homes, public works, market systems where goods are exchanged, law enforcement, and the accepted values and beliefs about justice and moderation, the repercussions for breaking the rules, the notions of good and evil, ideas about the good life, ideas about sacrifice and greed, ideas about war and peace, curiosity, and a fear of the unknown. However, the influences of *civism* are not obvious to the casual observer, but are subtle and hidden within the full range of cultural elements.

In this volume, I have taken the position that modern democratic *civism* most likely had its origins in ancient Athens because of its citizens' creativity and their love of freedom. In addition, ancient Athenian *civism* found its expression in the development of the Athenian democracy and its eventual decline and fall. The spirit of that democratic movement was well expressed by Donald Kagan (1991) when he encapsulated the Athenian love of freedom: "Citizens should be free in their persons; free to maintain their own constitutions, laws, and customs; and their cities should be free to conduct their own foreign relations and to compete with others for power and glory. The Greeks also believed that the freedom made possible by the life of the polis created a superior kind of citizen and a special kind of power" (p. 96).

The ancient Athenian Greeks eventually realized that citizenship could be shaped through educational means or what they called *paideia*. Since the time of Homer, the ideal man was presented in the image of the ideal community, and as the community evolved, so has the image of the ideal man. "We have pointed out that the essence of education is to make each individual in the image of the community; the Greeks started by shaping human character on that communal model, became more and more conscious of the meaning of the process, and finally, entering more deeply into the problem(s) of education, grasped its basic principles with surer, more philosophical comprehension than any other nation at any other period in history" (Jaeger, 1945, vol. I, p. xxiv). The great achievements of ancient Athenian politics and philosophy related to *civism* would become diffused and then muted by the historical movements, but its inspiration would continue to live on in dusty library shelves and in other hidden places. The smallest fragments of this ancient heritage have become the treasure troves of scholars who have spent endless years in search for the artifacts of the glorious age of Athens and its political accomplishments.

The evidential remains of ancient Greece are fragmentary and scarce, so it might be asked: "Why go on and attempt to search for the origins of *civism*?" The answer to this question lies in the fact that for over two thousand years, scholars have attempted to reconstruct the culture and the history of the ancient Greeks, and out of this effort have come some revealing assertions that have become accepted. This acceptance is based on research findings that have been reinforced by cross-referencing procedures, in addition to archeological findings of ancient remains. These findings have been used to help scholars to conclude that there were real places and real people similar to those places and people described by Homer, Herodotus, and Thucydides. Even Protagoras left some fragments of his philosophical writings that have led to new insights on his thoughts and speculations. Plato left behind several of his dialogues, and they have been used to advance the development of western philosophy and mathematics, as well as to develop a school that served as the origin of the ancient university. Aristotle's work led to the formation of libraries, and his *Politics* and *Ethics* has been a source for the social sciences, while his scientific work advanced the development of the liberal arts and the separate scientific disciplines.

Although the main focus of this volume rests on the body of scholarship that already exists, this volume also contains some new implications regarding what might pass for elements of an ancient Athenian *civism*. The elements that are identified and described are based on the premise that the literature strongly suggests that the Athenians were well aware of the importance of citizenship and were concerned about the development of moral education and character development. For example, the fourth century Athenian scholars argued over the development of idealized virtues and whether they could be taught by parents or in schools. By examining some of the issues related to *civism*, it is the author's desire that this study will reveal some new insights about the ways in which cultural forces have been used to create a civic mind-set among the ancient Athenian Greeks that allowed them to advance their culture to new heights of political understanding.

THE REAL EXPRESSIONS OF CIVISM

Part I
The Origins of Ancient Greek Civism

The age of revolution in the Aegean Sea region, also known as the "archaic age", is described as a time when Mesopotamian and Egyptian influences reached the Ionian Greeks. Cities located along the Eastern region of the Aegean coast in Asia Minor were being influenced by the diffusion of ideas as early as the ninth century BCE. As the villages of Ionian Greece began the process of evolving into larger urban centers, they attracted an intelligentsia from the older centers of civilization. This diffusion of cultural influences had the effect of carrying advanced ideas that, in time, would contribute to the eventual development of a natural philosophy. In addition, this diffusion also would include ideas pertaining to character development.

For example, one of the most interesting developments in Egypt was a form of instructional literature called the "instructions" (Kuhrt, 1995, vol. I, p. 146). It was a child rearing tradition (*paideia*) dating back to the Old Kingdom in which a father instructed his son by teaching him to memorize prudent maxims regarding good conduct and by establishing the habits of good living. The father, according to this instructional tradition, provided the son with those lessons containing guidelines designed to insure his success as a member of the ruling elite. In Athens, maxims often served as the content of copy exercises in the teaching of writing skills. Consequently, moral lessons aimed at advancing character development were routinely included as a exercise in city–state schools.

In addition, character development in pre–Hellenic Greek culture was closely associated with religion in the Mycenaean era. Character education also was based on those values related to the knightly virtues, which were expressed in Homer's epic tales. The formation of the Greek polis gave rise to new forms of character education that became associated with citizenship in the city–states.

The founders of city–states developed their political systems based on political *constitutions* that came to define their ruling institutions. Each polis devised its own unique formula of rule, but most allowed for some form of assembly or court and for the maintenance of military orders in defense of the homeland. Differences between multitudes of city–state political systems often were determined by circumstances from within the culture and from historical influences related to the founding of the city–state.

The city–state was that result of a *cultural revolution* that began to take place following a Dark Age that destroyed the old Mycenaean civilization. During the Dark Age (see Starr, 1961, chapter 3–5), the Mycenaean civilization was extinguished as the Greeks were forced to revert back to a basic subsistence form of existence. After more than two centuries of social and political decline, new political orders began to appear, based on a city–state pattern of urban development. The social and political order of most early city–states were, at first, based on monarchies that eventually were replaced by the most powerful families of a landowning aristocracy.

In the Early Hellenic period, the Greek city–states experienced internal cultural developments that created a new social order that also gave rise to distinctly different ruling models. These differences were reflected in the formation of city–states that emerged in Sparta, Athens, Crete, and elsewhere, which were due to their historical, religious, tribal, and geographic distinctions. The Athenian polis emerged as the central or mother city of the Ionian Greeks who had migrated and settled in Attica, the offshore islands of the Aegean, and along the west coast of Asia Minor. The Spartan polis was located in Peloponnesia as a land–locked stronghold of several united villages. The Spartans formed a powerful league in central Greece and their citizens were required to spend their time honing their martial skills; consequently, they also enslaved other Greeks, who were forced to farm their lands as helot serfs.

The origins of *civism* could be traced back to tribal sources, and especially those ancient tribal customs and tradition used for making important decisions and judgments regarding such issues as migration, war, and peace. In addition, *civism* was derived from religious interpretations of man's relationship to a designated god(s), as well as to the nature or characteristics of that god or goddess. "Religion could hardly be separated from everyday life when the gods took such a detailed interest in, and played so important a part in human affairs" (McClelland, 1996, pp. 7-8). Following an important cultural revolution of the ninth century BCE, the Greeks began the process of organizing city–states according to their law-based constitutions. In addition to establishing the basis for city–state constitutions, the city–state founders, prior to the process of codifying their laws, were required to address and identify those cultural virtues that would serve as the core values for their respective societies. These institutionalized values would provide a source of instruction for polis citizenship and as a means of uniting an increasing diverse urban population.

ONE

The Mycenaean Greeks

Civilization is always older than we think; and under whatever road we tread are the bones of men and women who also worked and loved, wrote songs and made beautiful things, but whose names and very being have been lost in the careless flow of time.

—Will Durant

The source of Athenian city–state *civism* has its origins in the Neolithic past when family and tribal membership was based on close kinship relationships and individuals could trace their ancestry to a patriarch. Tribal lines of descent often included mythological tales about ancient times when giants and heroes were locked in a battle of survival. The Neolithic Age in Greece also was a time of cultural advancement when human endeavors led to significant inventions, including the domestication of plants and animals, the smelting of metals, wheeled chariots, and the beginning of massive stone works. More important still, was the eventual development of important human institutions of religion, government, law, and alphabetical and counting systems. Combined together, these achievements allowed migrating tribes to establish settled territories, which encouraged the process of an advanced cultural development under the supervision of powerful kings and a warrior class of associated knights. By the fifteenth century BCE the Greek tribes had migrated into the Aegean Sea region, which led them into a closer proximity with the highly developed ancient Mesopotamian and Egyptian civilizations. Through the processes of diffusion from Asia Minor, the Greek tribes acquired some of their advanced cultural characteristics; consequently, the Greeks were able to produce a unique civilization known as the *Mycenaean Age*. By the thirteenth century BCE, the Mycenaean culture had spread from southern Greece to the central region and to the Islands of Crete, Rhodes, and beyond. During this time, the Mycenaean Greeks encountered the Minoan culture, which had dominated Crete for many centuries. The result of this encounter led to the further advancement of the Mycenaean civilization, which, for example, was illustrated by the Treasury of Atreus, the *tholos* tomb, which became Europe's first great monumental work.

By the early Mycenaean age, clusters of small communities were established as clan settlements, which were under the administration of an *archon* (a governor or chief magistrate) and his treasurer. The archon's responsibility was to administer the communal lands and to see that these lands were defended by the mutual obligations of every tribal group. Tribal Attica was composed of three phratries or brotherhoods; each phratry consisted of thirty clans or *gentes (gene)*, and each clan consisted of thirty heads of families.

Mycenaean civilization first emerged some time in the Late Helladic epoch (the Bronze Age), and the early settlements were located in the vicinity of castles and often situated on defensible sites. To protect their strongholds, Mycenaean kings sometimes built their residential villages inland or on natural promontories near the sea that could easily be defended. Other centers were built at an appropriate distance that allowed them security from sudden attack, yet near enough to launch their vessels on short notice. It was an age of kings in which burials were found to contain objects of bronze, gold, and silver with some inlayed jewels.

Mycenaean civilization was named after Mycenae, which was the largest urban center in southern Greece, located just north of Argos. The Mycenaean civilization was influenced by the Minoan civilization that was located on the Island of Crete. While the Minoans did not speak Greek, they had wide contacts throughout the Mediterranean world that helped to bridge the divide between the Egyptians and the Greeks. As a seaborne trading people, the Minoans spread elements of their civilization to mainland Greece that had an important impact on the Greek kings and their courts. Mycenae became famous as a stronghold that contained a royal palace and a place of tombs. According to Homer's *Iliad*, Mycenae was the residence of King Agamemnon who had launched a ten–year attack against Troy in 1194 BCE. Agamemnon's court consisted of heroic knights whose occupation was to serve as the king's sea raiders, or to serve in his defense when attacked by enemy clans or tribes.

The wealth of artifacts found at this center suggested a growing sea travel, as the Aegean Sea served as a highway for Mycenaean Greek pirates who plied their warships in search of opportunities to capture merchant vessels, to raid villages, or to lay siege to unsuspecting coastal towns. Also at this time, Crete was a powerful magnet for seagoing mainland Greeks who obtained their goods by barter or raid. At the height of Mycenaean power, Greek merchant fleets were able to set sail from the mainland and to defy the Cretan rulers in order to participate in long distance trade. Prior to this time, the Cretans held a monopoly on goods destined for trade in Egypt. To break the Cretan hold on Egyptian trade, the mainland Greeks may have fought and destroyed the palace at Knossos. At this same time, written records describing the appearance of seafaring Greeks began to appear around the coastal regions of the eastern Mediterranean and also in Egypt.

Late Mycenaean times, however, were not conducive to forms of formal learning; the Achaeans had little use for scribes and writing, although some written elements did exist. At this time, citizenship and *civism* in Mycenaean Greece were based on knightly virtues such as courage and loyalty, and the only skills required of young men were those connected with combat. The Achaean Greeks loved competitive games and sports, which provided them with a means for conditioning their young men for war, and included various ball games, dances, races, discus and javelin throwing, archery, wrestling, and chariot races. In addition, youthful boys would participate in one–on–one combat with mock or real implements of war.

The Nature of Mycenaean Civism

Within the Mycenaean feudal setting, *civism* relied on an oral tradition that thrived because there were no schools or special teachers of letters, nor were there any books or libraries. *Civism* came in the form of political relationships within each tribe, and it was based on a strict loyalty to family, tribe, and king. Therefore, an important role of the noble families was to prepare young men for their participation in the courtly life of the king.

During the Mycenaean Age, centers of political and cultural development also served as the residences of ruling kings and their companions. The village residence of the chieftain or king was called a *basileus*, which began to exhibit some of the early characteristics of the *polis*. The *basileus* was the homeland of a single tribe, which was made up of several clans and was a civic center. These centers were not true cities, but massive building complexes that were comprised of courts, palaces, temples and *tholos* tombs (circular tombs of heroes that were in the shape of a beehive). Religious cults were a part of the shared culture of the early Greeks. Later, the vestiges of religious cults would become ritualized into a Panhellenic religion that was celebrated at specific centers such as the worship of Apollo at Delos, the Apollo Pythios at Delphi, and Apollo Karneios at Sparta.

Mycenaean *civism* consisted of two important elements. On the practical side, boys at about the age of twelve were prepared for aristocratic knightly life and its responsibilities within the tribal community, and on the moral side, selected boys of noble families were inculcated in the values associated with the male role of the warrior society. Loyalty was to the family, clan, and king and the social foundation of the tribal social order. While boys practiced the martial arts, noble daughters were expected to learn household skills from their mother. They looked forward to the day when they would be "purchased" by a suitor so that they could begin their own families within the homeland territory of the clan.

The shared meals between younger and older men became an arena for shaping the mind–set or *civism* of young warriors. It was in the shared meal setting that the feats of the ancient heroes were recited as an ideal model for living a life of courage and nobility. To acquire the martial skills of the knight, young boys in military training often fell into intimate relationships with older men in a bond of affection and love that was designed to protect the youth and to motivate him to win recognition, which could be acquired only on the field of battle.

Citizenship was associated with tribal membership and a youths' status depended upon the reputation of his father and his family. Wars were fought to uphold the reputation of the tribal king. At this time, some of the more wealthy kings increased their reputations by building elaborate palaces. In addition, some wealthy kings employed scribes as courtly record keepers who kept trade accounts, recorded tax receipts, and recorded important events such as raids and wars, as well as important events in the life of the court. Mycenae scribes wrote on clay tablets in a script that represented an early form of Greek writing. While the evidence is thin, it appears that some form of the scribe culture was present in the Mycenaean or the Late Helladic Period from 1400 to 1200 BCE.

The Heritage of the Mycenaean Age

By 1200 BCE the Mycenaean culture entered a new phase of transition, which signified that it was slowly declining, and by 1100 BCE the Dorian invasion may have helped to devastate central Greece. The Dorian invasion, along with other complicating social, economic and social factors, ushered in a period that would become known as the Dark Age. It was not until the eighth century BCE that a new age of cultural development would slowly lead to a new age.. The disruption in culture caused by The Dark Age, however, did not entirely destroy the heritage of the Mycenaeans. Once the new age, the Hellenic Age, began to appear it was accompanied by a search of the historical past for those virtues and values that could be used as guidelines for social living in the new civic setting of the emerging Greek city–state.

During the Mycenaean period, reading and writing was not taught to youth, nor was it an expectation for social or political advancement, but following the Dark Age (900-800 BCE), syllabic writing developed into a powerful new technology, which may have originated in Cyprus. It appears that syllabic forms may have been used earlier in the Minoan writing system, whose signs and symbols were known as Linear A (the script of the early Minoans) and Linear B (the script of the mainland invading Greeks). Later in the *revolutionary centuries*, the ninth and eighth centuries, writing systems may have been employed to transcribe the oral stories of the gods and the great heroes of legend. The histories of families were needed to trace the generations back to the originating god(s) as a means to establish citizenship status and legitimacy in association with the formation of the polis. Youths also might be taught to make eloquent formal speeches as a means of enhancing their status, and while there were no schools of eloquent speech, there were heroic examples in which celebrated, seasoned, and successful warriors were held up as examples of individuals who had become persons of great public distinction.

In addition, rhapsodists were at the center of the ancient oral tradition that had emerged long before the early poets and they traveled from court to court to extol the knightly deeds and virtues of mythical heroes. Poems were memorized to celebrate great warrior deeds, which became the source of moral lessons of courage and daring, which also may have carried the notion of advancing the use of reason over brute force. For example, according to Homer's *Odyssey*, men are not the victims of the gods, but are responsible for their own fate, or sometimes their own misfortune. The gods did their best to save humankind from its own folly and to help them help themselves. The First Book of the *Odyssey* presents a prescribed practical Mycenaean education for Achilles, but this education is more characteristic of a new age, an age of cultural revolution that emerged in the eight century. Homer's prescribed curriculum consisted of the art of healing, music, reciting, choral singing, and so forth, which provide clues that revealed something of his own times and possibly his own education.

Homeric Civism and Citizenship

Homer's epic tales were a compilation of ballads in the oral tradition that described the heroes of the Trojan War and their homecoming. Homer's particular focus was the Late Mycenaean period, or that time of decline just prior to the Dark Age that has been called The Achaean Age. According to Homer, the Achaeans were a Greek–speaking tribal people who lived in the area of southern Thessaly and were considered the most powerful tribe among the Greeks. Homer used the name Achaeans for all Greeks who were under the command of Agamemnon. By focusing on the Achaean Age, which was a growing time of conflict and chaos, Homer was able to focus on those ideals related to excellence (areté), thereby producing his standard for excellence in life and in citizenship.

Homer's *civism* elevated the poet to the position of teacher of morals, whose mission it was to articulate a standard of social and political morality and citizenship. This standard was based on the deeds' immortalization of the mythological heroes since they provided an expression of those ideal civic virtues of the noble class. *Civism* during the eighth and seventh centuries BCE, therefore came to consist of social values that were established in the minds of aristocratic boys as a part of their military training to become knights for their respective city–states. The virtues of knighthood were contained in the recited poems of Homer, and later Pindar and others, who celebrated knightly manliness with courage and physical vigor. The celebrated deeds of the Greek warriors at Troy were repeated and memorized as a part of religious devotion to the gods.

Through the above described means, heroic poetry would set forth civistic examples before youth of a more modern age, which allowed Mycenaean virtues to continue to serve as critical aspects of the Greek ideal, an ideal that was celebrated by many future leaders, including Alexander the Great and Caesar. Homeric *civism* became based on the knightly virtues of excellence in bravery and in courage (*areté*), which were expected in the face of an ever–present insecurity at home and danger abroad. According to Homeric *civism*, returning sea raiders created great excitement, as all the members of their community would share in the distribution of their plunder. Celebrations were held in the honor of successful voyagers whose exploits and bravery were noted by wandering minstrels who recounted their exploits to the accompaniment of the string lyre. In actual reality, some of these conquering heroes were not above embellishment, exaggeration, and boldface lying about what they had encountered based on the idea that the better the story, the greater the victory.

The eventual destruction of the Mycenaean culture swept away many of the older tribal traditions and patterns, but as we have seen, not all the old virtues for civic living. This transition had the effect of clearing the way for a new civic age and a new *civism* based on the formation of the city–state. In this same process, many of the Oriental influences, influences that had helped to shape Mycenaean civilization, were no longer influencing the new urban cultural development. These more modern Greeks were turning inward to their own culture as the means to build the foundations of a new civic culture and *civism*. By 850 BCE, the age of Homer, Greek agriculture was becoming more efficient and the herds of domestic stock were larger, which created a greater prosperity and this prosperity led to a growing population that fueled a new *Cultural Revolution*.

Two

The Dawn of the City–State

The POLITICAL MASTERPIECE of the age of revolution was the creation of the Greek polis or city–state..
—Chester Starr

The "archaic" phase of the development of Greek civilization produced a new Hellenic outlook that was characterized by a sense of self–consciousness that manifested itself in a growing individualism. Intellectually, this new awareness suggested that this was an age of changing attitudes that included a new self–assuredness, as well as an awareness of a community-based citizenship. The formation and the development of the polis, or independent city–state, began to appear at this time, and the polis was destined to become one of the greatest political advancements of the ancient Greeks. This cultural advancement gave rise to an urban revolution so that by the eighth and seventh centuries BCE a multitude of city–states dominated the political landscape of the Greek mainland, its off–shore islands, and along the coast in Asia Minor. At its core, the formation of the city–state was the result of an awakening of a more efficient cultural pattern that grew out of an expanding agricultural base.

The polis offered a new and a better means of organizing the relationship between citizens and its political order; consequently, the formation of the city–state, over time, became a means of re-ordering Greek society. This new order included a new set of social and political values that began to weaken tribal power and leadership, although kinship relationships remained the most important consideration for qualifying an individual for citizenship. Furthermore, the city–state, including its constitutional foundation and its codified "legal systems", would change the basis of citizenship participation according to the degree to which power was concentrated or distributed among individuals and social groups. As a consequence, the appearance of the city–state produced new forms of *civism* that relied on a demand for a type of "education" that could be used to justify and unify a more diverse population based on new philosophical, social, economic, and political understandings.

The New Literacy

Historians often credit the re–appearance of writing to the return of commerce, although simple tradesmen of this era easily transacted business without the need for records or elaborate contracts. However, a more reasonable explanation may lay within the need to provide a better set of tools to express human experience and to explore intellectual themes related to religion and politics. Greek writing also was a cultural statement about a growing awareness of the cultural changes that were taking place in many human endeavors. It also may have suggested that something new was in the wind, something that was not northern or eastern, but something that was distinctly Greek in character.

By the eighth century BCE, the creative features of the archaic revolution could be detected in many elements associated with language, religion, literature, art, architecture, ceramics, and intellectual attitudes. The Aegean mainland, with its offshore islands, turned into a Greek pond, allowing the mainlanders to influence the entire Aegean region. At this time, pockets of isolated Greek speaking peoples were beginning the process of adopting writing systems. New forms of literary expression had already emerged, one being the introduction of the literature of the poets, including Homer and Pindar, who were declaring the ancient glories of the Mycenaean warriors, while Hesiod was espousing the virtues of hard work and daily living.

The Greek alphabet emerged from many modifications of the expansions and contractions of consonants and vowels, which first emerged as a product of the new archaic culture. Writing was spreading throughout the Aegean region, as local or varied alphabets were used in different regions of Greece. For example, writing systems of the eighth and seventh centuries were different in the cities of Melos, Thea, Crete, and Rhodes. Local variations of the alphabet, once established in a Greek city–state, were spread to foreign lands through the processes of diffusion and colonization.

City–states sent colonists to distant parts of the Mediterranean world as a means of dealing with over–population. Colonists carried local writing systems to their new homes in an attempt to replicate the culture of the mother city. Mother city–states and colonial city–states often formed a system of mutual support and dependency, which relied on well-known shipping lanes that had developed by this time. The mutual support system began to produce a new system of trade and defense that would, in time, become an important aspect of a process of empire building.

The process of founding and populating new city–states would be an ongoing process that allowed a city–state to balance its population with its local resource base and food supply. Diffusion and colonization also advanced a standardized Hellenic culture throughout the Mediterranean, which had the effect of spreading literacy, as well as architecture and the dawning elements of a new intellectual outlook. By 750 BCE the population of Greece had increased to the point that migration was an essential means of avoiding social stress and hunger. Under these conditions, the restless Greeks had always migrated to more promising frontiers. The Ionians moved to the region of the Black Sea, the Dorians established settlements in Sicily and the southern region of Italy, and the Aeolians moved west until they had reached the shores of France and Spain. Migration became a source of Greek cultural diffusion, as the immigrants carried their culture along with their households and agricultural possessions. The ties between mother city–states and colonies were recognized annually in various activities, including religious ceremonies.

Foundations of the Greek Polis

The city–state emerged as an extension of the ancient *basileit* (the village or central stronghold of the fourteenth century king or clan leader), which was feudal by nature; however, there were important differences. Greek society would no longer be built on the basis of a heroic kingship, but on the basis of a city with an agricultural and trading orientation. In the transition from tribal stronghold to city–state cosmopolitan center, certain important functions were transferred from tribal leaders to urban leaders. The attraction of the emerging city–state unit of social organization grew so strong that other forms, such as monarchy or cantonal federalism, were simply absorbed within the city–state. Despite the importance given to the Greek polis and all of its institutional developments, there is great disagreement pertaining to its rise and fall and some have claimed that it continued beyond the Classical period for many more centuries (see, Hansen, 2006, pp. 38–39).

Because of the importance of the polis as a political unit, a powerful aristocracy, out of necessity, came to rule the polis through its councils or assembles. Consequently, elements of the ancient aristocratic codes of conduct were adopted as a part of the evolving cultural life. The aristocratic codes of conduct came to be expressed in emerging educational forms that advanced as a part of the new urban setting that also contributed to new forms of city–state citizenship.

At this time, agricultural wealth was becoming concentrated in the hands of a landed elite, and the wealth of this aristocracy gave rise to other city–state groups such as merchants and craftsmen, smiths and free labor. These groups of freemen were attracted to the most prosperous city–states, especially those situated in strategic locations. As these groups prospered with the development of the city–state, new social classes eventually gained enough influence to affect the development of the characteristic polis pattern of urban development.

In addition to groups of freemen, the aristocracy owned or controlled large numbers of slaves. Slaves usually consisted of defeated peoples who had been sold into slavery as a consequence of war. The slave population consisted of Greek and non–Greek men, women, and children who had been members of foreign tribes. Most slaves were located on large farms, but some served in the growing merchant trade, in the mines, or as household workers for wealthy families, which included caregivers. Slave merchants were attracted to the battle sites to await the outcome of a conflict and to pay for, and carry away a large portion of the losing population to slave market centers. These centers were sometimes located at the site of sacred places, such as the island of Delos. For example, on important religious days the Ionian tribes gathered at Delos to participate in certain religious ceremonies, and at the same time many of these visitors attended the lively slave auctions.

The pattern of a typical city–state design included an urban center consisting of a central marketplace, temples, and palaces, all of which were sometimes situated near a defensive promontory. In its physical setting, the polis had become a specific geographic unit in which the activities of citizens were concentrated within the boundaries of the "asty", or polis precinct (see Starr, 1961, p. 338). The territory of the larger poleis also contained smaller agricultural villages that often served as the residence of small farmers and their agricultural workers. The typical pattern of the agricultural village consisted of a cluster of homes that were surrounded by plots of land that were cultivated by families and a few slaves, according to the seasonal nature of their crops. Many of these farmers maintained olive groves as a supplement to their row crops, and it was not uncommon for wealthy citizens to maintain residences in both the city and in the countryside. This dual residency allowed the aristocrats to help govern the polis and to manage their many other economic activities related to agriculture, trade, and sometimes banking. For example, one very famous Greek family was involved in the construction of important buildings, such as temples, palaces, and marketplace structures.

The Greek polis continued to reflect its village origins in that it was not a product of careful planning. The streets were disorderly and followed the meandering paths that had been simple footpaths of an earlier time. Buildings were not arranged in orderly settings, but over time, the temples and other public buildings slowly acquired their elaborate form, scale and decor. As was previously stated, the polis often was close to an ancient citadel or fortress as a point of retreat in times of crisis, but also came to include assemblies and courts, or public spaces, where citizens could assemble for a variety of activities. A common architectural feature became the temple and the *stoa*. Typically, the temples were distinguished by their colonnaded entry with assembly space in front of the structure. Public buildings, such as the stoa, consisted of a long portico and a rear solid wall in back of its colonnaded open front. It was designed as a public meeting place where friends could gather and where politicians addressed the assembled crowds. Because of their expense, protective walls usually were not built until interstate warfare made them a requirement for survival.

Civism and City–State Citizenship

The process of transformation from tribal village to urban center also created a new civic outlook that accelerated changes and served as an incubator of creative ideas and expressions. Above all, the city–state was a local dynamic, which became the pride of its citizens and was the source of political and economic well-being. "The divisions within cities made them hard to govern, and there was never any certainty that the future was going to be like the past" (McClelland, 1996, p. 9). The civic spirit that evolved was patriotic as well as exclusive, which had the effect of creating an unreasoned pride that sometimes led to competition between city–states. Internal competition also led to intensive rivalries that drove protagonists to excessive displays and unfair actions to gain the upper hand economically; but at the same time, this new civic spirit could evolve into powerful new concepts regarding justice and the role of the citizen as a person of rights and responsibilities. "Citizenship above all carried certain legal rights, such as access to courts to resolve disputes, protection against enslavement by kidnapping, and participation in the religious and cultural life of the city–state" (Martin, 2000, p. 61). It soon followed that to maintain civil order, judicial codes were needed to deal with the abuses and mistreatment that had accompanied the process of social stratification. "The rallying cry for this spirit was *dike* (justice), whose sister was *eunomia* . . . the maintenance of traditional right" (Starr, 1961, p. 343). This desire would soon become expressed in the movement that had replaced the monarchs with a more broadly based political order. This trend reflected the cultural changes that were taking place in artistic and literary expressions, social stratification, and new developments in class relationships, as well as a religious outlook and a new civic spirit.

Each city–state was a separate sovereign entity that usually was controlled by local aristocrats, although government systems varied and some were under the rule of a king or tyrant. By seventh century BCE, the Greek landscape was covered with thousands of city–states that were jealously protective of their own sovereignty and ready to go to war against any neighboring state that looked threatening. While the Greeks shared the same language, religion, literature, and aristocratic outlook, local interests dominated their sense of identity, and city–state identity encapsulated their sense of loyalty and citizenship. Civic patriotism kept the city–states from blending into a greater territorial unity. Inter-polis alliances were possible only when powerful city–states, were able to forge a league against another powerful league, aggressive city–state or invading foreign power. Separatism was reinforced by competition over trade and dominion over the seas. In addition, the Greeks were well aware of their differences, including their ancient tribal divisions as Aeolians, Ionians and Dorians. In addition, even though all Greeks shared a common language, they spoke it with distinctive dialects that spoke volumes of their alien differences. Ancient historic conflicts were never forgotten, which led to a natural suspicion and dislike on both sides of their social divide.

Three

The Spartan Constitution

By constitution we mean, whenever we speak with propriety and exactness, that assemblage of laws, institutions and customs, derived from certain fixed principles of reason, directed to certain fixed objects of public good, that compose the general system, according to which the community hath agreed to be governed.

—Lord Bolingbroke

According to Aristotle's understanding of the human condition, as stated in his *Nicomachean Ethics*, man is, by his nature, a political creature, and his highest good is expressed in the creation of the polis. Human statecraft within the polis was aimed at creating the greatest good as its realizable goal. Aristotle's ideal polis was organized in such a manner so that every citizen would have a greater possibility of expressing his potential according to his special capabilities. Moreover, the relationship between the citizen and the state was to be grounded on a moral foundation of justice aimed at promoting the happiness of its citizens. Polis citizenship, in other words, was the highest expression of individual human good. It was to be found in the expressions of ideal virtues in a states' constitution; therefore, the good state was organized according to those virtues that promoted the moral advancement of its citizens so that they could obtain a higher level of happiness, which meant a higher level of excellence (aretê).

An important assumption of *civism* is that political, social, and economic virtues differed according to each states' culture as reflected in its constitution; therefore, political designs, political structures, and political institutions, including its educational institutions, are the products of state constitutions. In other words, the constitution was the essence of the city–state, as it prescribed the nature of the state and the relationship between the state and its citizens.

The formation of the city–state meant a shift in traditional kinship relationships associated with the tribe to a new arrangement that allowed "outsiders" or foreigners, traders, tutors, and the like, to reside within the prescient of the polis. For this reason, the rulers of the polis were forced to clarify one's social and political status as residents of the polis. More important yet, leaders of the polis were forced to clarify the relationship between those who were empowered to rule and those rights and obligations of the ruled. The need for this clarification led to the laws that addressed the power of the state in its relationship with the residing polis population. As time passed, a mixture of laws and decrees were formulated to address issues pertaining to the means for resolving social, political, and economic disputes between polis citizens.

As these laws accumulated, discrepancies arose and also had to be clarified, leading to the desire for some type of orderly system that led to the codification of existing laws, and this desire gave rise to the notion of the polis constitution. The formation of the polis constitution came about as a result of the need to identify those ideal values and virtues that would distinguish the nature of a particular city–state. Polis constitutions, in other words, were more than an organized body of civil laws; they were a declaration about the nature of states according to those core cultural and political values and virtues. The polis and its constitution, therefore, became the main source of polis citizenship and the main source of polis *civism*. *Civism* was the state's means for communicating those core constitutional values and virtues to its citizen body. The goal of *civism* in the ancient Greek city–state was for the purpose of unifying or solidifying its growing and diverse society.

Polybius (c. 200–c. 118 BCE) in his *The Rise of the Roman Empire* describes in book IV an interesting analysis of city–state constitutions. He dismisses the Athenian constitution as a failed state because of its democratic system. He wrote, "For the Athenian populace is always more or less in the situation of a ship without a commander" — but he reserved his greatest praise for the Spartan constitution when he wrote — "It seems to me from the point of view of ensuring harmony among the citizens, keeping Spartan territory intact, and preserving the liberty of his country, Lycurgus' legislation and the foresight which he displayed were so admirable that one can only regard his wisdom as something divine rather than human" (Polybius, 1979, pp. 339 & 342). Polybius, while strongly opinionated, recognized the importance of the constitution in the success of the city–state. He suggested that there were two basic ways of organizing the city–state according to constitutional types: one type of constitutional state promoted a strong collective citizenship, and another type of constitutional state allowed for a greater degree of individualism. Polybius preferred the *collective constitution* that Lycurgus formulated for the Spartans to all other constitutions, especially in preference to the constitutions of the Athenians and the Cretans. This preference was based on his conviction that the Spartan constitution promoted the civic qualities of courage in battle and harmony in social relationships. On the other hand, Polybius failed, or refused to consider the importance of individualism as a source of advancing the culture of the city–state through a greater grant of freedom, which might lead to a greater creativity and higher cultural attainment.

The Spartan Civic Culture

Spartan civic culture, by the eighth century, was believed by Plato and Xenophon to be the creation of the legislator, Lycurgus (living sometime between 900 BCE and

600 BCE). He was a member of one of Sparta's most powerful aristocratic families and was in a position to become its lawgiver, (however, historically there are some good reasons to believe that the Spartan *constitution* was a work of centuries). According to legend, Lycurgus was motivated to design the Spartan constitution based on the belief that defective or physically weak children were destroying the vitality of the Dorian race. This concern led him to search for social practices that might be used to physically strengthen the Spartan population.

According to legend, Lycurgus traveled to Delphi where he received a set of ideas that could serve as the basis for a set of new principles to reform Spartan society. In addition, he also traveled to Crete to observe their ways of dealing with newborn children. Upon his returned to Sparta, Lycurgus formulated a set of legislative reforms designed to draft a set of laws that would define the nature of the Spartan constitution. Before retiring to Delphi, Lycurgus obtained a pledge from tribal leaders that none of his laws would be changed in his absence; he then committed suicide as a deliberate act of his civic responsibility in order to preserve his constitution.

Between 800 BCE and 600 BCE the Spartans refined the work of Lycurgus in which the Spartan constitution became completely intertwined with the Spartan lifestyle so that it regulated every aspect of public and private life. The Lycurgus constitution had the effect of destroying old kinship relationships by creating a new structure of government, which was based upon geographical divisions that dispersed the power of the aristocracy and led to an extreme form of citizenship that was designed to establish a greater sense of loyalty to the state. According to the constitution, a new government was formed through a process that combined elements of various political systems including democracy, monarchy, and tyranny.

These elements were recombined into a new arrangement in which political interests were kept in balance so as to neutralize troublesome excesses between the classes. A *dual monarchy* was included to neutralize the power of competing ancient royal families, and the two kings were limited mainly to ceremonial or religious activities, except in times of war, when they were in command of the armies. In addition, the kings were subordinate to the *senate*, which slowly became the most powerful political body.

The *Senate* consisted of older aristocratic men whose main task was to formulate policy and legislation and to serve as a high court in cases of treason or capital murder. The *apella,* or popular assembly, consisted of male citizens who had served the state and who were thirty years of age. The *apella* was a very large body of warrior–citizens, which met on the day of the full moon. Its powers included the acceptance or rejection of all new laws without discussion, but it could discuss any contemporary issues concerning Spartan society. Originally Lycurgus designed the *apella* as the sovereign body of the state, but as a result of a post–Lycurgean amendment, it was reduced to a secondary body, and the real power resided in the *senate*. In addition to these bodies, Lycurgus continued the office of the *ephors*, overseeing administrators, who had existed in Spartan society as tribal magistrates. After the adoption of the constitution, the *apella* chose five *ephors* and only the *senate* could check their power.

As time passed, however, the *ephors* became so powerful that they might be compared to that of the *consuls* of Rome. Their tasks included receiving foreign diplomats, deciding disputes in law, commanding armies, which allowed them finally to become more powerful than the kings. Following the Persian Wars, the *ephors* gained absolute power because of their control of the armies of Sparta.

Lycurgus' constitution had led successfully to the development of the new military state. The army and a special police force, whose task it was to spy on the population and to kill helots who might be considered a threat, enforced domestic law. The army was the most powerful institution in Spartan society and its military activities dominated almost every aspect of daily life. According to the Spartan moral code, to die in the service of the city–state was the highest good and the highest honor that one could attain in life. Polybius claimed that the success of this model was based on several constitutional elements. "First of all, there are the land laws according to which no one citizen may own more land than another, but all are to possess an equal share of the public land" (Polybius, 1979, p. 340). Lycurgus also attempted to reduce jealousy by eliminating money or the accumulation of money from Spartan society. Finally, the officials of the state, the kings and the Senate, held permanent or lifetime offices, thereby eliminating aspects of political ambition. Therefore the greatest goal of the Spartan citizen was to work collectively for reputation, honor, and the glory of the city–state.

Spartan Civism

Spartan *civism* was derived from its Lycurgus constitution and its state–sponsored citizenship training system. The aim of education was to produce the patriotic soldier–citizens; therefore, the Spartans ignored almost all forms of higher learning, as Sparta was committed to limited military goals. The main tenants of the Lycurgus constitution was aimed at excelling all other Greek cities in the virtues of courage, tenacity, physical strength and endurance, and fearless self–control in the face of danger. Subsequently, Spartan education was organized to produce a collective heroism in the face of a painful discipline and the greatest fear was a fear of cowardice in the face of danger. Mothers admonished sons to be brave in battle and, if necessary to die for Sparta, but they also warned them that if they displayed fear or cowardice in battle, they would be without their mother or a safe return to Sparta.

Spartan *civism* produced a rigid military society that did not support those individual capacities aimed at cultural refinement in the arts and sciences. Consequently, Spartan culture did not possess creative or intellectual cultural movements that would distinguish it as a center of learning, nor would it attract individuals of talent, which stifled its capacity to develop progressively beyond its fierce reputation on the battlefield. Unlike many other city–states, Sparta was never a consolidated center, nor did it possess splendid temples or lavishly decorated buildings; instead, it consisted of four scattered villages that were archeologically representative of an earlier age. While there was an acropolis and stoa, the remains of the stoa never have been found. There were shrines to Apollo and Artemis, as well as a hero's shrine.

Much of Spartan *civism* rested on the state's ability to produce efficient hoplite military units, and it became a society in which the family was reduced in importance, as the purpose of marriage was to rear healthy children to become citizens of the state. "First and foremost Lycurgus considered children to belong not privately to their fathers, but jointly to the city, so that he wanted citizens produced not from random partners, but from the best" (Plutarch, 2005. P.19). Marriage was the only acceptable status for men over the age of thirty and for women over the age of twenty; bachelors were despised and celibacy was considered a disgrace.

Lycurgus forbad citizens from participating in the vulgar occupations associated with the common trades; therefore, the helots did most of the laborious work, moneymaking was deemed an occupation left to foreign merchants. Young men, men under the age of about thirty, were restricted from the market place, and old men were encouraged to spend their time in conversation and in attending the places of exercise where they could instruct the youth or discuss issues pertaining to the city.

In addition, Lycurgus had advised against the building of a fortified city wall; the lawgiver preferred a wall of men to a wall of bricks, or men who were obedient to the law. Youth were taught to fear the law more than they would fear an enemy, and the only intellectual aspect of their education was the memorization of the laws and some excerpts from Homer. Young boys mainly were taught what the law commanded and the law forbade them to flee in battle regardless of the consequences. Fidelity to the law took precedence over all other virtues and proof of this virtue was illustrated at the Battle of Thermopylae (480 BCE) when the Spartan King, Leonidas, and his three hundred warriors died attempting to hold off the invading Persian hordes. From a Spartan warrior perspective, a time of war was preferred to the time of peace, for the time of war also was a time when the diet was less restricted and the discipline was more relaxed. It was a time of comradeship when military units marched to the beat of military rhythms accompanied by pipes, which were sounded as they advanced on their enemies. As a part of the preparation for war, excerpts from Homer were memorized and chanted to the accompaniment of the lyre. The rhythms were simple Doric measures that were known to most adult warriors. The purpose of rhymes and rhythms were to exemplify honor and courage and to instill an exaggerated *patriotism*. Virtues, introduced in the classroom, were reinforced in the mess hall as the youth listened to the stories and admonishments of the old warriors. Spartan musical accomplishments also were based on military themes that centered on songs about great men who had died for Sparta. In addition, their dance was in the form of gymnastic exercise that represented the combative movements of the battlefield. "Within their limits both songs and dances were excellent, and their value as a moral discipline was recognized by the best educators of the other Greek States" (Boyd and King, 1995, pp. 14-15). Wrestling was popular, as it developed the skills for individual combat and conditioned the body for the physical endurance needed in hand-to-hand fighting.

Boys, after the age of seven, were encouraged to form relationships with older men, ideally seasoned warriors, as a means of military bonding in which both parties were encouraged to support each other in battle. This was considered a perfectly honorable association and was designed to strengthen the boys' moral character. "The older men, too, showed even more interest, visiting the gymnasia frequently and being present when the boys fought and joked with one another. This was not just idle interest: instead there was a sense in which everyone regarded himself as father, tutor and commander of each boy" (Plutarch, 2005, p. 22). Youth were not trained to serve as foot soldiers in the regimented infantry or the cavalry corp., but were shaped into a unified group whose solidarity became the essential feature of their warrior–citizenship. "In short, the common mess in many ways served as a boy's school and even his alternate family while he was growing up, and this group of males remained his main social environment once he had reached adulthood" (Martin, 2000, p. 78). While some boys were given lessons in reading, most remained barely literate. According to Plutarch, boys learned to read and write no more than was necessary (Plutarch, 2005, p.21). Those that could read only cared to read about the exploits and the genealogies of great heroes; the goal was to instill the *areté* of the knightly warrior as a mind-set for a fierce and fearless infantry.

Girls also were trained in the mission of the collective state and were allowed to remain at home, but also were expected to participate in a vigorous form of physical training. "He made young girls no less than young men used to walking nude in processions, as well as to dancing and singing at certain festivals with the young men present and looking on" (Plutarch, 2005, p. 17). Girls were taught to praise the manliness and the rivalry of boys and to jibe the timid and withdrawn personality. Female exercise also was aimed at inspiring an exaggerated gallantry in young men and their physical regimen included bodily conditioning through such activities as running, jumping, and leaping. Older girls were instructed in military exercises such as throwing the discus and javelin and combative sports including wrestling. The physical nature of this education greatly impressed Plato, who would incorporate the education of women into *The Republic*. Among the Spartans, it was commonly believed that physical training contributed to the production of healthy babies who could pass the inspection of the elders. Girls, prior to marriage, also were expected to participate in public ceremonies and festivals in celebration of religious occasions. Their dances and choral hymns of the Spartans were designed to engender that sense of *patriotism* that translated into a family duty to raise loyal and patriotic sons who would not disgrace them on the battlefield.

The Spartan School of Citizenship

To attain military goals and virtues, the total control of Spartan education was in the hands of a warrior elite under the authority of the state. Under this system all males received a complete, universal military training. The family surrendered their boys to the government, which directed every aspect of life until they reached adulthood.

This process actually began when all newborn Spartan children were examined by a group of elders, who decided their fate. Those accepted were returned to their mothers, while those rejected were subjected to death by being hurled off a cliff or by being exposed to the elements. In some cases, exposed children were adopted by non–citizens or helot families, and in marginal cases, the children might be returned to their mothers for further development and a later re–examination.

State sponsored education began at seven years of age and ended at about the age of fourteen. The boys were organized into local units or groups, which became subject to the severe discipline of their trainer, a state official called a *pædonomus* who was responsible for the boys who now lived in barracks. Boys were organized into units according to age, and each unit was under the control of an older boy, or captain, who supervised them and rendered punishment to those youths who were guilty of disciplinary offenses. Spartan leadership consisted mainly of the threat and the use of force. The purpose of early training was to instill discipline and to physically toughen the young lads. They had few comforts, not even bedding or sandals, and were expected to travel in all seasons and through all climatic and geographic conditions. By about the age of twelve, they were allowed a simple garment and were taught to endure hunger. They foraged in the countryside where they stole food or whatever was needed; if caught, they were routinely flogged by their captain.

Actual instruction consisted mainly of physical drill and gymnastics, or physical play in which the youths were allowed to participate in competitive ball games before they were taught to throw the javelin and discus. Older boys participated in more demanding physical contact sports including wrestling and boxing and, on certain festival days, they participated in the brutal *pancratium* (combat game), which was fighting without restraint or rules. This was a bloody affair, which included biting, hitting, kicking, scratching, and gouging. When a boy was bloodied, he was not permitted to cry or complain, nor was he allowed to show any signs of weakness. Because this contest was open to the public, reputations were made and lost here. Physical form, dexterity and poise were not at all involved in such a free–for–all; it was simply a battle of the fittest and was training for actual combat where rules and civilized behavior had no place.

One of the main purposes of unit learning was to develop a strong *esprit de corp* that was the result of common hardship, as well as a shared religion and a love of the city–state. These feeling were expressed in unison chants, war dances, displays of arms or athleticism, all of which were demonstrated in various religious ceremonies. Boys in the company of men might be interrogated for their attitudes and common knowledge, or they might be required to sing a warrior's song and give an opinion on an issue of current concern. An inappropriate response would be chastised, and a young man might be physically punished for his stupidity. Apollo was their golden god, son of Zeus and Leto. He was deemed the god of purity and light, could foretell the outcome of future events, and was considered a good and loyal friend of the warrior. He was depicted as fierce in battle and merciless in war, a god who killed without remorse and stood his ground to defend a fallen friend.

At eighteen years of age, young men became cadets and were sent out to perform soldiering duties, which included garrison responsibilities and spying on helots. Training focused almost exclusively on the strategies of field warfare. Between the ages of 18 and 20 the cadet was given specific training in infantry arms and movements. A scourging on the altar of Artemis Orthia tested every cadet (Artemis Orthia was the sister of Apollo and the goddess who was depicted in the form of a virgin huntress of the field). This test of their manhood and endurance was similar to the tortures of the flesh performed in a right of passage in other warrior cultures. The youth who endured the greatest number of stripes also was given the greatest honors in the form of a prize.

At the age of twenty, the youths lived a military lifestyle in which they took the oath of loyalty, which was followed by ten years of service in the field and on the borders, where they lived a "Spartan existence". Manhood arrived at the age of thirty, when the mature citizen was allowed membership in the Assembly. The physically strapping man now in his prime was expected to marry and to visit his wife on those occasions of off–duty leave. The main responsibility of the mature warrior–citizen was to contribute to the training of the next generation of Spartan male youth who would be trained to follow in his footsteps and to replace him in the ranks when he fell in battle.

Aristotle wrote that the Spartans were not superior in their training, but in the fact that the other Greek states could not compete with them as robotic soldiers. When the other Greek states finally defeated the Spartans, their veneer of superiority quickly faded. History demonstrated that the viability of Spartan society was fairly secure as long as it stayed within the bounds of its own neighborhood and adhered to its common military and educational traditions so rigidly reinforced by religious law.

Four

The Athenian Constitution

The Greeks recognized a close analogy between the organizations of the State and the organism of the individual human being.
—Sir Paul Vinogradoff

In the early decades of the eighth century, the city–state of Athens consisted of the area around the Acropolis, or *upper city*, and the agricultural lands that surrounded the city. Urban development formed a mile–wide band that skirted the Acropolis, which was located five miles inland from the natural harbor, called Piraeus, which made Athens an ideal site with the advantages of inland security and easy access to the sea. The agricultural lands, which dominated the economy, consisted of large aristocratic holdings and the smaller private plots, which were owned by freemen. As the result of agriculture and a growing overseas trade, the Athenian Greeks were slowly becoming a powerful Aegean power. By the seventh century, the landowning aristocrats, identified as the *eupatrid* oligarchs, served as Athens' most powerful political elite.

Origins of Athenian politics and government can be traced back to Theseus, who, according to legend, brought the people of Attica into one political organization with one capital. This occurred some time in the thirteenth century BCE, when the process of a tribal consolidation began, and was completed in the ninth century. After Theseus' death, the people of Athens thought well enough of him that they worshiped him as a hero and god. In 476 BCE, city officials brought the bones of Theseus from Scyros and deposited them as sacred relics in the Temple of Theseus. Long before this time, the oldest noble families (those with the largest landholdings) began to wield oligarchic power within the Athenian precinct that had been created by Theseus.

For a time, the landed aristocracy tolerated a kingship, especially when disorder threatened, but they were quick to reassert their feudal domination once peace was restored. The central government of the Athenian precinct under the monarchy, and later the oligarchy, had evolved into the form an *archonship*. Some scholarly sources claim that the office of *archon* can be dated back to at least the seventh century BCE. By this time, there was a list of *archons* posted in public on a stone monument and also by 650 BCE there were nine *archons* that served as the executive and judicial bodies of the oligarchic government.

In addition, the control of the city's military resources and the responsibility for military decision making also was under aristocratic control. This was the time when the "special" office of the *archon* was created in which the responsibilities of the chief archon included the management of his Council (*boulé*), which consisted of the ancient *ecclesia*, or the heads of important noble families. (In the fifth and fourth centuries the *boulé* met in a building or bouleutêriorn located in the public market area of Athens, and was made up of representatives from each of the *demes*.) The powerful noble families continued to tinker with the government by changing its form and the rules that it followed.

The Oligarchic Constitution

Some time in the eighth century BCE the powerful leaders of Athens replaced its ruler, or *basileus*, with three civic officials that were called *archons*. Each archon was assigned an important responsibility for the management of Athens. One of the archons was given the old title *basileus* and his responsibility was to manage the cults of the city, as well as to sit in judgment of conflicts pertaining to cult affairs and religious lawsuits. Although the military affairs of Athens were the concern of all of these *archons*, they assigned a powerful noble military commander to serve as commander–in–chief, rendering him the title of *polemarch*. In times of war the *polemarch* was responsible for planning military strategy, as well as for commanding the structure of the army. In addition, the *polemarch* served as a judge in law cases that involved citizens of foreign cities or in cases involving trade and exchange. Of the three offices, the most prestigious office was that of the *eponymous archon*. He was assigned the task of presiding over a council, but in addition, his duties included the supervision of the public affairs of the city and he served as a judge in nonreligious or civil law cases. The prestige of the eponymous archon was greater than that of the other archons because his name was given to the year of his rule. Six additional individuals were named *thesmothetai* to serve as a judicial panel or court ("those who laid down the law"), and their main function was to insure that community moral standards were observed. The entire body of nine archons was elected annually from the eupatrid families and they would serve as officials of the Athenian city–state for one year.

The *archon court* was presided over by the *basileus* or religious leader, which was a carry–over from the days when the king would serve in the capacity of political and religious leader of the community. "From pre–Solonian times on, there were in Athens two kinds of law court. Most private litigation fell within the jurisdiction of one of the nine archons, each in charge of his own tribunal, and each within a well–defined sphere of competence. . . . Other cases regarded as private were tried before the Areopagus, which had, at all times in Athenian history, jurisdiction in all cases of homicide, of wounding or poisoning with intent to kill, of arson, and such religious matters as the care of the sacred olive trees" (Ostwald, 1989, p. 6). The archon court often ruled on issues related to social conduct according to tribal custom. Because the population consisted of separate tribes and clans with differing customs the court served as an important means of maintaining unity and social harmony within the city–state.

The ruling archons also served as a council called *boulé* and became known as an ancient council called the *Areopagus*. When the *Areopagus* sat as a council, it became the decision-making body in the service of powerful landed *eupatrid* families. The name was derived from the Ares' hill where the archons assembled to conduct business in the cool of the evenings. Politically, the *Areopagus* was responsible for making informal laws and decrees that governed commerce, religion, customs, and military activities, and thereby combined the powers of the executive, judicial, and legislative activities of city–state government. In 621 BCE the function and the responsibility of the Areopagus became more directly judicial as a result of the adoption of *Draco's Code*, thereby making the Areopagus a court as well as a council. Draco was an aristocrat and he favored the large landowners over the other classes (see "Social Class Conflict").

As time passed, ex–archons were allowed to attend and to vote in the Areopagus alongside those currently serving their one–year terms as archons. This eventually would lead to the formation of a tradition that gave rise to an *archonship* political class of nobles, thereby making the office of archon more prestigious and more political. From time to time, charges and suspicions about misconduct in public office would cause the Athenians to establish traditions that were designed to review the behavior of the archons during their one–year term of office. Automatic lifetime membership appointment to the office of the archonship was changed so that each person nominated to an archonship would be submitted to public scrutiny. It was decided that each person appointed to a position of public responsibility must undergo public investigation regarding his qualifications for office. This investigation for fitness was called the *domimasia* and this review focused on the past conduct of the candidate. Fitness for an archonship was based on three criteria that included the candidate's health, reputation in the treatment of his parents, and record and reputation in military activities. Upon completion of a specified duration of time in office, the archon again was reviewed according to his conduct while in office, which mainly focused on his fiduciary behavior. This test of conduct was called the *euthyna,* and was used to determine whether the archon would be appointed to the Areopagus for life.

Aristocratic Citizenship and Social Stratification

The social classes of sixth century Athens reflected an ancient social stratification in which distinct levels, or layers of society evolved out of the Athenian agrarian base.

By this time, a fixed class system had evolved, which was subsequently modified by the formation of the polis. The primary levels of social classes included large landed aristocrats, medium and small farmers, craftsmen, merchants and traders, and free hired labor. The solidification of the socio–economic classes resulted from the need for military resources that could be used in offensive or defensive warfare. As warfare evolved into a pattern of components, it depended on a king, his oligarchic leaders who often served as generals, a cavalry consisting of nobles who were wealthy enough to own and raise horses, and a heavy infantry that fought in close phalanx formation as hoplite soldiers. Hoplite nobles became a sort of evolving middle class consisting of medium and smaller landowners with the ability to acquire the armor and weapons for close rank frontline warfare.

The aristocratic control of the city–state was built on a military class system that consisted of aristocrats, knights, hoplite infantry and non–citizen freemen. The *hippes* were a knightly class of moderately wealthy landowners who provided horses to the state, and in times of trouble, served as a cavalry that worked behind the infantry or on the wings of its formation. In Athens they were the only class from which the archons, judges, and priests were selected. The *zeugitai* were common citizens who provided oxen in times of war, and who could equip themselves to serve as heavily armed hoplite infantry. Hoplite soldiers were equipped with helmet, shield, cuirass, greaves, sword, and spear and worked in a tightly formed infantry line, which moved as a solid wall against the enemy. The *thetes* were non–citizen freemen who served as a light infantry in exchange for certain protected rights.

Athenian society also was stratified into three socio–economic classes that placed the landowning elite *eupatrid* aristocrats at the top layer of the class structure. These landed aristocrats lived in town villas, and their fields were tilled by large numbers of agricultural workers consisting of slaves and hired labor. The *demiurgoi* emerged as a body of middle class professionals with relatively high wealth gained from commercial activities within the city. As trade grew and coinage became the common form of exchange, and as the Greek colonies multiplied, the *demiurgoi* class grew in status and power. The lowest class, the *georgoi,* or the peasant class, owned small plots of land, which gave them a small degree of economic and social status.

Social Class Conflict

During the transitional years of the seventh century, clan ownership of communal property began to disappear, as agricultural land was falling into the hands of large landowners. This economic transformation created a situation in which many smallholdings were no longer able to support a family. As a consequence, the small plots were sold off, and many of the rural poor moved to Athens where they became disenfranchised freemen. Some of these freemen remained on the land and became *hectemoroi,* or landless, sharecroppers who worked smallholdings within the larger estates of the aristocrats. At this same time, the growing urban middle class used their increasing political power to reduce the wages of free labor to a state of poverty, which, in part, resulted from a growing use of slave labor. The growing influence of the upper classes and emerging urban middle classes, along with the disenfranchisement and increasing poverty of the displaced farmers and free laborers, had the effect of increasing social stress between the social and economic classes of Athens. By 752 BCE, the power of the landed elites had grown to such a degree that they were able to replace the king with an archon system of rule, which gave the aristocrats almost absolute control of the archon government. Later, they used their power to limit the term of the archons to ten years, and less than a century later, the term of office was further limited to one year. The aristocrats also gradually removed the rights of the small landowners through their adoption of the Draco's laws.

In 621 BCE, when Draco was given the charge of preparing a codified written law, his task was, in part, to attempt to cool the threat of class conflicts. The result of these laws, however, had the effect of favoring the landed classes over the peasant farmers and of creating a feudalist society that did nothing to relieve the plight of the debtors. More importantly, the code helped to create the eupatrid noble class, who then became the absolute political and economic masters of Athens, according to the oligarchic constitution. The severity of the Draco's code was so extreme ("draconian") in nature that it created civil unrest because it upset centuries of traditional cultural or tribal relationships and understandings. Consequently, small farmers, emerging urban classes, and hired labor began to demand political changes aimed at those constitutional reforms that would begin under Solon.

Aristocratic Civism

The cultural transformation of Greece began with the archaic Cultural Revolution, which led to the formation of the city–state. The formation of the city–state created an increased prosperity that had the effect of increasing the number of aristocratic families. By the eighth and seventh centuries, aristocratic families began to hire tutors to help educate their children. Aristocratic education reflected the general cultural understanding that human beings possessed a dual nature consisting of a *soul* (spiritual nature) and a *body* (physical nature); therefore, in order to produce a "good" man, a citizen of the city–state, both aspects of his dual nature must be brought into a harmonic balance through education. Music was expected to help shape the soul of the citizen, while exercise was to help shape the body of the citizen. Consequently, by the seventh century, achieving this harmonic balance between soul and body became the overall mission of aristocratic education, which was very limited. "Only well–to–do families could afford to pay the fees charged by private teachers, of whom they sent their sons to learn to read, to write, perhaps to learn to sing or play a musical instrument, and to train for athletics and military service" (Martin, 2000, p. 140).

The foundation of aristocratic *civism* that emerged at this time was grounded in an elitism that was produced by both religious and social factors that combined to create an international aristocracy. Elite families that made up the international aristocracy assembled every four years at the site of important religious shrines to participate in athletic contests that served to reinforce their class identity. Delphi and Delos, for example, became associated with religious prophecy and places where treasuries housed the wealth of their associated tribes. In addition, these and similar sites contained monuments celebrating great historical events, temples to mythological gods, and monuments dedicated to important families and individuals. The most important of these religious sites would eventually become the Olympia site containing shrines for Zeus and Hera located in the vicinity of western Peloponnese. In the fifth century this site become the most important gathering place for the celebration of aristocratic games. The Ionian tribes periodically assembled on the island of Delos as a means to reinforce their common kinship ties and to worship at the temples dedicated to Apollo and Artemis. In addition to recognizing the status and the importance of the noble families, the ceremonies held at these sacred places were used to recognize and reinforce those commonly shared virtues that characterized the aristocratic class according to those Homeric virtues celebrated in the *Iliad* and the *Odyssey*.

More important yet, these gathering places reinforced the notion of an international aristocratic identity called *Panhellenism*. "Panhellenic festivals fostered a sense of Greek identity, reinforcing a feeling that Greeks everywhere shared a common heritage, language, and religion" (Pomeroy, et.al., 2004, p. 59). Aristocratic citizenship was grounded in a strong sense of loyalty to the family, to ancestry, to the gods, to the refinements of aristocratic social class, and to the recognition that all aristocrats shared a common identity and bond. Aristocratic families often intermarried with other families from distant city–states in order to form political and diplomatic alliances, but another important reason was to help consolidate a family's wealth as a means to solidify their local and foreign prestige and status.

Although the Athenians expected their youth to be trained to defend the city and its territory, and while they owned slaves, they had not subjected neighboring tribes into a state of serfdom, as the Spartans had done. In addition, Athens was the oldest and most important city of the Ionian people in all of Greece, which meant that it was the beneficiary of constant contacts with other Ionian cities in the Aegean and in Asia Minor. The easy flow of ideas among the Ionians had the effect of feeding the Athenian love of learning. Athena, their goddess of wisdom and war, allowed the Athenians to advance their *civism* on the foundations of mind and body, which was organized around music and gymnastics to reflect this important balance.

Unlike Sparta, where education was a public affair, the city–state of Athens placed the responsibility for education on the shoulders of the parents, and it was considered a private matter. The Athenian father ruled his family with absolute authority and he alone determined the fate of his family members. The father was expected to educate his children, but there were no laws that required him to follow the dictates and customs of tradition. However, there was a degree of social pressure applied to the aristocratic father to provide some form of education for his children. For example, if a father refused to meet his responsibility to educate his son, the son, according to tribal law, was freed from his responsibility to support his parents in their declining years.

Within the home, childrearing was the responsibility of the mother and she might delegate that responsibility to a household servant. In some homes the mother, or a female slave, was expected to provide the children with basic instruction in the fundamentals of the alphabet, as well as the elements of literature. Typically, an aristocratic child heard nursery rhymes, folklore, and stories about gods or heroes from the works of Homer or from the works of Hesiod. It was not uncommon for children to be expected to memorize and to recite them as a demonstration of their education. Early childhood education was used to help to establish, or to cultivate, a love and respect of Greek culture as something of great value. The result of family education was indirectly aimed at cultivating within children a creative imagination that caused them to be curious about the world. In addition, this form of education helped to cultivate a poetic feeling that shaped and typified the Athenian culture. Hesiod, for example, employed the use of myth to reveal the sources of divine justice in order to demonstrate the notion that justice was an aspect of the divine order of the universe and not an invention of man or society. As a consequence, Hesiod planted the notion that justice was a natural element of human nature and human affairs. His poem, *Days and Works,* reflects rural life and the struggles of the peasant farmers, as well as the injustices created by social and economic life in a stratified city–state society.

At the same time, young Athenian men were given military training and were sworn to oaths of loyalty to the polis before they were granted citizenship status. Athenian *civism* required a certain amount of service to the state in exchange for political rights. The idea of an exchange of service for rights helped to establish the idea that Athenian citizenship was individualistic in nature; it was a partnership arrangement, or an agreement between the citizen and the state.

In sum, Athenian *civism*, prior to the rise of democracy, was family and tribal centered according to religious and social custom. Furthermore, this *civism* required a commitment to community based on those standards of excellence that the poets had identified as exemplary. For the Athenians, this meant that each individual, while seeking to be true to him or her self, must contribute to the advancement of the ideals of the city–state. Both the Spartans and the Athenians had adopted Athena as their patron goddess (see Martin, 1996, p. 52), and Athena represented ideals and virtues related to wisdom and war. The Spartan Athena placed a heavier civic emphasis on the virtues of war over wisdom, while the Athenian Athena placed a heavier civic emphasis on the virtue of wisdom over war. This civic emphasis made a very a large difference in the advancement of their respective forms of *civism*, which in turn made a large difference in the means that were used to advance their respective forms of citizenship. The Spartans developed the most powerful land army in Greece based on a totally dedicated hoplite infantry, while the Athenians slowly assembled the greatest intellectual resources for the advancement a new golden age of cultural development.

The Real Expressions of Civism

Part II
The Athenian Democratic Constitution

Solon established a constitution and enacted other laws, and the Athenians ceased to use the ordinances of Draco apart from those concerning homicide. The laws were inscribed on the kyrbeis and set up in the Portico of the Basileus, and everyone swore to observe them.
—Aristotle

The beginning of the constitution in Athens cannot be dated to a single event or person, but it is generally agreed that its origins can be found in the reforms of Solon in 594 BCE. By this time, as the result of the Draco Codes, the Areopagus consisted of a *Council of 400*, whose members were chosen by lot from the large landowning eupatrid families. From Draco's time, laws and decrees had been written and posted in public places such as central marketplaces, which suggested that there was a growing literacy among the upper classes. In 594 BCE Solon became a powerful political leader, archon and reconciler, and he began a process of replacing the Draco codes with a series of his own reforms, which led to the beginning of the end of the oligarchic constitution; over time, it would be replaced by the evolving democratic constitution. Solon's reforms would be followed by the reforms of Cleisthenes in 508 BCE, the reforms of Ephialtes in 461 BCE, and the rule of Pericles from 443 to 429 BCE, a period known for its high cultural achievement that has been called "the Golden Age of Athens", or the "Age of Pericles". The end result was a political system that began with Solon that replaced aristocratic rule with the rule of the *demos* or "the people." As a result of this transformation, citizenship values and understandings underwent radical changes, as did tribal and social class relationships. The new focus of political power shifted away from the Council of 400, the Areopagus, to the Assembly (*ekklesia*) of the people. Citizenship in ancient Athens was restricted to male citizens eighteen years of age who were born of Athenian parents.

Democratic *civism*, as a result of the democratic constitution and the establishment of a democratic citizenship, came to be focused on the techniques of *persuasion* as a means of gaining and maintaining political power. For example, Pericles used the reconstruction of the destroyed temples and public buildings of Athens to communicate his vision for an ideal democratic society and state. The skills of communication, in its many forms of political and artistic expression were used to "educate" the public in the new democratic civic virtues. These new virtues were designed to dominate the political mind–set of the Athenian citizen according to those behaviors that would balance individual self-interest with the collective interests of the community. In addition, these new virtues also demanded that the Athenian citizen become more involved in the affairs of the city–state. As these virtues became accepted, political power became more broadly distributed, and as a consequence, educational resources also became more attractive. However, despite a growing literacy, most of the voting population did not have an adequate educational preparation in the knowledge, skills, and values needed to meet the demands of their democratic civic duties and responsibilities.

FIVE

The Democratic Reforms of Solon

The paradox in democracy is that it must depend on citizens who are free, autonomous, and self–reliant.

—Donald Kagan

Solon (c. 638-558 BCE), during his lifetime, gained the reputation of one of the Seven Wise Men of Greece because of his extraordinary gifts as a literary figure, his fiscal integrity, and his political leadership. His father was a direct descendant of King Codrus, the legendary king of Athens, and his family was a distinguished member of the exclusive eupatrid noble class. Solon's mother was related to Peisistratus, who became the tyrant of Athens between the rule of Solon and Cleisthenes. In his youth, Solon became a popular poet and his poems were copied and memorized by schoolboys for generations. His fame as a poet led him into public life and opened the way for him to impact the culture and the politics of his age. Solon's father suffered financial losses in attempting to help his neighbors and friends who were in debt. He may have lost his estate and his wealth, which may help to explain the reason for Solon's turning to commerce and trade. In the process of rebuilding the family fortune, Solon was able to establish a reputation for honesty and integrity. Among Solon's accomplishments was the re–occupation of Salamis, which established his reputation as a commander in war, earned him fame and led to his exceptional political career. Salamis, an island forty miles off the coast of Attica, was the subject of his early poems and was used to help to stir the Athenians to reclaim the island from Megara.

The Solonian Revolution

In 594 BCE Solon become a candidate for archon and this important position allowed him to use the powers of the Areopagus to reform the monetary system and modify the social, economic, and political structures of Athenian society in order to head off class-strife that was threatening civil war. The changes became known as *Solon's Constitution*; some authors have termed it "the Solonian Revolution." His reforms included the cancellation of mortgage debt, personal debt, debt enslavement, as well as the recall of those who had been banished for financial reasons. At first these reforms caused the eupatrid creditors to grumble over their loss of property and to charge that Solon had encouraged fraudulent mortgage dealings; however, it was soon realized that he had personally lost a fortune in loans and mortgages. The nobility soon understood that Solon's reforms had saved Athens from civil war and that they led to a greater social harmony between the classes. Solon encouraged landowners to specialize in olive oil and wine as products for export and also advanced a ceramic industry, which helped the Athenians to establish a stronger economy. As a result, the poverty of the lower classes was eased and the urban commercial classes gained in wealth, causing them to support Solon's democratic political reforms.

Economically, since ancient times, the Athenian population had been stratified into three economic classes that included: the *eupatrids*, who lived in relative luxury in town, while slaves and hired men tilled their holdings in the country; the *demiurgo*i, or public workmen, who worked as craftsmen, traders, and free laborers living in the precincts of the city; and the *georgoi*, or free land workers, who lived on small plots of land as peasants and made up the debtor class. The debtors lost out because of the custom of dividing the land among their sons and the decline or loss of the collective clan lands, and as a result, some became traders, some became tenant farmers, some descended into serfdom, some were sold into slavery, some starved to death, some sought opportunities abroad, and some turned to violent protests. The growing protest movement had the effect of pressuring the need for social reform, which gave Solon his challenge. As class conflict grew, the archons sought relief in the law, but soon realized they had to find saving grace in a redirection of the institutions of state and a new and different kind of leadership.

Solon's new economic classes included: the *Pentacosiomedimni*, whose lands produced at least five hundred measures of produce; the *hippes*, whose lands produced three to five hundred measures of produce; the *zeugitai*, whose lands produced two to three hundred measures of income; and finally the *thetes*, who produced some level of income. Income determined honors and taxes, with the fourth class, the *thetes* (mainly a landless group), exempted from both honors and taxes, and they were not eligible to hold office or to serve on the juries. Political honors, a vital element of aristocratic status, now was determined by economic grade and took the form of a constitution based on a "timocracy," or government based on honors, as determined by taxes. According to this system, eligibility for military and political service was without salary, but was rich in social status and reputation and could lead to higher political office. The *Pentacosiomedimni* classes (the *eupatrid* families) were eligible for the archonship and to serve as military commanders, while the second class served as low–level officers and made up the cavalry; the third class made up the heavy infantry, and the fourth class served as a light infantry.

Solon's greatest contribution put Athens on the road to the formation of a democratic political system. This system began in 594 BCE when he extended membership in the Areopagus to the two top social classes in Athens. Solon also expanded the legislative machinery of government by creating a second *boulé* in the form of the *Council of Four Hundred*, which consisted of one hundred representatives each from the four tribes and served the task of preparing legislation for the Assembly. The Assembly became a reconstitution of the ancient *ecclesia* that had existed as a king's council. The appeals court, called the *hêliaia*, was transformed into a people's court or a popular jury system or *dikastêria*, which consisted of six thousand jurors drawn by lot to serve on various courts. Every citizen gained the right to attend the sessions of the Assembly and to join in its deliberations. The Assembly had gained the power to pass laws and decrees, powers previously reserved for the Areopagus, however, most of the powers of the Areopagus remained in place, providing the aristocracy with a continuing powerful political influence.

In addition, the Assembly was granted the right to elect officials and hear the pleas or the complaints of citizens who believed that they had been wrongly or unfairly treated in the people's courts (*dikastêria*). The people's court met over one hundred fifty times a year and was made up of citizens who were thirty years of age and were drawn by lot. The courts heard grievances between individuals and also became a place where politicians exchanged charges and counter-charges with one another about each person's conduct. The courts also became a place where public policy could be explained to citizens, and thereby the courts helped to educate the public about the law and various political issues. All citizens were eligible by lot to serve in the Assembly and on the jury's list for a term of one year. It has been estimated that the Assembly met about forty times a year on the hill called Pnyx. "Meetings were typically held in the Pnyx, a theater-like area built and used exclusively for meetings of the Assembly" (Ober, 1989, p. 132). During the fourth century it was estimated that the theater held from 6,000 to 8,000 citizens.

Solon's Civism

Solon's *civism* was based on his belief that polis life should stress the enhancement of simple joys a shared citizenship, as well as the importance of justice and seeking to live a productive life. He promoted the notion that every boy should learn to swim and to read. His influence also extended to the idea of regulating the private schools for the purpose of community well-being. His ideal community was grounded in friendship and love of self and neighbor; therefore, the good life included a balance between private and public life, which allowed time for wine and song, as well as hunting and sport. While Solon did not interfere with the content or the methods of instruction, he did address the rank and the age of pupils, the moral character of the servants who supervised children, the operating hours of the schools, and the protection of students while attending school.

He imposed severe punishments for those who might molest youths attending school. Solon also attempted to define the role and the moral character of the *paidagogos* by establishing standards to be applied to their conduct.. The *paidagogos* accompanied the pupil to and from the school and often remained in the classroom to, among other things, monitor the conduct of the class and the master and to report back to the parents. As a consequence of this practice, the family was better able to make judgments regarding the education and welfare of their sons. Sometimes the *paidagogos* was a slave who had been educated or had previously served as a teacher. In addition, Solon set the standard of justice as the city–state criterion that would ease the social and class conflicts that threatened to destroy the social, economic, and political cohesion of the Athenian city–state.

More important still, Solon's *civism* attempted to address a growing perception that social injustices were a result created by the economic excesses allowed or embraced by the oligarchic constitution. Therefore, Solon's *civism* was based on his recognition that Draco's laws were the source of a great social, economic and political injustice that communicated the message that the state and its laws favored one group over all others. He recognized that the way to correct this sense of injustice was to create a mind–set based on the understanding that justice and the law must become blind to the affairs of the social classes. The only way that the state could herald this message was to make radical changes in the current economic direction of the Athenian city–state. Mortgages and debts had to be erased so that Draco's injustices could be ended, especially those injustices that allowed the power of the state to align itself with the aristocrats over all other sectors of Athenian society. In other words, Solon's *civism* represented one of the first political experiments to recognize that justice, in all of its forms — economic, social, and political, must be safeguarded within the state's constitution. Without this safeguard, the state was destined to fail based on the reasonable assertion that injustice leads to social stress, and stress produces civil conflict, which could possibly erupt into civil war.

* * * *

Following Solon, the nobles worked to undo his reforms, while the middle classes, having whetted their appetite for power, sought after more changes. The desires of the city-dwellers and the poor farmers found a possible champion in the form of a nobleman by the name of Peisistratus, who swept into Athens in 560 BCE claiming to be the champion of Athena, and seized power to rule as a tyrant. For a time, Peisistratus was willing to share power with the Alcmaeonid family, the family of Cleisthenes and Pericles, but in 546 BCE, the Alcmaeonid clan attempted to overturn Peisistratus, and as a result, they were forced into exile.

Six

The Democratic Reforms of Cleisthenes

Thus the people obtained control of affairs, and Cleisthenes became leader and champion of the people.

—Aristotle

Cleisthenes (c. 570 – 508 BCE?), the son of Megacles and Agariste, along with his influential Alcmaeonid family, obtained a contract to rebuild the temple of Delphi that had been destroyed in the 584 BCE Sacred War. The family won the favor of the priests by using the best materials in the reconstruction of the sacred shrine. Using their good will, the Alcmaeonids were able to rid Athens of Peisistratus' son Hippias, who was evicted when the Spartans were persuaded to occupy the city. The Spartans intended to restore the old aristocracy, which allowed the Alcmaeonids to return to Athens and to possibly rule. But following the departure of Hippias, Athens fell into a political struggle in which Cleisthenes lost in his bid for power against Isagoras, who won the election for chief archon. In response, Cleisthenes triggered a revolt against Isagoras and turned to the people of Athens to join his cause with a promise to reform the political system through a people supported dictatorship. For a second time, the Spartans occupied Athens in an attempt to restore Isagoras by driving Cleisthenes and his family back into exile. A popular rebellion followed in 507 BCE that drove the Spartans from the city, which led to the recall of Cleisthenes. Back in Athens (c. 500 BCE), Cleisthenes became chief archon and began a program to establish a stronger democracy about 500 BCE.

The Cleisthenes Constitutional Revolution

Cleisthenes continued the democratic constitutional reforms that began with Solon, which had been interrupted with the rule of the tyrant Peisistratus and his sons. Once in power, Cleisthenes reorganized Athenian society through territorial divisions that formed ten new tribes consisting of ten trittyes or counties based on geographical location, which replaced the political structure of the original four tribes of Attica. Each of the new tribes was made up of *demes* or districts from within the city, the coast, and the interior areas of Attica. New religions were formed around the *demes* and new ceremonies were used to hold the *demes* together. Foreigners were given citizenship according to the district of their residency, and almost overnight, the number of those eligible for participation in civic activities increased, as citizenship was granted to many who had previously been excluded. Through the policies of the Assembly, local villages and city districts (*demes*) became the basis for *citizenship*. *Citizenship* was bestowed on eighteen-year-old males whose fathers presented them to the *deme* bodies. In effect, the granting of citizenship now by-passed traditional clan and religious leaders, placing the granting of citizenship in the hands of the political leaders of the new political districts. Instead of being known by the name of his father, the citizen became known by the name of his district, or his *deme*.

Military structure was reformed with the addition of ten *strategoi*—one general selected from each of the ten new tribes. The *polemarch* and the ten generals became a command structure for the army. A *Council of 500*, made up of fifty representatives from the new mixed tribes, replaced the *Council of 400 (boulê)* that had been created by Solon, and gathered most of its powers from the Areopagus. Members of the *Council of 500* were selected by lot to serve for a term of one year. The process of selection was called *sortition,* as names or numbers were placed on shards and then drawn at random from among the eligible citizens who were thirty or older; henceforth, every citizen had an equal chance of serving in the government. During Solon's time, the *sortition* (selection by lot) was a means of resolving conflicts between ambitious individuals and groups who were competing for select positions such as magistrates.

During Cleisthenes' time, selection by lot was used to choose among all citizens to serve in the Assembly and in the *Council of 500,* and also became a popular means for jury selection in the people's court. However, five hundred was difficult number to manage so it was decided that each tribe would represent the whole Council for one tenth of the year. During each tribe's term of service, its members were given the title *prytaneis*, which designated a period of time somewhat like a month, and each day that the Council was in session a new president and secretary were chosen by lot. "The Council, or executive body of the Assembly, was composed of men chosen by lot, and a new *epistatês* ("president") of the Council was chosen by lot daily" (Lanni, 2006, p. 31).

The Assembly, made up of all eligible citizens, was so large that should everyone eligible actually attend, it would consist of over thirty thousand individuals. The *thetes*, or the fourth class, was the excluded group, while the archonship and the Areopagus remained as the stronghold of the aristocracy, but its power to act or to direct the affairs of state was taken away. The archons (the magistrates) were elected directly by the *Assembly* and would be chosen by *lot* from the 500 candidates who had been previously elected, and in 457 BCE the office of *archon* was expanded to include members of the third class. The election of magistrates was an important step toward democracy, as it was used to shift control of the government from the aristocrats to the citizens. This expansion meant that the office of archon had lost much of its influence and had become mainly ceremonial. The only remaining power of the archon was to serve as a type of grand jury that conduced preliminary duties called *anakrisis*, but despite the diminishing powers of the archon, it continued to exist as an office in other cities in Greece, and in some cities, continued to exist into the Hellenistic Age.

The work of stripping the aristocracy of its exclusive political power would continue under Pericles, but the Areopagus continued to exist for another seventeen years after the Peloponnesian War. This indicated that the political strength of the citizen masses had increased, and attacks against the power of the aristocracy continued to grew. The administrative power of the ruling class was charged with corruption. During in the archonship of Konon (462/1 BCE) the Areopagus was stripped of all its acquired prerogatives, which were now assigned to the Council of the 500, to the Assembly and to the law courts.

The Civism of Cleisthenes

Besides the creation of an expanded and strengthened democratic system, Cleisthenes centered his new citizenship on the principle of *equality* (*Isonomia*) or the equal rights of all citizens. This right was so powerful in its *civism* perceptions that even Alexander the Great would find it impossible to discount. To establish this principle, Cleisthenes had to create a broad power base in Athens by convincing the masses of the lower classes that he would help them to gain political power. He began to build this power base by pledging that he would become the champion of the people over the aristocrats. This commitment created a new understanding that political power was to reside in the hands of the citizens, which would allow them a greater participation in the affairs of the city–state.

Cleisthenes' laws created a new democratic *civism* that became grounded in the idea that common citizens were capable of ruling themselves. Henceforth, huge numbers of citizens were admitted into the Assembly on designated days to hear speakers argue for and against issues submitted by the Council. The final decisions on these matters were determined by the casting of citizens' ballots. The most serious actions of the citizens' Assembly related to issues of war and peace and the voting of resources in support of their decisions. While the influence of the aristocracy still carried a great deal of influence, the new democratic *civism* projected a shared perception that the common people were now in control of the state's destiny.

In addition, citizens were chosen by lot to serve as officers of the Council and Assembly, which included those officials assigned to keep order over a somewhat unruly crowd in the Assembly. More important, those serving in the Assembly were required to render their votes based on the merits of the arguments made by different sides supporting or opposing an issue. The rendering of such judgments required knowledge of past events and the skills of logic. This requirement could, under some circumstances, prove to be a very dangerous precedent since such complexities required an advanced civic education. In other words, most of the citizens of Athens serving in the Assembly were not prepared to analyze or to judge the merits of complex arguments, and therefore were in danger of rendering faulty decisions. In most cases, however, the issues before the Assembly only required a general knowledge, or a decision based on common sense. It also became a common practice in the Assembly to have complex issues or problems presented by "experts" in the hope that they could help educate the citizen audience before they voted.

In the course of time, Cleisthenes' *civism* began the process of changing the mind–set of the people from a tribal mind–set to a citizenship mind–set. In other words, each individual citizen, regardless of tribe, was to participate in making decisions that could affect the fate of the entire community. This important change impacted the individual's social and political psychology (*civism*), which could only take place through a reorganization of Athenian society. Cleisthenes thereby mandated the creation of ten new tribes so that the citizens of the demes would follow one another instead of following only the leaders of their own particular kinship group. The reformulation of the tribes was intended to broaden the individual's perception of his kinship ties beyond the traditional localism, as well as to weaken family influences in political matters. This reform was implemented by expanding the importance of those relationships to more distant tribesmen, especially those relationships that would develop into new social, economic and political linkages. These changes were necessary in order to modernize Athenian society to meet the growing complexities of urban and cosmopolitan developments, but these changes did not alter the sanguine nature of Athenian citizenship.

In addition, the *civism* of Cleisthenes required that citizens accept the perception that they were the defenders of the democratic constitution, which caused them to establishing the law of *ostracism*. According to this law, powerful individuals could be forced into exile for a long duration of time as a means of protecting the state. This law was first used against the relatives of Peisistratus, and over time, it became applied to any individual deemed by any citizen to be a threat to the welfare of the state. Therefore whenever a vote of ostracism was called, it was for the purpose of removing an internal threat to the democracy. Normally, such a vote was taken in the Assembly without provision for appeal; however, exiled citizens could be recalled because of changes in citizenship body sentiment. Sentiment, an important result and expression of *civism*, also was a factor related to politics and to the changing perceptions regarding what was good for the welfare of citizens and for their city–state. Cleisthenes' reforms led to the formation of a strong democratic sentiment that would be more powerfully expressed in the fifth century following the defeat of the Persians.

Cleisthenes *civism* was expressed in a series of checks and balances, which also included a randomization process through the application of an allotment. Selection by lot was a means of insuring that the various schemes of powerful individuals could not succeed in exercising an unfair political influence through such means as bribery. Bribery was a common means of securing a favorable outcome in politics and was used in the ancient world to influence elections, as well as jury selection. The selection of a jury was an attempt to make sure that jurors could not be bribed. The allotment was a reform that was based on a new democratic *civism* that created the perception that any citizen selected by lot for jury duty was capable of serving on a jury and was capable of honestly and fairly deciding the outcome of a conflict between citizens.

Indirectly, democracy, combined with the allotment, helped to fuel a new demand for additional educational resources, and these resources would become aimed at developing skills related to public speaking. This demand resulted from placing citizens in a position where they might be called on to ask questions, to explain their opinions, to make an argument, to present a proposal, or to challenge a proposition. In addition, this demand had the effect of attracting ambitious individuals to the city, including teachers who were enticed to come to Athens by the growing demand for higher forms of education. With the advent of the democratic system, oral communications and skills associated with argumentation were becoming critical aspects of a "good" education, which helped to establish the perception that a good leader was a good speaker. Consequently, the new *civism* created by Cleisthenes' democratic reforms included the perception that leadership required oral communication skills; therefore, leadership skills could be acquired through educational means.

Despite his best intentions, Cleisthenes did not foresee the vulnerabilities that would arise when an uneducated population took the reigns of political power, as citizens now became subject to the various influences that they had never experienced before. Nor did Cleisthenes realize that his reforms would lead to new and unexpected changes that would begin to appeal to the public in unanticipated ways. For example, Cleisthenes did not recognize the extent to which his reforms would create new forms of *individualism* that would overpower the collective foundations of the tribal state.

After Cleisthenes retired from public office, the leadership in the polis embraced new classes of politicians that served various interests and clienteles. Many of these politicians had become educated in the skills of public speaking, but not in the morals and ethics of self–sacrifice for the good of the state. These men would use their oratory skills as the basis of their political power, and in some cases they would use their talents to beguile the citizen body into making some very bad decisions, which could lead the Athenian democracy to the brink of extinction.

THE REAL EXPRESSIONS OF CIVISM

Part III
The Golden Age of Athenian Democracy

The history of the democratic doctrine furnishes a striking example of an intellectual system blown about by the social wind.

—Bertrand de Jouvenel

Pericles presents life of Athens as an ideal balance between private and public, and also between cultural and political. The Athenian citizen, it is said, is well informed about public affairs and brave in war, but also loves the beautiful and things of the mind. He enjoys a vigorous public life, of contests and festivals, but also grace and beauty in domestic life (Burrow, 2008, p. 31).

Anaxagoras, an Ionian philosopher from Clazomenae in Asia Minor, arrived in Athens shortly after the end of the Persian War. As a scientist, Anaxagoras probed into every issue and idea about human and natural life and he gained a reputation for raising questions that challenged traditional and religious beliefs. In addition, he had a style and manner of conducting himself with great dignity, giving the impression that he had great confidence as expressed through his bearing. Anaxagoras' manner of speaking, as well as his thinking on political and social issues, cast a long shadow of influence over Pericles. During his life in political office, Pericles, at times, was criticized for his style of addressing every issue from a rational perspective. At the same time, Pericles was flexible in that he encouraged citizens to think for themselves as a characteristic of their democratic citizenship in order to help them to sort out issues, even if that meant that citizenship reasoning created a degree of social and political disunity. This notion suggested that Pericles was one of the world's first political leaders to become a teacher of *civism* through his attempt to model himself as an ideal democratic leader. The leadership of Pericles may be contrasted with that of Cimon, who represented a conservative and ancient *areté* of the Homeric tradition. From a personality perspective, Pericles was deliberate, cautious, and reflective in his reactions, while Cimon was dashing, daring, and reckless.

Pericles' vision of a new Athenian society helped to shape the classical enlightenment, which came into full fruition at this time. His favorite activity was to use his home to assemble his friends, as well as those who assisted him in the political affairs of the state or in his political duties, for discussions of an artistic or intellectual nature. His inner circle of friends included his teachers Damon, and Anaxagoras, as well as leaders of the Enlightenment, including Protagoras, Zeno of Elea, and the tragic poets Aeschylus and Sophocles (also a co–general), as well as the historians, Herodotus, and Lampon (the mystical seer and high priest of religion). These individuals alone helped in planning an ideal city in Italy. Protagoras and Pericles may have held extensive discussions on the moral implications of citizenship and the nature of an ideal citizenship education (*civism*) for creating the proper mind–set for democratic individuals living in a democratic society.

The expanded democracy in Athens had the effect of energizing its citizens in the defense of the city, and gave the Athenians a reputation of power and strength. As time passed, the laws of citizenship became more exclusive so that only one fifth of the population could acquire that status, as Athenian citizenship was ancestral or kinship (sanguine) in nature. Because kinship was the basis of citizenship, Athenian *civism* was both racial and ethnic in its perception and in its expressions, but it also acquired some of the elements of rational reasoning that were derived from philosophical influences that had arrived in Athens in the sixth century from the Ionian cities of Asia Minor.

SEVEN

Prelude to the Golden Age of Pericles

The citizens of the polis shared their ethnic identity (language, culture, history, religion) with the citizens of other city–states within the region, whereas their sense of political identity (including patriotism) was centered on the polis itself and separated any polis from all its neighbours..
—Mogens Herman Hansen

In the 10th century BCE a group of indo–Europeans had settled in Asia Minor in the region known today as Iran. In 612 BCE, a related people, known as the Medes, laid down the foundation for a Persian empire when they joined forces with the Babylonians to defeat the powerful Assyrian empire. A new empire would emerge under Cyrus II, who staged a successful revolt that created the province of Media, which was the first province (satrapies) of the Persian Empire. In 546 BCE, Cyrus extended his empire to include the lands of the Lydian King to the west, which brought the Greek cities in Asia Minor into conflict with the rising Persian Empire; however, due to intervening confrontations this collision of cultures would be delayed until the rule of Darius I (522–489 BCE). King Darius, "the Great King", decided to expand to the west after the Ionian cities within his domain staged a revolt in 499 BCE. The decision to invade Greece was triggered by the intervention of main land Greeks who attempted to aid their Ionian kinsmen within Darius' domain.

King Darius I of Persia invaded the Greek mainland in 512 BCE, which was caused by his determination to subdue the rebellious Greek cities within his domain and by the wealth of the mainland Greek city–states. Wanting to punish the Greeks for their interference, Darius now decided to expand his empire to the west to include the mainland Greeks across the Aegean Sea. His decision to conquer the Greeks may have been influenced by Hippias (the son of the tyrant Peisistratus), who arrived in Persia in 506 BCE, and who urged the king to expand his empire on the Greek mainland in a bid for his own return to power in Athens.

Darius landed his naval forces at Marathon, where he believed the Persian cavalry would have an advantage. The Athenians under the leadership of Miltiades, the father of Cimon, engaged invading forces and managed to defeat them in this great heroic battle. This embarrassing setback would lead Xerxes, the son of Darius, to plan a greater and overwhelming invasion consisting of tens of thousands of men and hundreds of invading ships. He built a bridge across the Hellespont and forced alliances with Thrace and Macedon. The threat of invasion had the effect of forcing the Greek cities into a united front to drive the Persians from Greece. The final turning point of the war occurred in 480 BCE when a Greek fleet, under the leadership of Themistocles, defeated and destroyed a larger Persian fleet at Salamis.

Factional Politics in Greece

The outcome of the Persian War led to some important political and economic repercussions, which allowed the Athenians to begin to develop a trading–empire. Internally, the Persian War would instigate a great struggle for the political control of Athens between the conservative forces of Aristides and the democratic forces of Themistocles. The aristocratic families mainly allied with Aristides, but some (the Alcmaeonids, the family of Pericles) allied with Themistocles. As a result, a struggle for power set aristocratic family against family, which led to the formation of two powerful political factions or blocks. The Alcmaeonids, under the leadership of Pericles, opposed the conservatives who had lined up under the leadership of the noble Cimon.

Aristides was moderate in his views and had been aligned with Cleisthenes, also an Alcmaeonid descendant. At this time, Aristides had concluded that democratic reforms had gone too far. Themistocles, also of noble background, helped to create the naval resources that were credited with the defeat of the Persians at Salamis. In addition, Themistocles had helped to create the harbor at Piraeus, and was credited with convincing the Athenians to use the accumulated wealth from their silver mines to build war vessels to defeat the Persian navy. In the process of building the parallel walls around Athens and Piraeus the Athenians managed to enflame the jealousy of the Spartans.

Themistocles proved to be a genius, but also a treacherous manipulator. He arranged for the ostracism of Aristides, which would allow him to freely pursue his plan to defeat the Persians by building Athenian naval forces; however, once the war threatened the survival of Athens, he recalled Aristides. After the war, the Athenian and Spartan oligarchs conspired to drive Themistocles from Greece. The enemies of Themistocles successfully exiled him when it was discovered that Themistocles had been involved in a scheme to embezzle funds and when the Spartans found evidence that he was planning to commit an act of treason against the Athenians. Themistocles fled Greece and entered the service of the Persian king, where he contributed to a scheme to subjugate the Greeks. After Themistocles' death in 449 BCE, the leadership of the democratic forces in Athens fell to Ephialtes, who opposed Cimon, in part, because of Cimon's Spartan connection.

Cimon lost his popularity in Athens when he recommended reconciliation with the Spartans. Cimon's downfall came when he convinced the Athenians to aid the Spartans in putting down a helot revolt. The Spartans dismissed Cimon and the Athenians, which was viewed as an insult to the Athenians. This insult led to Cimon's disgrace and to his political downfall. He was ostracized in 461 BCE and fled Athens. Pericles, who may have helped to engineer the ostracism of Cimon, was working to reduce conservative political influence so that he and the democrats could secure a more powerful political foothold in Athens.

The Reforms of Ephialtes

Little is known about Ephialtes, except that he came from a poor family and that he was considered to be an incorruptible politician who represented the political interests of the democratic classes in Athens. With the passing of Themistocles and Aristides, Ephialtes came to power for a short time to lead the government in Athens; however, he engaged in a bitter feud with the Areopagus aristocrats, which cost him his life. In 462 BCE he sentenced some of the Areopagus members to death and further weakened what remained of Areopagus political power. At this time, the lower social classes, the *zeugitai* and the *thetes,* were pressuring for a greater voice in the Athenian government. In response to this pressure, aristocratic resentment grew so intense that Ephialtes was assassinated in the public market place, which was a shocking event in Greek politics. The assassination of Ephialtes had the effect of opening the way for Pericles to take over the democratic leadership movement in Athens.

Before he died, Ephialtes helped to expand the power of the people of the lower classes by forcing changes that allowed juries, chosen by lot, to rule on the actions of the magistrates and the generals. The lower classes also gained the power to judge the conduct of politicians by forcing them to appear before the popular court, the *dikastêria*. In other words, the *dikastêria* became the place where officials (magistrates and military commanders) were examined after serving in public positions. This examination, the *euthynai*, was aimed at uncovering any irregularities that may have occurred in fiscal accounts and also judged any or all allegations of misconduct. Of equal importance, this court also heard the *euthynai* of the Athenian generals who led armies in battle. This hearing was very threatening to those military leaders who had lost men in battle or commanders who were accused of dishonoring Athens on the battlefield. As a consequence of this court, it was not uncommon for military commanders to voluntarily go into exile rather than to return to Athens. In addition, this court conducted the *dokimasiai*, which was an examination of officials that was held between the election to office and the beginning of the official term of office. The establishment of this court had the effect of advancing the Athenian democratic system by placing the fate of magistrates and military commanders in the hands of the *demos*, which gave the common classes virtual control over the Athenian government.

The power struggle between the oligarchs and the democrats in Athens remained unsettled for the time being, while under the surface these social class conflicts would continue to smolder, but those citizens who were discontent with the growing democratic political movement in Athens had other choices. These choices consisted of moving to other city–states. Greece contained more than fourteen hundred city–states with alternative forms of government that characterized the differences between one city–state and another. Citizens disgruntled with their form of homeland rule could relocate to another polis from within that same tribal identity. "Law was always the law of a regime, regimes change overnight and a disgruntled oligarch or democrat could always find a regime that suited him by walking up the road to a more congenial *polis*" (McClelland, 1996, p. 11). The opportunity to change city–state citizenship could provide the means for a voluntary exile, and this condition served as a safety valve that helped to relieve the pressure of civic unrest and to bring about a degree of social harmony.

The Delian League

The Golden Age of Athens (480-399 BCE) began with the defeat of the Persians and the supremacy of the Greek navy, which now ruled the waterways and controlled much of Mediterranean trade and commerce. This hegemony was strengthened with the further development of the Delian League, which derived its name from the Ionian treasury located on the island of Delos. The original purpose of the league was to provide for a common defense and for shipbuilding activities for its member cities. As the danger from Persia diminished after the war, some members of the league began to question the role and the need to continue such a league. While intermittent warfare would continue between the Persians and the Greeks, the Persians would never again be able to muster such resources as it had in 480 BCE.

For the Athenians, the end of the Persian War did not suggest that the Delian League should be weakened or terminated. Shortly after the war, the Athenians were moving into a possibly dangerous military conflict with the Spartans. At this time, the Spartans began to view the rising wealth and the growing naval power of Athens with suspicion. The Spartans did not possess warships, nor did they surround their city with defensive walls. As resentments and suspicions grew, the Athenians looked to the Delian League as an important source of their economic and military power, while at the same time, the Spartans were being driven to a state of hostility by their league allies.

The Sources of Democratic Civism

The two invasions by the Persians (at Marathon and by land invasion over the Hellespont) had a dramatic effect on the Greeks that would change their perceptions about themselves and about the outside world. According Greek perceptions, the Persians represented a barbaric people and an "Oriental despotism." As an imperial power, they intended to destroy the Greeks and to enslave their city–states. Because the Persians represented a much larger and more powerful military force than any combined force that the Greeks could assemble, victories in Marathon and at Salamis stood as divine proof of Greek superiority. This perception had the effect of advancing a powerful sense of a Panhellenic shared identity and patriotism. This *civism* was based on a mind–set that stated that regardless of Greek differences and their past grievances, the Greeks would, in times of danger, replace provincial hostility with Panhellenic unity in order to oppose external threats.

Temporarily, the war with the Persians united all political factions in Athens, but the victory over the Persians also produced a new political factionalism and a renewed inter–city–state struggle to control the Athenian government, which was expressed by the ongoing class war struggle. "To judge from our sources, most poleis were split into two rival poleis, one of the rich, who supported oligarchy, and one of the poor, who preferred democracy" (Hansen, 2006, p. 125). This class struggle in Athens was illustrated by the competing views of Aristides and Themistocles.

Once political leadership in Athens fell to Ephialtes, he promoted political reforms that exasperated conflict between the conservatives and democrats, which became centered in the popular courts. Because of the accountability requirements associated with the *euthynai* and the *dokimasiai*, the courts, made up of juries appointed by lot, allowed the democrats to gain a great advantage over the oligarchs. "Vigilance was clearly a necessity. After all, most of these citizens were pure amateurs, and, even assuming their essential honesty, the likelihood of an irregularity of some kind must have been very clear" (Jones, 2008, p. 34). Citizen's accountability contributed to a new democratic *civism* based on the perception that all citizens were politically, constitutionally, or legally equal. *Equality*, the democratic demand for equal political and legal rights, was an attempt to balance the influence of opposing social or economic groups in the hope of achieving a higher level of social justice aimed at producing a higher level of social harmony. In other words, democratic forms came to rely on certain built–in checks and balances that had the effect of preventing the concentration of power from getting into the hands of one person or a single social group. Democratic *civism*, according to these checks and balances, came to rest on the idea that every social class should have a voice in politics and some means to defend itself against constitutional defects. This *civism* created a commonly held perception that institutional reforms could be applied to remedy social injustice.

Democratic citizenship, in other words, was accompanied by a unique expression of a new democratic *civism* that was aimed at correcting perceived, as well as actual social injustices. This transformation indicated the great distance to which Athenian society had moved in just two centuries. Earlier in its history, Athenian polis citizenship, like that of almost all of the Greek city–states was associated with military service, or the military classes; however, in the Classical period of the fifth century BCE, Athenian democratic citizenship would include all native–born citizens. "In the Classical democratic polis political rights were granted to all native–born citizens, so that not only the hoplites but also the light–armed and the rowers had access to the political institutions" (Hansen, 2006, p. 117). This radical political change opened the way for the establishment of the first democratic political system in Europe, and as a result, almost every free person living in Athens gained a stake in the future success of the Athenian polis.

Eight

The Golden Age of Pericles

When Pericles, Aspasia, Pheidias, Anaxagoras, and Socrates attended a play by Euripides in the Theater of Dionysus, Athens could see visibly the zenith and unity of the life of Greece—statesmanship, art, science, philosophy, literature, religion, and morals living no separate career as in the pages of chronicles, but woven into one many–colored fabric of a nation's history.
—Will Durant

Pericles (c. 494 – 429 BCE) was born three years before the battle of Marathon to Xanthippus and Agariste. Agariste was the niece of Cleisthenes and was the namesake of Agariste of Sicyon, the wife of Megacles. "In the first decade of the fifth century, about 494 BCE, the pregnant Agariste, daughter of Hippocrates, dreamed she gave birth to a lion. In a few days, as Herodotus tells the story she presented her husband, Xanthippus, with a son, whom they named Pericles" (Kagan, 1991, p. 11). Pericles was caught up in politics that would change the course of Athenian history and the development of democratic citizenship; his life, however, became one of contradictions. The question remains: Who was Pericles? Most ancient sources agree that he was a man of rank, ability, and integrity who completed the democratic reforms and led Athens to its greatest heights of power and cultural achievement in which the Age of Pericles became known as the Classical or Golden Age of Athens. Thucydides called him one of the Athenian generals. He was described as honest, devoted to politics, an excellent speaker, dedicated to the reconstruction of Athens, cautious in military and foreign affairs, a gentleman, and a rational thinker.

As a youth, Pericles received every educational advantage; for example, he formed a friendship with the philosopher Anaxagoras, who helped to develop his keen interest in ideas; consequently, he learned to approach politics with deliberation and with great care. His music teacher, Damon, had the reputation of being a most accomplished man in every way, as well as a musician, and a companion of inestimable value for young men, and Plato described him as "the wisest of all citizens." According to Kagan (1991), "Damon taught that different kinds of music express different elements of human character, and Plato reports his observation that 'when modes of music change, the fundamental mores of the state always change with them'" (Ibid., p. 22). Music and gymnastics had been the foundation of Greek education, and music was taught as a means of developing the moral character of young men. Music combined with gymnastics may have been one of the oldest forms of ancient *civism*. Damon used music to shape Pericles' attitudes on life and on practical political issues. Some scholars have suggested that Damon was the source of the idea of paying jurors for their daily service to the state, which allowed the lower classes to take part in the politics of Athens.

Pericles first gained notoriety in association with the public arts as a patron who was selected to help produce a festival in 472 BCE. At this time Pericles was recognized as a person of considerable wealth who was obligated to provide a portion of it for the public good in a type of wealth tax called *leiturgia*. Pericles was selected to assemble the chorus for the *Persians* by Aeschylus. The play depicted contemporary life and illustrated the suffering of Persian wives in the great defeat and loss of lives at Salamis. The play reminded the Athenians of their great victory and the glory that had come to them despite their destroyed city. Aeschylus won first prize for his play, and Pericles' successful association with Aeschylus made him a man of influence. To further his career, Pericles turned to military service, which led him to be elected to the position of Athenian general. Pericles gained further notoriety as one of the public prosecutors of Cimon in 463 BCE, and this role allowed Pericles to demonstrate his moderation in politics. Shortly after coming to power, Pericles recalled Cimon from his exile after his conviction and allowed him to return to military service. Pericles rewarded the service of Cimon after his death with a state funeral and full military honors, which had the effect of lessening tensions between the democrats and the oligarchs.

After securing an honorable reputation as one of the ten generals, Pericles became the most powerful politician in Athens, a politician willing to use honorable and expedient means to persuade others to help achieve his desired goals. Because of his political skills, Athens was provided with a mixture of democratic privilege, which was combined with efficiencies of an enlightened authoritarian executive. Some might say that he was a dictator who was willing to act without hesitation. The result was a long period of good government that came to rest on a growing body of enfranchised free citizens.

Periclean Civism

The Periclean democracy was based on the assumption that politics was a natural aspect of human nature and that man was designed by nature to live in a community setting. The rise of democracy that accompanied the development of the polis required modifications in traditional social understanding to accommodate the growth of a broader and more inclusive community, and the Assembly and the courts reflected these advancements. Democratic participation in the affairs of the polis required the citizens to exercise their judgment within the decision–making process that determined the action and even the fate of the polis. "Rather, that faith was grounded in the assumptions that the collective wisdom of a large group was inherently greater than the wisdom of any of its parts. This conviction is one of the central egalitarian tenets of Athenian political ideology" (Ober, 1989, p. 163).

While equality was the basis of democratic rule, not all individuals shared in their ability to discriminate between alternative arguments or actions to be taken to resolve public issues or conflicts. Pericles was aware of the need to advance the civic education of Athenian citizens, and he did all that he could to set an example and to encourage a new form of *civism* based on his example and his public works. He was hampered in this work by the fact that education was the exclusive domain of the aristocratic classes and that he was not able to change this condition. At the same time, his vision for the future of the Athenian democracy may have included some form of an advanced *civism*. During his lifetime, he was willing to encourage experiments with planned urban development and the development of ideal laws and constitutions. His discussions with his friends may have included topics pertaining to moral and character education and to whether or not virtue could be taught to all citizens through some form of universal public education. He devised programs for the migration of Athenian citizens that helped to spread the idea of democracy to the outlying Greek colonies.

By 440 BCE Pericles had been in power for two decades. He was at the height of his influence and was at the center of the Greek Enlightenment. By this time his leading critics had been exiled and he felt free to give full reign to the glorification of Athens as the beacon of civilized life in the Aegean world. Some feared that his power was so great that he could become a tyrant or a king, and some called him a dictator. His critics chastised him for his virtues and his public image was that of an arrogant aristocrat because of his seemingly detachment from the social affairs of the city. He avoided drinking parties and stayed away from the activities of the upper classes.

Pericles envisioned a reshaping of the Greek world in which a more orderly and a more rational society would emerge based on ideals of a complete democracy. The free citizens, whose sovereignty allowed them to exercise their will according to ideal polis civic virtues, would be used to create the ideal state and would create this new order based on education. According to this vision, the community or state was to serve as the source of virtue and not the family or the tribe, nor was Homer's ideal of individual courage and heroism sufficient for this new age.

The virtues of an ideal community were reflected in the laws of the state and in the actions of the people as expressed through the Assembly. The polis, community or state, would guarantee each citizen protection against injustice, factionalism, and civil strife. Ideal democratic citizens would be dedicated to the polis, which would give them their sense of identity and direction. Although free to act in their own self–interest, the citizens would be educated to sacrifice for the collective good and to forego a life of self–indulgence. The leaders of the state were to be the educators, who would teach the people to act in accordance with the virtues of democracy.

Pericles realized that there must be some form of education to prepare citizens for citizenship and he looked to Protagoras for his recommendations in this regard and rejected the severity of the Spartan system, which was completely dedicated to a *civism* of a military type. In its place, he favored an indirect *civism* that allowed for freedom of choice while surrounding the citizens with models of virtue, not too far removed from some of the ideas of Plato.

Pericles was determined to "teach" the citizens of Athens to work together for the good of the city and to convince individuals that they were dependent upon each other for the success and the defense of the city. In addition, he worked to advance participation in the affairs of the community by shaping the democracy on a decision making model that required citizens to develop their skills in rational thought and the application of good judgment. Knowledge and informal forms of education were the pillars of his vision for the advancement of the civic community that he hoped to build. He would teach the people through his speeches, deeds, and his public works that would dominate the public spaces in Athens. In the Funeral Oration, Pericles is reported to have used the burial of the men who fell at Samos to explain why democratic citizens must be willing to sacrifice for their city. He compared the educational system of the Spartans with the freedom of the Athenians and claimed that the Athenians were superior to the Spartans because their choice to sacrifice for the community was based on rational thought and a willingness to take risks to preserve their freedoms.

He argued that the excellence of the polis was an excellence of *equality* in the political affairs of the state and that all citizens must be prepared to perform their duties of citizenship as a democratic *areté* based on political rights and responsibilities. He explained that citizenship must not be based on class or clan, but on the good reputation of their city, and that democracy was to be used as a means to elevate all citizens to the level of nobility that had previously been reserved for the aristocracy. In other words, human beings possessed a divine nature that could be strengthened through appropriate means. Like the philosophers, he was thinking in terms of a form of moral and character education.

According to Pericles' unfulfilled vision, the citizen was not to be educated as a generalist, but was to be good at many things, including the art of war and peace. This education would require learning in speaking, reasoning, aesthetics, athletics, and military science. More important still, they were to learn to work together as a collective solidarity that required the sacrifice of self–interest and greed to the call of a higher order of accomplishment.

The highest reward for the citizen was to die in the service of the state, as that represented the virtue of the common good, and freedom demanded such a sacrifice in times of danger and threat. Virtue and immortality were no longer to be expressed in terms of individual recognition, but in a collective understanding related to citizenship and democracy. In a democracy all citizens are equal before the law and there is no superiority in regard to kinship or class. But at the same time, democracy must make space for individual expression, privacy, freedom from suspicion, and a wider acceptance of personal behaviors. Respect for the law was the highest civic value, and respect was based on thoughtful reasoning, rather than fear or forced obedience.

Civism as Public Works

For four decades, Pericles attempted to give direction and form to the Athenian democracy before he died in the plague. During that time, he strove to educate Athenian citizens through his example and through his vision as was expressed in his public works. His goal was to help advance rational thought as a means of preparing the citizens of Athens to exercise their civic responsibilities. His only political power was his persuasive skills and the application of rational argument to the issues and problems facing Athens. The Assembly decided almost everything by a majority vote, but for thirty years, the Athenians kept re-electing Pericles to a position of leadership, and even when they dismissed him, he was soon recalled. By 448 BCE Pericles and Athens were at the height of prestige and power. The "first" Peloponnesian War was coming to an end and Athens was in possession of a powerful navy that insured the solidarity of its empire in the Aegean Sea. The rebellious cities of Samos and Byzantium had been returned to the alliance and Pericles was about to deliver his famous Funeral Oration that extolled the virtues of democracy and democratic citizenship. Tribute from the empire flowed into Athens and was to be used to rebuild the city, especially the temples and the acropolis that had been destroyed by the Persians.

The vision of Pericles demanded that Athens become the teacher of the Greek world, which was to become a new world of the mind and the spirit that would be advanced through a collective intelligence. Pericles had launched a great experiment in civic achievement that was aimed at establishing a higher level of education, citizenship, *civism*, and civilization. The reconstruction of Athens provided Pericles with an opportunity to express his democratic vision for the city through great public works. The Athenians swore an *oath at Plataea* that they would not rebuild their temples as a tribute to those who died in the war of liberation to free themselves from the Persian aggression. Following the peace with Persia, the Panhellenic Congress had issued the Papyrus Decree that allowed Pericles to free the Athenians from the oath at Plataea and to use the Delian treasury to honor the oath. Pericles would not only reconstruct the destroyed temples, but would transform Athens into a great city as the leader of a great empire. The building program was to become a means of educating the citizens of Greece in the virtues of the polis, to celebrate democracy as superior to oligarchy, and to advance Panhellenic relationships. In particular, the reconstruction of the Parthenon was to express the virtues of democratic rule. The building and art were to glorify a political ideology, along with its religious implications. In addition, the Parthenon would house the treasury, which was the symbolic center of the empire.

Athena, depicted as the virgin warrior, came to represent the changing role that the empire played in the city-state. She signified a greater naval power, which also fostered trade, commerce, and wealth. In addition, she was the goddess of the enlightenment in which the arts and sciences were emphasized as an aspect of reasoned thought and wisdom. "The Parthenon was meant to achieve visually what the Funeral Oration aimed at orally: the depiction, explanation, and celebration of the Athenian imperial democracy" (Kagan, 1991, p. 161). It was to be *civism* in a visual form that was applied as a means of constantly reinforcing the virtues of the new state. This suggests that learning in the fifth century was not dependent on literary forms, but relied on hearing and seeing. In addition, there were many other forms of *civism* including poetry, song, playacting, religious festivals, competitions, speechmaking, assembly meetings, and statues and monuments based on heroic expressions.

These forms of expression were found everywhere within public spaces and their messages were repeated a thousand times a year and many times a day. They could not be avoided as they were expressed in a language that could not be mistaken or misinterpreted. Moreover, they were associated with religion and religion dominated ancient society. "From this point of view, the juxtaposition of human beings with divinities may be seen as part of the patriotic symbolism that dominates the temple, connecting all the people of the Athenian democracy to their heroic ancestors and the victorious goddess who is their patron and symbol of wisdom and intelligence" (Ibid., p. 166).

Literary expressions of *civism* also were found in the writings of Protagoras, the close friend of Pericles, who incorporated civic education into aspects of the school education, which also was designed to advance the virtues of democracy. It may have been Protagoras who convinced Pericles that democracy must be grounded in classroom instruction, thus suggesting that Protagoras was one of the fathers of *civism* as it was expressed in lower and higher education. Despite his belief that political virtues were unequally distributed within the population, he, like Pericles, was convinced that education was the best means of preserving and advancing the democracy. "Not only did he believe such education to be possible, he felt it necessary for a healthy political society" (Ibid., p. 167). Protagoras' instruction was aimed at advancing the reasoning powers of the average person, which would encourage him to become involved in the affairs of the polis. This type of education was to extend from cradle to grave and was to immerse the citizen in ideal models of what was expected within the polis.

Pericles built a music hall called the Odeum, close to the Acropolis, to celebrate victories over the barbarians and the forces of darkness. The décor of the Odeum included masts of destroyed Persian ships at Salamis. Damon, as was previously stated, had convinced Pericles that music had a great influence on the moral fabric of the society and changes in musical styles would change the values of the culture. With this in mind, Pericles wanted to present the best music that would inspire patriotism and to ban music that retarded the culture, or brought about its moral decay. Music and play performances, as aspects of *civism*, impacted those emotions, which could be used to inspire or retard patriotism so that they were deemed important aspects of ancient civic lessons.

The public appearances and the public performances of a leader were a means of affecting public perceptions and thereby they became an instrument of *civism*. The leader's ideal vision for the state was communicated to the public, in part, through the images that he used to communicate it to the public. The leader's vision suggested that certain values were worth striving toward, and such a vision, while it might never be attained, transformed the state into something that was either noble or base. Athena, for example, represented an early vision for its Athenian citizens of an idealized notion related to wisdom and war. The goodness of the Good state was found in these ideals and the strength of this vision could be used to transform the mind–set of its citizens.

In other words, Pericles would use many forms of *persuasion* to bring his vision of the state to fruition through a willing compliance of the people. He would allow the people ample freedom to make up their minds, but would use the resources of the state to direct their attention toward those virtues that he was attempting to engrain into the culture. He sought to inspire the citizens of Athens to seek a higher level of civilization through a new secular religion of the state without offending traditional values. He believed that the common man could be elevated to become more god–like through the processes and practices of an enlightened rationalism.

* * * *

The Golden Age of Athens would last for only seventy-five or eighty years, but within its timeframe in the western world the notions of *citizenship* and *civism* transformed Athens into a new civilization, which began to reshape notions related to the role of education in the development of *citizenship*. *Citizenship* continued to rely on a form of character education as prescribed by the poets, but it also contained a stronger emphasis on literacy, or the skills of reading and writing. With the increase of citizenship participation came the need to read public laws and decrees that were posted in the marketplace. *Civism* related to citizenship, required that individuals listen to counter arguments related to the actions of government and to make wise decisions if they chose to exercise their franchise.

Although *civism* was an idea that had not arrived institutionally, it was embedded in educational changes that emerged in the fifth and fourth centuries BCE. Pericles and his intellectual friends detected the seeds of *civism* in the ideas that they were discussing, especially in regard to the recommendations of Protagoras. The ideas of a political power would be established through the education of youth, and would become the focus of important intellectual debate that would reappear in the fourth century in the dialogues of Plato and the philosophers, who were interested in the idea of whether virtue could be taught or whether it was an innate aspect of a person's inherited nature.

During the fifth century, it was generally agreed that political virtue (*civism*) was a matter of class and good breeding and was mainly within the domain of the noble classes, despite the attempts of Pericles to elevate all citizens to this level of refinement. In the fourth century, the common citizens of Athens controlled the institutions of the state, the Assembly, the Council, and the courts, and the new elements of *civism* appeared in the arguments of the politicians and orators. *Civism* was found especially in the exchanges that took place before the people's court, as an expression of polis *dēmokratia*. Although the ruling power of the aristocracy remained an important aspect of political power, this power would soon fall to the growing middle class commercial interests within the urban setting of Athens. According to the ideology of the Athenian democracy, the people ruled through the Assembly, and at times it seemed to work as intended, but at other times the people were controlled by demagogues who intended to assert their will over the nebulous will of the people.

THE REAL EXPRESSIONS OF CIVISM

Part IV
The Decline of the Athenian Democracy

My own opinion is that when the whole state is on the right course it is a better thing for each separate individual than when private interests are satisfied but the state as a whole is going downhill.
—Pericles

Over time, the Athenian democracy expanded to include the lowest social classes, which included hired labor, or the class that served as rowers for the fleets that were used to expand and maintain the Athenian Empire. As the lower classes gained access to the participatory democracy, nothing was done educationally to prepare the new citizenship body for their civic responsibilities. As a consequence, the Athenian Assembly, the sovereign power of the state and the empire, was in danger of being manipulated by *demagogues* who used their speaking skills to whip up emotions in support of their aims. "Among their objections to the demagogues was that the latter did not appeal in their speeches to the rational intellect but to irrationality, in the form of the baser emotions and ingrained prejudices of their audiences" (Ober, 1989, p. 123). Weakness in the first democratic system of rule was caused by many social, economic, and political issues, including those related to a need for some type of state–sponsored civic education for the lower classes.

The Peloponnesian War was the culmination of the long brewing struggle between the two most powerful leagues in Greece under the leadership of Sparta and Athens. It became a war of empires and a war of attrition. For more than thirty years, the war encompassed many phases of fighting with some intermittent periods of calm and recuperation, as the balance of power and alliances shifted from one side to the other. The effect of the war was to reorganize the entire Greek world and its international relationships with its member states and more distant foreign powers.

The outcome of the struggle had the effect of weakening both sides, but in the long run the Spartans would emerge the military victors only to lay the ground–work for its own ultimate destruction. For the Athenians, the war meant opportunity to expand its naval empire, but politically it tested the flexibility of its democratic system, which caused some scholars to suggest that its excesses led to its own lack of self–restraint and moderation. The most shameful consequences of the war were the inhumane atrocities that were committed by both warring leagues and the devastation that destroyed cities and the civilization that had flowered just prior to the war. Due in part to the tremendous loss of life and property, the Greek city–states would never again fully recover its prosperity, political power, cultural drive, or creative energy.

The war placed a great strain on the Athenian democratic system, which had the effect of placing Athens on the road to ruin. This destruction caused Athenian society to degenerate into a class warfare that eventually led to an oligarchic coup and a dictatorship of tyrants that ended in a civil war.

Nine

The Athenian Empire

For almost three decades at the end of the fifth century B.C. the Athenian Empire fought the Spartan alliance in a terrible war that changed the Greek world and its civilization forever.
—Donald Kagan

The conflict between Athens and the Peloponnesians began almost as soon as the Persians had been driven out of Greece in a period called the *Pentecontaetia*, or the first phase of the larger and longer war. The conflict between Athens and Sparta grew more intense when the Athenians attempted to build defensive walls around Athens and Piraeus, as these walls threatened the ability of the Spartans to exercise the power of its land armies to settle disputes. In 465 BCE, a helot revolt was so severe that the Spartans were forced to call on their allies to re–establish their internal civil controls, but fearing an Athenian change of sides, the Spartans dismissed the Athenians in a disgraceful manner. These events set the stage for future conflicts that would begin in earnest starting in 459 BCE.

Conflicts with Peloponnesian allies had dragged on throughout the 450s and the 440s, and it eventually was ended by the thirty-year peace that was established in 446 BCE. During these troublesome decades the Athenians attempted to line up more allies and to continue to weaken the Spartan League. The rise of Athenian naval power caused concern in Persia, and in 457 BCE the Persian king sent an ambassador to bribe the Spartans to invade Attica as a means of drawing the Athenians away from Egypt. The growing fear of Athenian power in the Aegean, central and western Greece, and Sicily would eventually force the Spartans to abandon the peace and to end their isolation in 431 BCE. The end of the Pentecontaetia marked the beginning of the greater Peloponnesian War, as Athens and Sparta would enter a new stage of direct confrontation.

The source of this confrontation began when the Persians had looted and burned Athens and destroyed the Acropolis, including its temples and shrines. These sacred ruins remained untouched until 447 BCE, when Pericles began the reconstruction of the Parthenon, a symbol of the power of the city and a monument to its democracy. To finance the reconstruction of the sacred temple area of the acropolis, Pericles had the treasury at Delos moved to Athens so that he could use its wealth in the reconstruction. Pericles reasoned that Athens was the mother city of the Delian league, and as such, it represented all of its member city–states. But in reality, the reconstruction of Athens actually had the effect of reducing league member states to a state of subjugation in the service of the interests of Athens. Consequently, when some member city–states attempted to defy the authority of Athens or to withdraw from the League, they were severely punished and sometimes occupied.

The Delian League began as a voluntary alliance of approximately 140 city-states of various sizes based on tribal and/or commercial relationships. The underlying principle of the alliance was the agreement that the allies would share the same friends and the same enemies, making it a defensive and offensive league. The Athenians had long claimed leadership of the Ionian cities as the oldest center of the Ionian people. The relationship between the Ionian peoples was recognized in religious celebrations, which were celebrated on Delos and at Athens. The fundamental basis of the league was blood ties rather than political ideology, as the Athenians were willing to recognize any constitution as long as each entity stayed within the aims and organization of the league. As long as Athens, a democracy, was successful and strong, other states came to embrace its political system, allowing democracy to spread to other cities, including some cities in Peloponnesia.

Initially, league members were considered equals, but as time passed, the Athenians used their control of the votes of the smaller city–states to control the larger city–states' members. During the war, the league was deemed essential in the face of Persian military power, but when this threat diminished, some cities sought to reclaim their independence. The Athenians considered withdrawal from their league the same as reneging on a sworn oath. They refused to allow it and they were willing to use force to prevent it. Those seeking to reinstate their independence from Athens sometimes chose to associate with the competing Peloponnesian league, or attempted to establish some form of cross-league relationships to guarantee their neutrality.

The transformation from league to empire was triggered by the disastrous expedition to Egypt. Upon hearing of this fiasco, some of the allies used the crisis to rebel and to declare their independence. In 465 BCE, Athens laid siege to Thasos, a league member, which caused other league members to begin to fear the growing power of Athens as a threat to home rule. During the early phase of the Peloponnesian War, Athens became even more determined to keep its League intact and to gain greater control over the affairs of the member states, especially in regard to the payment of tribute. The Thasos rebellion, in particular, signaled the end of the confederation of cooperating city–states.

The Athenians reacted to the threat of withdrawal by attacking the rebel cities and punishing them by forcing democracies upon the rebel oligarchs who often ruled the local polis. In some cases, Athens confiscated lands and sent colonies made up of Athenians called *cleruchies,* and in other cases they established occupying military garrisons. Newly installed democratic regimes were required to swear an oath of loyalty to Athens to insure that the Athenians could enforce agreements and tribute. Over the years, more than twenty–four colonial settlements were established by Athens as a means of fortifying the league and in securing the shipping lanes to protect the corn route from the Black Sea. The Athenian empire became a reality by 440 BCE and constituted an extensive territorial domain. "It included large portions of what is now Libya, most of Cyprus, a more or less continuous strip of land up the western coast of Turkey from Rhodes to Hellespont, scattered settlements all around the Black Sea, the Gallipoli peninsula, a strip along the North Aegean coast, scattered settlements up the east coast of the Adriatic as far as Albania, most of the toe of Italy and most of Sicily" (Davies, 1993, p. 9).

The Civism of Might

Thucydides created speeches in which Pericles justified the empire as the means of providing Athens with pride, status, power, and wealth to become the greatest city of Greece. Aristophanes, in the *Wasp,* claimed that Athens had earned the right to an empire by defeating the Persians. The Athenians also claimed the right to enforce the empire, which meant that they were allowed to punish rebellious cities for failing to assert their freedom against the Persians and for refusing to make their required sacrifices on behalf of the empire. Pericles' Funeral Oration, as created by Thucydides in 431/0 BCE, asserted the rights of empire based on Athenian cultural leadership of the Greek world. The Athenian envoys to Sparta in 432 BCE justified the empire based on a despotic *civism* that claimed that Athens was less brutal than it might otherwise have been. Finally, the Athenians were willing to assert the argument of the dictators and tyrants, that "might makes right" based on the argument that powerful men and cities rule others when they can as it is "the rule of nature". The problem was that domination was equated with slavery and slavery was for barbarians and not for Greeks. "The contradiction was fundamental: Athens could not subject the Aegean states to what was widely called 'slavery' while simultaneously claiming them as fellow–members of a community" (Ibid., p. 107).

Membership in a fifth century Greek community usually was based on *citizenship*, but the Athenians were not willing to hear this argument; instead, they used force to maintain the empire and to make it a fixture of the Athenian world. Because of these policies, the leaders of the empire planted the seeds of their own destruction. In 454/3 BCE the treasury at Delos was moved to Athens and housed in a treasury located on the Acropolis. "From that year until late in the Peloponnesian War, the Athenians took one–sixtieth of the tribute paid by the allies as first fruits for the goddess Athena Polias, patroness of the city and, now, the reconstituted league"

(Kagan, 1991, p. 95). Pericles was free to use the money as he pleased and he used it to glorify Athens as the first city among the Greeks. But the Athenians had taken an oath not to rebuild their temples that had been destroyed by the Persians, which forced Pericles to find a way to relieved honorably the city from the oath and to allow it to begin his rebuild. This was accomplished through legal channels and the rebuilding program began.

Once the Athenians gained power, security, and wealth from the empire, they could not let it go. The tribute also paid for public services that had allowed the Athenians to build the most powerful navy, which could be used for expansion. For Pericles, the empire was the strength of its democracy, which fueled the new age that he had envisioned. Because of the empire, the Persians could not enslave the Greeks and the Athenians now had the means to advance trade and commerce in protected waters. Athenian power and wealth were attracting scholars from around the Greek world and Pericles was determined to encourage this development. He also believed that Athens could become the aesthetic and intellectual center of the universe. "Athens was to be the 'education of Greece,' and toward that end she had to attract the greatest poets, painters, sculptors, philosophers, artists, and teachers of every kind" (Ibid., p. 111).

Athens was to become the beacon of intelligent life, the cutting edge of advanced thought, and the "school" that would lead the Greeks into an advanced world of a new and higher civilization, as a stream of knowledge would flow from Athens to far corners of the empire to inspire others to emulate its greatness. Pericles' vision demanded an empire that would bring law and order, which was needed to promote industry, arts, and intellectual pursuits. The Athenian empire was a sea empire that relied on a great navy, which meant that for the time being, most of the resources from the empire would be used for a strategy that was fortress–bound on land and flexible at sea. At the same time, Pericles wanted to limit the expansion of the empire. The defeat in Egypt had taught Pericles not to reach too far away as it was a threat to the Aegean Empire. "He plainly believed that intelligence and reason could restrain unruly passions, maintain the empire at its current size, and use its revenues for a different, safer, but possibly greater glory than the Greeks had yet known" (Ibid., p. 115). A solidified league was the preamble of the Great War that was to follow in the decades to come.

TEN

The Tragedy of the Peloponnesian War

If one has a free choice and can live undisturbed, it is sheer folly to go to war.
—Pericles

Some historians divide the Peloponnesian War (431 – 404 BCE) into three phases that include: The Archidamian War named after King Archidamus of Sparta, which lasted from 430 to 421 BCE; The Desultory phase of the war, which lasted from 421 to the Athenian defeat in Sicily in 413 BCE; and The Ionian War, which lasted from 413 to 404 BCE and ended with the defeat of Athens (Davies, 1993, p. 117).

The Peloponnesian War began between Athens and Sparta when civil war broke out in Epidmnus located in Peloponnesia. The Epidmnus democrats drove the aristocrats from the city and the allies of the aristocrats returned to lay siege to the city. This city was a colony of Corcyra, an island state located off the western mainland in western Greece. Corcyra had been a Corinthian colony, but had fallen into bad relationships with the motherland. The besieged democrats of Epidmnus called on Corcyra for help but were refused forcing the democratic leaders to appeal to Corinth knowing that it would cause war. The Corcyraeans were angered by the call for help and warned the leaders of Epidmnus to dismiss the Corinthians and sent a fleet to besiege the city. The Corinthians responded by organizing a new colony at Epidamnus and calling on its Peloponnesian League allies to send settlers. The Spartans refused to be dragged into the conflict; however, the conflict threatened the stability of Peloponnesia and they asked for a negotiated settlement after Corcyraean leaders called on the Athenians to intervene. The Corinthians set sail for Corcyra where they were defeated in the battle of Leucimne, causing the Corinthians to return home to build a greater naval fleet.

War clouds grew more intense in 433 BCE, as the Athenian Assembly debated an alliance with Corcyra. The Athenians feared the possibility of a combined Corinth/Corcyra fleets that would upset the balance of power between the two Leagues. Pericles, having been convinced that the current peace was about to end, sent a small fleet to patrol off the coast of Corcyra to ward off a Corinthian invasion. In September the battle of Syota commenced when a Corinthian fleet arrived to attack the Corcyraeans. The Corinthians routed the Corcyra fleet and the Athenian fleet moved in to force the Corinthians to break off the attack. This action humiliated the Corinthians and caused them to conspire to bring Sparta into the conflict: consequently, Pericles was now forced to end his reconstruction program for Athens in order to finance the growing conflict.

The war had officially started in 431 BCE, as Plataea, a small town between Thebes and Athens, became an issue of contention. Plataea had rejected Theban advances and had called on Athens for help, as its democratic leaders had refused to accept the Boeotian League and Theban aristocrats who dominated the league. Thebes in alliance with Sparta could not tolerate the alliance between Plataea and Athens, as the town was located on a critical road that ran from Thebes to Athens. After having been defeated by the Athenians in the preliminary phases of the Peloponnesian War, the Thebans were determined to take the town. The attack took the form of a sneak night attack aided by local aristocrats; however, the citizens resisted and the main army was blocked by the swollen Asopus River. The democrats took their revenge by executing all of their Theban prisoners, causing the first atrocity of the war and setting up conditions for a nasty revenge. The Theban failure at Plataea would force King Archidamus to invade Attica to ravage the countryside surrounding Athens, but his delays allowed time for the Athenians to evacuate their livestock to Euboea, which for now served as a safe haven.

The Potidaeans' rebellion took place in 432 BCE based on a promise that Sparta would intervene and help the city gain its freedom from Athens. War threats had increased when Potidaea, located in northern Greece, began to rebel against Athens and to build defensive walls. The Athenians ordered the destruction of the walls and the dismissal of the Corinthian magistrates, but the Potidaeans petitioned the Spartans for help. The Athenians made peace with the Macedonian king and sent a force to surround Potidaea, which began their two-year siege. Also at this same time, the Athenians passed a set of decrees that barred Megarian merchants from the league ports of the Athenians. Megara was on the border of Attica, which had long been a region of dispute, and the decrees were designed as a warning to other city–states who might enter into conflict with Athens. The Megarians also appealed to Sparta for help against the Athenians.

At this time, the Spartan ephors called on the Spartan Assembly to review the issues and the complaints that had been registered against the Athenians causing the Athenians to send envoys to Sparta to plead their side in these conflicts, and they also called for these issues and complaints to be submitted to arbitration. Under pressure from the Corinthians and other allies, the ephors called for a vote of war and King

Archidamus was ordered to invade Attica and to destroy the Athenian army and the defensive walls that protected the city. Pericles offered arbitration of the Megara decrees and prepared for war by recalling the Athenians to move off their lands and into the defensive walls for the duration of the war.

The Athenians attempted to strengthen their league and to protect its grain shipments coming in through the Hellespont by preventing the Peloponnesians from gaining a foothold in Potidaea and elsewhere. The Athenians used diplomatic means to make friends with King Sitalas of Thrace and King Perdiccas of Macedon. At this time the Spartans had suffered few losses in the war, while the Athenians had lost their crops, vineyards, and olive production. The siege at Potidaea came at a high price and Sparta was planning another raid into Attica to cause more destruction. Pericles was under attack from Cleon, who wanted a more aggressive war and a more severe policy toward rebellious League members. The Assembly sent a war fleet north in an attempt to force the surrender of Potidaea, but again failed to accomplish its goals with heavy loss of men and materials.

The Plague

The Spartans returned to Attica to continue their devastation of the land and remained for 40 days; in response, Pericles sailed for Peloponnesia to establish a presence in order to force the Spartans to return to their homeland. Pericles attempted to demonstrate that he was willing to carry the war to the Spartans if they refused to withdraw. It was at this time that a plague arrived in Athens and began to kill great numbers of the Athenian population. The Athenian hoplite army was struck down in great numbers, perhaps close to 5,000, as well as the Athenian cavalry, and the rowers who manned the warships. Finally, the Athenian Assembly decided to send envoys to Sparta to seek an end to the conflict. The Spartans demanded an end to the siege of Potidaea, the restoration of Aegina, withdrawal of the Megarian Decrees, and the dissolution of the Athenian Empire. The Athenians could not accept these terms and returned to the business of war by relying on its powerful navy and defensive walls. The enemies of Pericles had finally brought him to trial on a charge of embezzlement and he was forced to pay a heavy fine that would be paid by his friends. In 429 BCE Pericles contracted the plague and died, leaving the Athenians without his moderate leadership.

The Spartans, fearing the plague, stayed out of Attica, but decided to move against Plataea in support of the Thebans, who were still angry over the execution of their prisoners. The siege of the town was preceded by an offer of neutrality, which was refused by the Plataeans, and the women and children were sent to Athens. The men of Plataea called on Athens for help, but the Athenians would not face the Spartans in a land battle. The crisis came in the summer of 429 BCE when the Peloponnesians built a siege wall around the town and destroyed the town. As the siege proceeded, the Athenians moved to the northeast to deal with the rebellions in Chalcidice.

The Athenians arrived in Chalcidice to face a rebellion in Spartolus that threatened the region of the Hellespont and the flow of grain from the Black Sea. The Athenians met defeat, which created crisis. The Peloponnesians attempted to set up a rouse to keep Athenian ships out of Peloponnesia by an attack on Acarnania, but the attempted ploy failed at Stratus, forcing the Spartans to move away. The Athenians arrived to attack Spartan ships and captured some of their crew, which handed the Spartans a humiliating defeat. Other naval stand–offs followed in Crete when Phormio attacked the Spartans forcing them to flee, abandoning some of their ships and crews. The Peloponnesians' allies continued to pressure the Spartans to push the attack as they attempted a raid on Piraeus, which was mainly undefended. The surprise attack failed, forcing the Spartan commanders to raid Salamis on their way to Piraeus, which alarmed the Athenians and forced the Spartans to sail home.

The New Politicians

As the Athenians crowded into the zone between the two Great Walls, as a means of avoiding Spartan attacks, which caused anger to set in and Pericles fell under the political attack of Cleon. Cleon was from the merchant class and had operated a tannery in Athens; his growing political power signified that a leadership change was taking place in Athens, as tradesmen and other middle class leaders came to challenge aristocratic leadership. These new leaders, so–called *demagogues* of the war years, included Cleon, Hyperbolus, Androcles and Cleophon. Cleon served as a regular member of the Assembly where he led blistering attacks against Pericles and his supporters, but Pericles was able to continue to persuade the people to follow his lead and his co–generals lent their support to turn the *prytanies*, officers of the Assembly, to take no action. Pericles used the Athenian cavalry to harass the occupying Spartan army under the Spartan king, Archidamus, and after a few months the army returned to Sparta and Pericles was able to order his fleet to raid Peloponnesian coastal towns in a hit–and–run tactic. The Athenians attacked Aegina and removed its population to protect Piraeus; the Spartans resettled its refugees near Argos to spy on the democrats.

By 427/8 BCE the leadership of Athens was no longer in the hands of the aristocrats, as new political leaders from the middle ranks of Athenian society had come into their own and were challenging each other for influence and for political power. At this time a rivalry was set up between Nicias, son of Niceratus, and Cleon. Nicias was a slave trader, who supplied the mines. Cleon and Nicias were alike in that both had opposed the peace party and both wanted to win the war. Nicias presented himself as a pious wealthy gentleman, while Cleon was considered a political activist whose enemies viewed him as a mean–spirited, vulgar loudmouth.

Rebellion within the Athenian Delian League would advance the power struggle for political leadership between these two images of popular rule. At this time, Athens was free of Spartan invaders, but was in serious financial difficulties. The war parties were in control of the political debate in both Athens and Sparta and they were willing to punish their rebellious enemies with a bloody retribution. For example, the islands of Lesbos and Chios had their own fleets and were autonomous members of the Delian League. In 428 BCE the oligarchs again decided to declare their independence from Athens and fomented rebellion and appealed for Spartan support. The oligarchs in Lesbos, located in the city of Mytilene, built defensive walls and set up a blockade of their harbor. The Mytilene oligarchs told the Spartans that the Athenians were too weak to react to a rebellion backed by Spartan resources.

The Spartans sent envoys to Mytilene with the message that, should they rebel, the Spartans would relieve them by invading Attica and by sending war ships to Lesbos. The Spartans were now under the leadership of King Agis, son of Archidamus, who devised a new plan to fight Athens on land and at sea, which sparked more rebellions throughout the empire. However, the Spartans were weak at sea and though they sent a fleet to Lesbos, they soon saw that the fleet was in danger and it had to be recalled. These decisions caused the leadership of King Agis to be brought into question, as was the strength of Spartan military forces. In the meantime, the Mytilene oligarchs planned to break out of their surrounded city, by arming the lower classes, but the lower classes rebelled against them and they demanded military stores, which forced the oligarchs to surrender the city. Terror was becoming the new policy of the war party in Athens, but at this time the Athenians were not ready to render wholesale slaughter on their enemies, while the Spartans were more so inclined.

At this point, Cleon and the war party demanded the death of all adult males and the sale of all women and children into slavery. A ship was sent to Mytilene with orders to carry out the mass killing, but just in time, the Athenians recalled the order and saved the population when the more moderate generals prevailed in the Assembly. At this time, Plataea surrendered to Sparta and was promised fair treatment, but instead, the Plataeans were all put to death, the town was leveled, and the land was given over to the Thebans, which spoke volumes about the intentions of the Spartans as the savior of the Greeks. Factionalism between the oligarchs and the democrats threatened to destroy the Greeks unless cooler heads could prevail. "Party membership and loyalty came to be regarded as the highest virtues, overshadowing all others and justifying the abandonment of all restraint of traditional morality" (Kagan, 2003, p. 117). This new state of terror also was fueled by greed, ambition, a hunger for power, and a will to destroy all opposition regardless of the means. The war parties in both Athens and Sparta would allow a systematic mass murder to replace the common sympathy that the Greeks had traditionally shared in calmer days.

In 417 BCE the Athenians attacked Melos, which had enjoyed the benefits of the confederacy without paying tribute. The Melosians were accused of aiding the Spartans with resources and with their sympathies. Doric oligarchs controlled the government so that the Athenians deemed it necessary to starve the city into submission. In 416 BCE the Athenians, under the leadership of the war party, committed one of the worst atrocities of the war. They killed all of the captured adult males, sold their women and children into slavery, and replaced them with Athenian colonists. The atrocity occurred at a time when Nicias, Hyperbolus, and Alcibiades entered into a competition for the leadership of Athens. Nicias portrayed himself as a pious man devoted to the temples and the gods. He used his wealth to donate a bronze tree and land to the priests in an extravagant ceremony to demonstrate his favor with the gods. In 416 BCE Alcibiades countered Nicias by entering seven chariots in the Olympic games and dedicated them to the glory of Athens. At the same time, Hyperbolus plotted to pit Nicias against Alcibiades and to force one or the other into exile so that he could gain political leadership at their expense, but this plot failed when Nicias and Alcibiades united to have Hyperbolus ostracized from Athens.

The Syracusans

Syracuse had been established as a Corinthian colony and the people were ethnic Dorians, which allowed them to call on the Corinthians for help and to use their influence with the Spartans for military assistance. At this same time, Alcibiades was in Sparta urging the Spartans to aid the Syracusans. He argued that the Athenians had planned to conquer Sicily, Italy, and Carthage and to use their captured resources to win the war. He recommended that the Spartans build a fort at Decelea in Attica as a threat to force the Athenians back to Athens. Because of their distrust of Alcibiades, the Spartans were only willing to send a token fleet to Sicily; Gylippus, the commander of the ships, was a most unusual and effective commander. He was a *mothax*, or a person of inferior status, because of his lack of wealth and because of his helot mother. He would prove to be a brilliant field commander who possessed an iron will and a determination to defeat the Athenians.

The Athenians began an attempted siege of Syracuse in 414 BCE, requiring the control of the harbor and the building of siege walls around the interior borderlands of the city. Nicias, however, was not enthusiastic for this task, as it came at a time when he had fallen ill. The Athenians would make advances only to be driven off by the Syracusan cavalry. The Syracusan forces destroyed the Athenian siege walls, forts, and supply centers before they retreated behind their city walls in a hit and run fashion. In addition, they made friends of the Sisals, the local tribal people, and called on other island cities for help in their defense. Meanwhile, Gylippus had arrived to lend his tactical support for the relief of the city, and soon additional reinforcements arrived from Corinth. Gylippus issued an ultimatum, which was not answered, and then he seized and captured the Athenian stores and built counter–walls to the Athenian siege walls. Nicias realized that he was in danger and contemplated a retreat back to Athens planning an escape route should the balance of force shift against the Athenians. The Corinthians entered the harbor and Gylippus built forts to counter the Athenians on land. Finally, Nicias wrote to the Assembly in an attempt to explain that the Athenians had lost the offensive initiative and were now in a defensive posture and asking to be recalled or reinforced. His illness grew worse and he asked to be relieved, but the Assembly refused to listen and instead of recalling the fleet, it sent another force under the command of Demosthenes and Eurymedon.

The Assembly assumed that the pious Nicias had the favor of the gods, and this assumption led them to send another fleet to Sicily. At the same time, the Spartans sent an army to Attica to build a fort at Decelea. The fort at Decelea was established to encourage slaves to run away, to encourage the Thebans to conduct raids into Attica, and to block the Athenians from traveling to Euboea. In the meantime, the Athenians in Syracuse became trapped on land and in the harbor, which forced them to attempt another breakout from the harbor, but they again were defeated and forced to shore, where they died in great numbers. When Demosthenes attempted to organize another breakout, his men refused and fled inland as a final act of desperation. Nicias now attempted to organize an orderly escape by land and moving to Catana by taking a route that avoided the cavalry at Epipolae. The surviving Athenians were divided into two bodies led by Nicias and Demosthenes. The Syracusan army arrived and trapped Demosthenes in an olive grove where he surrendered under terms that would save the lives of his men. He did not attempt to save himself, but attempted a failed suicide.

The Peloponnesian army caught up with Nicias, who attempted to negotiate a truce, which was refused. Out of desperation, he attempted a flight across the Assinarus River where his men were trampled and slaughtered. Thucydides declared the Sicilian expedition the greatest drama of the war, while many in Peloponnesia mistakenly celebrated the event as the destruction of the Athenian Empire and the end of the war. Thucydides summed up the total destruction of Athens' greatest army and armada: "They were beaten at all points altogether; all that they suffered was great; they were destroyed, as the saying, with a total destruction, their fleet, their army, everything was destroyed, a few out of many returned home" (Thucydides, *History of the Peloponnesian War*, 7. 87: 5–6). Much of the blame of this great disaster was laid at the door of Alcibiades, whose selfish and devious nature had helped orchestrate the circumstances that would destroy the Athenian fleet and army.

The fiasco in Sicily had repercussions in Athens, Sparta, and Persia that would change the conditions of the war. The Spartans realized that they had to challenge the Athenians at sea and that it was now possible to defeat them on land and sea. It was time for the Spartans to align themselves with the Persians as a means of gaining the financing for shipbuilding and to encourage the Persians to allow the Phoenicians to return to the Aegean region. The Athenians had lost over 216 warships (of which 160 were Athenian), as well as over 3,000 hoplites, 9,000 crewmen, and 1,000 foreign mercenary troops. The treasury was near empty and the Spartans were ravaging the countryside from their fort at Decelea. Inflation was out of control and taxes were not paid on time or at all.

The citizens of Athens were losing patience with the government and were concerned that the Assembly had made serious blunders. It was now decided that to survive, the Athenian government needed to be modified by adding of a panel of ten wise men. The purpose of this panel was to advise and to help control the decision making process of the Assembly. The new panel was called *Probouloi* and was selected from each of the ten tribes. The panel took over some of the most important tasks of the Council through its power to draft bills and decrees. Unlike the Council members, they were not limited to a term of office and their reputations gave them an important status in the affairs of state. The panel included such important men as Sophocles and Hagnon, the old generals who had served with Pericles. These wise old men ranged in age from sixty years of age to eighty years of age, and most were inclined to see Athens and the war from a Periclean perspective. The effect of the *Probouloi* was to restrain the Assembly and to force it into a more prudent form of deliberation. The problem now was to reconstruct the navy by building ships and protecting the grain shipments coming in from the Bosphorus through the narrows of the Hellespont. Soon, however, a new round of rebellions erupted to threaten the viability of the Empire and its democracy.

The Persians

The focus of the Peloponnesian War now shifted back to the Aegean region where the Persians were becoming more active in their attempt to regain their position in Asia Minor and its offshore islands. At this time, both the Athenians and the Spartans were courting the Persians for resources, as both had become financially weakened by the war. Following the death of King Artaxerxes, his son, Darius II, competed with his many half brothers for the Persian throne. Earlier the Persians and the Athenians had agreed to a treaty of peace, but following the Sicilian disaster, the balance of power had shifted. King Agis was in Attica at Decelea. Envoys were arriving from Lesbos pleading for Spartan help, the Euboeans were in revolt, and the Persians were involved in Chios and in the Hellespont. These critical events ushered in a new phase of the war that Kagan (2003) called "the Ionian War". At this time, the Spartan had emerged as a naval power and Alcibiades, who by this time had been driven out of Sparta, was now advising the Persian throne. A Spartan congress formulated a plan that was designed to destroy the Athenians at Chios and Lesbos and then to move to the Hellespont, but the Corinthians balked at the plan, which alerted the Athenians who made moves to counteract the growing Spartan threat. The Chians became fearful of the Athenians and were forced to forfeit ships to them who then set a trap for the Spartans, forcing them back to Peloponnesia. Before they reached safe waters, the Athenians attacked, destroying their ships and killing their commanders.

The Spartans worked to revise the proposed treaty with the Persians, but negotiations continued to favor the Persians and the Spartans appeared weak; meanwhile, the Athenians returned to Chios where civil war promised an easy victory. The Spartans were forced into action and they sent a fleet along with a panel of advisors to supervise Astyochis, the commander of the fleet. At this time, the northern satrap, Pharnabazus was calling on the Spartans to send warships to the Hellespont to help foment a rebellion of cities in that region. Spartan ships also sailed to Miletus at a time when Astyochus decided to abandon Chios, which stranded the Spartan army. The Athenians divided their fleet to confront Antisthenes, who was at Caunus, and sent ships to Miletus. The Athenians attacked Antisthenes at Miletus, but these forces were defeated when Astychus arrived and surrounded the Athenians, who managed to escape. The Spartans moved to Caunus to form a larger fleet to confront the Athenians; meanwhile, the Spartans sent Lichas as an emissary to confront the Persians regarding the details of their negotiations. He was a strong-willed diplomat, and he charged the Persians with duplicity and with having ambitions to enslave all the Greeks. This charge angered the Persian satrap Tissaphernes and he walked away from the negotiations. At this time, the oligarchs in Rhodes rebelled and contacted the Spartans for help in destroying the local democratic regime. The island fell in January of 411 BCE because the Athenians came too late to the rescue.

The Anti-Democratic Coup

A revolution occurred in Athens in 411 BCE in which the oligarchs violently deposed the democracy. Alcibiades attempted to influence these events to bring about the end of the democracy. "At that time he proposed the dissolution of the council of Four Hundred that had seized oligarchic power by violence and the restoration of the old council of Five Hundred" (Ibid., p. 366). In addition, he called for an end to the system of payment for public service, which had the effect of excluding the rowers (*thetes*) from office. He also called for the installation of a constitution of the Five Thousand, which restricted citizenship to the classes below the hoplites. As a result of the revolt in Athens, Athenian commanders Thrasybulus and Thrasyllus declared Samos independent to carry on the fight against the oligarchs in Athens. The *thetes* in Samos also opposed the oligarch rebellion as they had been stripped of their citizenship. The Samoan commanders came to believe that they could preserve the democracy and the empire. They believed the Athenian democracy depended on the strength of the navy and not on the self-motivated politicians in the Assembly.

The revolt at Byzantium threatened the Athenian grain supply and the Athenians had no choice but to respond. The Spartans were convinced that victory was at hand despite their recent loses at Chios, Thrance, and Heraclea. The Carthaginians entered the picture when they went to war against Syracuse in 409 BCE, which forced the Syracusan fleet to depart from Aegean waters and to return to Sicily, which weakened Spartan naval power. At this time the Athenians became involved in a civil war that broke out in Corcyra that moved it to neutrality, and the Spartans captured Pylos. The Spartan fleet was able to win back Chios and the Spartans still held important cities in the Hellespont. To add to the worsening conditions for the Athenians, the Persians were willing to finance another Peloponnesian fleet. The ability to defend the Hellespont was made more difficult by a growing bankruptcy that prevented fleets from sailing and by the disgruntled crews who refused to sail without pay.

The Athenian commander, Thrasyllus, was able to set sail for the Ionian coast and to reclaim some of the lost cities, but he was only moderately successful. He suffered loses at Ephesus, which forced him to move on to the Hellespont to join the fleet controlled by Alcibiades. A combined Athenian naval force moved to Lampsacus to raid against the Persians and to attack Abydos. Thrasyllus engaged the satrap,

Pharnabazus, when Alcibiades appeared with his hoplite troops and cavalry. The Persians were forced to retreat, which allowed the Athenians to loot the area before moving on to raid in Chalcedon in early 408 BCE. The Athenians built up a stronger force to siege the city and the two opposing sides met in the contained area. The Athenians defeated the Spartans in the open and forced them to retreat back to the city. The Persians interceded to negotiate a settlement that required the city to pay its regular tribute to the Athenians, and the Persians agreed to allow Athenian envoys to meet with King Darius II.

The Spartans had completed the construction of their new fleet. Cyrus, the son of Darius II, had replaced the satrap, Tissaphernes, to become the ruler of Lydia, Phrygia, Cappadocia and Ionia. He would prove to be a crafty and ruthless ruler, who planned to defeat the Athenians as a means to gain the Persian throne. He was in search of a Spartan commander who was capable of taking risks to defeat the Athenians. He soon realized that Lysander, a *mothax* with a Spartan father and helot mother, was a man full of ambition. Agesilaus, the half brother of King Agis, had sponsored Lysander, and Lysander was able to use his connections to form an alliance with Cyrus. In 396 BCE Agesilaus became Spartan king, and in 407 BCE Lysander moved a new Spartan fleet to patrol along the Asian coastline. He occupied the harbor at Ephesus where he could easily attack the Athenians at Samos. Cyrus provided the necessary funds to pay the crews and Lysander worked with the Greek aristocrats to form oligarchic alliances. "In the short run, the arrangement (between Sparta and Persia) gave Sparta what she wanted: the money to build, equip, and pay a fleet; the confidence to surmount early naval defeats; and the ability to carry the war into the Aegean against Athens' major island allies, to attack her corn–route through the Hellespont, and ultimately to annihilate the Athenian fleet at Aegospotami in 405 BCE and blockade Athens into capitulation" (Davies, 1993, p. 140). Cyrus promised that after the war Lysander would rule the allied Greek city–states of Ionia.

By now the Athenians grew desperate to confront Lysander, the Spartan commander at Ephesus, as their crews were deserting due to a lack of pay. The Spartans played a waiting game hoping that Athenian oarsmen would defect to them for pay. In February of 406 BCE Alcibiades left his fleet to join Thrasybulus, who was laying siege to Phocaea, located to the north of Ionia, in an attempt to confront Lysander. Canon was given command of Athenian naval forces when Lysander's term of office expired, and Callicratidas replaced him. Callicratidas set out to rival the achievements of Lysander, but his discipline was so severe that his crews threatened mutiny.

Callicratidas moved the Spartan fleet to Chios and Teos, where he threatened Lesbos, and secured a new rebellion against the Athenians. Callicratidas was ready to face Canon in a final showdown to end the war. Canon lost thirty *triremes* to Callicratidas and he was trapped. Meanwhile, Canon called for reinforcements, which forced the Athenians to take the gold from the statues on the Acropolis, and farmers and slaves were recruited as crewmen. Eight generals were sent with the inexperienced seamen to reinforce Canon. Callicratidas divided the fleet, leaving some of the ships to guard Canon, while others sailed to Cape Malea near the island of *Arginusae* to watch for the rescue fleet from Athens. Callicratidas attacked the Athenian fleet at dawn as both sides lined up with the Athenians in front of Garipadasi Island. This was a good defensive move because it restricted the ability of the Spartans to maneuver. The Spartan ships became scattered as the center of the Athenian's formation molested and destroyed them. Callicratidas was killed and the Athenians went about the task of destroying remnants of enemy ships and their crews. The Spartan ships blockading Canon at Mytilene learned of the defeat and fled, giving the Athenians one of the greatest sea victories of the war.

The Sacrilege and the Lost Peace

The victory was celebrated back in Athens until it was learned that the generals had failed to recover the bodies of the dead. An untimely storm, as well as a state of confusion that followed the engagement, had prevented the rescue operations. Commanders had attempted to pursue the fleeing ships and the confusion of the commanders had resulted in a situation where the normal and expected rescue was impossible. The main body of the Athenian ships had sailed to *Arginusae* to reorganize and to confer. Some ships were left behind for the rescue and recovery operation under the care of Theramenes and Thrasybulus, but the storm caused the men to fear for their lives, and they refused to obey their commanders.

The abandonment of the dead and dying on the battlefield was deemed a sacrilege and it created a furor, which led to accusations between the eight generals. The Assembly ordered a trial and some of the generals fled or went into exile rather than facing the charges. The demagogues prevented the remaining generals from defending themselves and prevailed in calling for the death penalty. By coincidence, Socrates was serving as the representative of his tribe as *prostates* and was presiding over the Assembly. He refused to allow the question to be put to the Assembly and was the only one of the *prytanies* who acted with such firm conviction. Assembly members threatened to indict him and he was overruled; the Assembly accepted the Council proposal to put the generals to death. The Assembly, whipped up by Cleophon, put reason aside and voted their passions. The fourth century critics of democracy were now in a position to declare rule by the people as a failed ideology, and an inefficient system of decision–making, a system characterized by a lack of effective leadership.

With their defeat at *Arginusae*, the Spartans were in desperate need of Persian money, but by now they despised the disgrace that came to them as a result of their dealings with the Persians. The pressure was great enough for the Spartans to sue for peace and to agree to abandon Decelea; however, under the leadership of the demagogue, Cleophon, the Athenian Assembly rejected the peace, as many had come to believe that the Peloponnesian leadership could not be trusted. Vocal critics of the peace argued that the Spartans sought peace as a means to reorganize their forces in preparation for a new war. In response, the Spartans returned Lysander to commander of the Spartan naval forces and ignored their own constitution by giving him the power needed to rebuild the navy and to cooperate with Cyrus.

This plan worked out well for the Spartans, as Cyrus was more than willing to use his own resources to end the Athenian Empire, but in a strange turn of events, Darius called Cyrus to account for the murders of his own cousins and he actually replaced him with Lysander. This action gave Lysander full access to Persian money and tribute, but before Lysander could exert his influence, he had to deal with a new wave of Panhellenic patriotism and anti–Persian feelings. Lysander talked of ending Greek factionalism, but then worked to destroy the democrats on Miletus by replacing them with pro–Lysander oligarchs. The generals at Samos had failed to prevent Lysander from reaching Miletus, and in Caria and Rhodes he was able to terrorize the populations by killing the men and enslaving the women and children. He attacked the Athenians in Aegina and Salamis and landed troops in Attica, but was driven out of Rhodes. In addition, he attacked the sea–lanes in the Hellespont in an attempt to cut Athens away from its food supply, and was able to retake the lost cities of the coastal region.

The Final Defeat

The Athenians were convinced that Lysander and the Spartans would not hesitate to kill them and to sell the women and children into slavery; therefore, they decided to refuse to surrender and to face the possibility of a Spartan siege. Lysander decided not to take revenge on the Athenian garrisons stationed in the occupied cities and allowed them to return to Athens. He now realized that more atrocities would strengthen Athenian resistance and that they would have to be starved into submission, which would be very expensive.

To enhance his own power base, Lysander established *decarchies,* or military juntas, in captured cities, along with Peloponnesian garrisons. The juntas consisted of hand–picked oligarchs who were anti–democratic and were out for revenge. He demanded tribute and laid the foundation for a Peloponnesian Empire similar to the one that he had just destroyed. He failed to dislodge the democrats in Samos who killed the aristocrats in preparation for a Spartan siege. Lysander moved to Attica and assembled a Peloponnesian force in the area of the Academy and moved to the walls of the city in an act of intimidation. The Peloponnesian allies, however, began to quarrel and the Thebans demanded the complete destruction of Athens. At this time, Pausanias (408-395 BCE), the Spartan king, grew suspicious of the ambitious Lysander. He was willing to allow the Athenians to survive as a weak city–state and to limit Spartan ambitions to the affairs in Peloponnesia. These divisions gave the Athenians new hope for better terms, should they resist surrender. Pausanias returned to Sparta and Lysander sailed for Samos, but left behind a naval blockade of Athens.

The Athenians sent envoys to the Spartan ephors and asked for better terms and agreed to destroy a portion of the walls, but the demagogue Cleophon rejected the idea in hopes of further negotiations. At this point, Theramenes offered to go to Lysander and to negotiate the stalemate. He returned to Athens in 404 BCE hoping that the Athenians were ready to compromise with Lysander. By this time, the

Spartans had lost some of their thirst for revenge and were willing to allow Athens to survive, provided the citizens were willing to accept a military type of junta made up of Athenian oligarchs.

This compromise was based, in part, on the growing fear of the ambitions of the Thebans. Athens was ideally located to serve as a buffer state between Thebes and Sparta. Lysander wished to install a decarchy, along with a Spartan garrison. Also at this time, Lysander was experiencing strained relationships with the Spartan kings, which may have allowed Theramenes to propose a moderate regime for Athens to ward off Spartan jealousy and to guard against rebellion in Athens. At this time, Darius II was dying and Cyrus was contending with Artaxerxes II, his brother, for the throne of the empire. Lysander feared that if Cyrus lost this power struggle and Artaxerxes II became king, the Persians might decide to punish Sparta and to support Athens, suggesting that Theramenes may have proposed a moderate regime in Athens along with a pro–Lysander junta to assuage the fears of Lysander before the death of Darius. Following his report to the Athenian Assembly, Theramenes was given the authority to negotiate a peace with Sparta, which allowed Lysander to signal his approval to the Spartan ephors.

The terms of the peace required the partial destruction of the Athenian defensive walls, the forfeiture of the cities of the empire, the return of exiled oligarchs, the revision of the old (Solon) constitution based on aristocratic rule, and a defensive alliance between Sparta and Athens. The demagogue, Cleophon, objected to these terms and led the Assembly to reject the peace and to the demand that the democracy be preserved. Cleophon and the radical democrats feared the return of the exiled aristocrats. The peace party decided to remove Cleophon and he was tried and executed, which opened the way for the peace agreement to be ratified, ending the Peloponnesian War in 404 BCE. The Spartans imposed an oligarchy, which set about taking revenge on its old enemies. They created a rule of terror based on murder and the confiscation of property.

Civil War and the Democratic Resurrection

The oligarchy consisted of Thirty Athenians who were aligned with the Spartans and were secretly working to destroy the democracy. Charmides, the uncle of Plato, Critias, the orator, and Theramenes, the statesman, became the leaders of the Thirty Tyrants. Critias was ruthless and he had the more moderate Theramenes executed. The Thirty Tyrants organized an army of upper–class hoplites as a means of hunting down the democratic opposition and of imposing absolute rule. At the same time, they proposed a constitution that was supposed to eventually replace the junta in the form of a conservative democratic regime consisting of 3000 wealthy citizens. Thrasybulus, the son of Lycus and naval hero of Samos, was living in Athens until he decided to oppose the Thirty Tyrants and to take his supporters to Thebes where he would organize a counter–revolution, civil war. The revolutionaries built a stronghold north of the city, which soon became a mecca for young men who had learned to hate this tyranny. In 403 BCE Thrasybulus and his revolutionary army of about 1,000 filtrated into the port city of Piraeus and defeated the army of the Tyrants. The encounter led to discussions between leaders of the two opposing armies in which the commander of the tyrant force actually was persuaded to return to Athens to reconsider the current political situation. The army of the democrats moved to Athens where their appeal forced the Tyrants into exile. The Spartans decided to remove their garrison and establish a general amnesty between the oligarchs and the democrats. Both parties were asked to swear an oath of reconciliation, which began a new era of civil harmony within Athens and throughout Greece. For the Athenians, this reconciliation laid a foundation for a new civility that would allow the Athenians to begin the process of establishing a second democracy and empire.

Within ten years, the walls of the city had been rebuilt, along with a new fleet of warships that were able to reassert Athenian power in the Aegean, thereby allowing for the creation of a new confederation of Ionian Greek cities. By 375 BCE the second Athenian Empire became a reality. After the amnesty, the democrats tried Socrates in 399 BCE because of his association with the leaders of the Thirty Tyrants and because he held unconventional religious views that were perceived as impious. Socrates could not be put on trial for being a friend of the Thirty Tyrants, as that would violate the amnesty, so he was tried on the charge of corrupting youth, Alcibiades being an example. This tragedy, along with the atrocities that occurred during the war, caused some of the most important fourth century philosophers to conclude that democracy was a flawed political system that had to be replaced.

Despite its growing critics, the resurrection of democracy came in the form of a reconstructed democracy that was led by Athenian patriots who were fed up with the tyranny. These "new" democrats were determined to end the class warfare that had produced the factionalism that had led to the destruction of the first democracy and empire. In 400 BCE Sparta had begun an empire–building program and following the death of Cyrus, the son of Darius II, the Greeks in Asia Minor called on the Spartans for protection. In 396 BCE King Agesilaus declared the Greek cities independent and they became hostile against the Persians. King Artaxerxes, brother of the now deceased Cyrus, sent the satrap Tissaphernes to rescue the situation, but he failed and was executed for his efforts in 395 BCE. The growing trouble between Thebes and Sparta would force the recall of the Spartans from Persia and fourth century city–state conflicts would grow in intensity for the next six decades, and would eventually open the door for aggressive neighbors to invade and eventually conqueror all of Greece and then Persia. Also during the fourth century, Plato and Aristotle re–examined democracy as a means of proposing alternative ways to establish a more just and virtuous society.

Eleven

Athens in Decline

The Philosophers bring us to an area of social change best explored in terms of the new or changed roles, which certain individuals or groups came to play in Greek society.
—J.K. Davies

In fourth century Athens, the political leaders were desperate to maintain the city's food supply and the Athenians again were willing to use force to maintain their critical sea–lanes. The leaders were more flexible in addressing these conflicts than they had been in the past and they periodically sponsored congresses and attempted to negotiate multilateral treaties to maintain the peace. These policies had the salutary effect of creating the Common Peace of the 370s and the 360s, but at the same time, the desire for city–state autonomy remained a powerful goal, as did the need for a mutual defense agreement. Military power remained the most important means of protecting city–state interests, but ambitious military leaders and armies were now replacing the citizen–soldier. Mercenary armies found ample opportunities for employment as aggressive city leaders, and monarchs began to seek opportunities to encroach on neighboring states. "Precisely because traditional republic Greek states found no way of reconciling the subordination of one state to another with the values which had come to matter, the monarchs on the fringes of Greek culture could move in successfully, filling the vacant role of leader and guarantor and exploiting them for their own purposes" (Davies, 1993, p. 156). Also at this time, rapid cultural changes were taking place throughout Greece.

The changing moral standards of the fourth century were expressed in various art forms related to literature and to fine arts; for example, vase paintings began to reflect a strong homosexual theme that was permeating the times. Drinking parties suggested that morality was becoming grounded in new excesses of human conduct, based to some degree on self–indulgence and moral decline. During the fourth century various forms individualism also become excessive.

The comedies of the times emphasized wealth and status over the themes of human frailty and the abuse of *hubris*, which first began to appear in the fifth century. The important poets and play writes of the fifth century were canonized in the fourth century as an indication that the fourth century was a post–classic era. By 330 BCE, statues were being erected in memory of the old classical masters, especially in memory of Aeschylus, Sophocles and Euripides. The original works of these great democratic literary playwrites were stored and guarded so that the current productions of their plays could not be corrupted by new interpretations. Display, in the fourth century, became more exaggerated, which was reflected in the theatrics of oratory that now became another source of public entertainment. The divinity of a living person, which may have first appeared in connection with Lysander, became more acceptable in the fourth century suggesting that the culture was in decline, as oriental religions and cults grew in popularity. At the same time, oratory was falling into disrepute as a result of the political orators who had led Athens to disaster during the closing years of the fifth century. "The greatest liability of all is to have a loud voice, like that of the 'new politician' and their successors" (Too, 1995, p. 87).

Orators, looking to advance their careers as politicians, were seeking to make money at public expense. In some cases, they damaged the reputation of the city. Some of the leaders of Athens, for example, were willing to take bribes from foreign governments. In addition, the laws of Athens allowed individuals to use the courts to bring charges against wealthy individuals, which made them prey to blackmailers and a variety of scams. In other words, by the fourth century, there was a growing number of individuals who used the courts for their own personal gain. These individuals were called *sycophants* and they operated somewhat akin to modern day bounty hunters. Only in ancient Athens they were often predators of the state. For example, in *Antiodosis*, Isocrates presents a view of himself as a victim of the unscrupulous sycophants who claimed that he had not paid his wealth taxes. "The sycophant was similar to a bribed politician. Both used the political apparatus of the state for illegitimate personal advantage, but, while the bribed politician sold his convictions for pay, the sycophants had no convictions in the first place" (Ober, 1989, p. 174). According to Ostwald (1989): "And above all, the institution gave rise to the development of Sycophants, that class of blackmailers and informers who specialized in prosecutions of cases in which an adverse decision of the jury would award a substantial part of the fine to the successful prosecutor" (p. 81). Also in the fourth–century rhetoricians attempted to displace the "loud–mouthed" demagogic politician with a new quietism in which writing trumped the oral tradition as democracy and classical Greek culture continued to decline. The written word, in other words, became a means that could be used to counter the scheming demagogues, but even more important, it became a more reflective voice for the philosophers.

The Second Athenian Democracy and Empire

The influences of the Peloponnesian War continued to shape the affairs of the city–states in Greece, as well as the relationships and the events in the regions surrounding

Greece. During the Ionian phase of the Peloponnesian War, Conon (Konon), who had served as an effective general in the sea battle of *Arginusae,* survived the political upheaval surrounding the Athenian reaction to the failed sea rescue that brought down the eight generals. In the year 404 BCE, Conon was able to find new employment as a Persian admiral, a mercenary general and as an Athenian politician. His reputation and the willingness of his soldiers and seamen to continue to follow him allowed him to enter the service of the Spartans and the Persians, while remaining loyal to Athens. "Konon used his three roles as Persian admiral, mercenary leader, and Athenian politician, to link Athens more closely to Persia, destroy the Spartan fleet of Cnidos in August of 394, and begin to re–create the Athenian Empire in the Aegean" (Davies, 1993, pp. 147-148).

Conon led the Persians against Spartan interests and he used Persian money to rebuild the Long Walls surrounding Athens and to re–establish the Aegean islands and the Ionian cities in Asia Minor as allies of Athens. To counter this growing threat, the Spartans attempted to negotiate with Artaxerxes by offering to forego their claims to the cities of Asia Minor and suggested that the Greek islands near the coast also be allowed to establish self-ruling constitutions. This ploy worked as the Persians arrested Conon in 391 BCE, which ended the Persian/Athenian alliance and, out of a fear of the growing strength of the Athenians, the Persians re–established their working relationship with Sparta. Artaxerxes wanted to control the Greek cities in Asia Minor as well as the offshore islands, including the important island of Cyprus.

As was previously stated, things had gone badly between Sparta and Persia, due in large part to the role that Sparta had played in supporting Cyrus against his brother Artaxerxes II. Consequently, Artaxerxes viewed the Spartans with displeasure and began to help Athens rebuild its strength as a counter–weight to Sparta. This change in diplomacy eventually allowed the Athenians the opportunity to reconstruct their lost empire and to begin the process of building a second Athenian empire. By 392 BCE the Athenians were rebuilding its navy in order to re–establish its dominance among the Ionian islanders and other holdings in the Aegean. At the same time, and the Corinthians now were willing to play an important role in preventing the Spartans from developing and expanding their empire. The nine–year peace, King's Peace, which had followed the ending of the Peloponnesian War, had the effect of realigning city–state forces that now were shaping Aegean and Greek affairs.

The last half of the fourth century BCE was a time of chaos, conflict, revolution, and interstate warfare. International problems also were pressing in on Greece because of the growing activities of the Persians and the increasing military power of the Macedonians. Cities were changing governments as tyrants, monarchies, oligarchies, and democracies ruled in some of the Greek cities; some cities attacked their neighbors to acquire their resources and Sparta continued to send governors and garrisons to rule by force. These new conditions and institutions drew their characteristics from both democracy and oligarchy. The second phase of the Athenian democracy continued to advance in the fourth century, as institutional developments of the fifth century were refined, especially in regard to the people's courts (*dikastérion*). Aristotle credited the judiciary power of the people as an important source of democratic rule. Throughout the fourth century, even after the defeat of Athens and their allies at Chaeronea in 338 BCE, the Athenians continued to embrace democracy for another sixteen years. Democracy, or elements of democracy, also lived after the Hellenistic dispersion, despite the despotism of Alexandrian monarchial dynasties.

The Spartan Hegemony

The Spartan king, Agesilaus, set out to free the Greek cities of Asia Minor from Persian control when he engaged the Persians and easily defeated them, causing Artaxerxes to bribe Athens and Thebes into a war with Sparta. Following the victory of Agesilaus over the Persians in 396/5 BCE, he was recalled from Persia in order to engage the Athenians and the Thebans, and he barely defeated them at Coronea in 394 BCE. The combined naval forces of Athens and Persia were able to destroy the naval fleet of the Spartans, ending their brief naval domination. Persia supplied the Athenians with fresh money to rebuild her Long Walls, however recall that the Spartans negotiated with the Persians causing their financial support to be withdrawn.

Under pressure from the Spartans, the Persian king forced all warring parties of Greece to sign the Peace of Antalcidas, or King's Peace, of 386 BCE. According to this treaty, Lemnos, Imbros and Scyros went to Athens, while the majority of the city–states were guaranteed their independence. The Spartans were allowed to build an empire in central Greece and to withdraw from Asia Minor. Sparta established a garrison in Thebes to break up its emerging power and then turned its back on the Greeks, who were rebelling against the Persians in Cyprus and in Egypt, allowing the Persians to gain all the Greek cities of Asia Minor along with Cyprus. Consequently, everything gained by the Greeks in the Persian War was lost to the Persians, who actually controlled many of the mainland city–states of Greece. Athens had suffered its greatest defeat and its greatest humiliation, while Sparta earned the enmity of her Greek neighbors.

By 378 BCE, Athens had reformed its alliances in the Aegean region by bringing Chios, Lesbos, Rhodes, Byzantium, and Thebes into a new confederation. Three years later the confederation included seventy independent Greek cities. The emerging empire posed a new threat to Sparta and the growing power of Athens forced the Spartans to agree that the city–states of Greece should be allowed to be autonomous and also to be free of foreign garrisons. In 375 BCE a renewed King's Peace was established, but it only lasted for 18 months. At this time Thebes was determined to gain control of all of Boeotia and a new peace between Athens and Sparta was concluded in 371 BCE.

Because of the King's Peace, Spartans were given the power to interpret and to enforce Persian treaties in Greece and they used this opportunity as an excuse to invade Boeotia. Sparta intended to establish a Lacedaemonian type dictatorship in Boeotia in order to extract taxes and wealth. Sparta also claimed that the Boeotian

Confederation had violated the King's Peace and ordered it dissolved. In 371 BCE King Cleombrotus of Sparta invaded Boeotia with an army of 10,000. The Thebans rose up to protest the intrusion and assassinated the four Spartans sent to rule their region. The Thebans reorganized their confederation and called on Epaminondas to prepare them to war against the Spartans.

The two armies met at Leuctra where the Thebans defeated the Spartans, which allowed them to march into Peloponnesus and to give the Messenians (helots) their freedom. Thebes gained in influence in Greece by serving as the guarantor of Greek freedom from Spartan intervention. Step-by-step the structure of Spartan control of Peloponnesus was being dismantled. At this time the Spartans' strength was reduced to about 1,000 full citizens and the reputation of Spartan military power was destroyed. Meanwhile, the Athenians were actively seeking allies, and in 370 BCE formed a defensive alliance with Elis, but after Leuctra, the Athenians were forced to defend Sparta, as Athens was now in opposition to Thebes.

Upon his return home, Epaminondas attempted to create a new Theban empire and planned a war of conquest against the Athenians. Under his leadership the Thebans proved to be despotic causing several Greek cities to look to Athens for leadership. A combined Athenian and Spartan force met the Thebans at Mantinea in 362 BCE. The Thebans won the battle, but Xenophon's son, Gryllus, ended the Theban threat by killing Epaminondas. Persia was growing more active in the Hellespont as Athenian shipping was now at risk. Soon the power of Thebes fell into decline, and in 357 BCE Theban control of Boeotia disintegrated. In 357 BCE several states declared a "Social War" of rebellion against Athens in which Athenians were forced to grant the rebellious cities independence, which left Athens without allies or financial resources. Following a brief respite after the Social War, Philip II of Macedonia defeated the combined Athenian and Theban armies at Chaeronea in 338 BCE. One year later Philip became the elected commander of Greece and Macedon.

The Mercenary Commanders

Military matters related to empire building in the fourth century became associated with the growing power of the mercenary commanders, who also came to represent a threat to Greek liberty and democracy. As warfare continued to dominate city–state relationships, private armies became an important political and military factor. Adventurers found employment by serving as hired soldiers for kings or commanders and became embroiled in wars in Sicily, central Greece, and Asia Minor. Xenophon, for example, hired out to the Spartans who had become embroiled in Persian/Spartan politics. These exceptionally capable mercenary commanders were able to operate independent of polis authorities and could move about from one opportunity to another.

Dionysius of Syracuse was an instance of a cavalry commander who gained political power through his resistance to Carthage. He built a powerful army that was independent of Syracuse and by 380 BCE he gained control of virtually all the Greek states in Sicily and Italy and was in a position to build a political dynasty. He lived in a fortified palace and conquered a large territory which incorporated previously independent villages, towns, and city–states into his dominion. Mercenary commanders needed armories and a fortified administrative center to serve as a capitol, which was sometimes created in the form of administrative cities. The traditional polis, as a self–contained political unit, was no longer able to compete with these newly organized territorial states and was losing its political importance.

Dionysius was one of the first commanders to establish a pattern of rule that would be followed by Philip II; it was a pattern that allowed him to move into the power vacuum created by the state of continuous city–state warfare that characterized fourth century Greek politics. But in addition to being a competent military commander with a large mercenary army, Philip was a skillful politician and diplomat, which complimented his military power. Philip was able to secure Greek support through a change in policy that allowed the defeated city–states to keep their government, their weapons, and their defensive walls. He won support among the masses by protecting the weak and destroying the powerful, and he presented himself as a friend to the common man. Philip also used his diplomatic skills to gain allies and only resorted to force when he met direct opposition. Both the Athenians and the Spartans were caught off–guard when Philip positioned himself to serve as arbitrator of city–state conflicts and at the same time was able to guarantee the independence of Peloponnesian cities from Sparta. Isocrates and Plato's nephew, Speusippos, viewed Philip as a protector against the radical forces that were threatening to bring chaos to Greece rather than its conqueror. In addition, Philip was perceived as the man who could use his mercenary forces to establish the long held dream of a Panhellenic united Greece.

The Macedonian Monarchy

Philip and his son Alexander had a long–standing connection with the Greeks and had adopted some of their cultural expressions. For a time Philip had lived with the family of Epaminondas in Thebes, where he studied military tactics and acquired some elements of Greek customs and manners, but at the core he remained Macedonian and expressed their rough ways. He preferred the company of military men who had been seasoned by years of campaigning on the battlefield. For many Greeks, Philip was considered the bravest of men and carried the wounds of battle that included the loss of an eye, a broken shoulder, and partial paralysis of an arm and a leg. Philip also acquired and retained the skills of a wily master diplomat who often preferred deal–making to war. When war was inevitable, Philip was generous in victory but treacherous in his negotiations.

Affable in most of his relationships, Philip was willing to make promises and agreements when it served his purpose, and to break them at his pleasure, and then he would willingly promise again. He did not recognize or apply moral standards to politics or to diplomacy, but he preferred negotiations to the slaughter of war. Once on the battlefield, Philip extracted a bloody toll on his opponents and after the battle, it was not uncommon for him to walk about among the dead and to lament the slaughter. Demosthenes, despite his opposition, respected Philip and many Greeks considered him the greatest military man of the day. During his lifetime he was the most admired and feared sovereign and his government reflected his personality. He was an aristocratic monarch that could call on the battlefield services of over eight hundred Macedonian noblemen.

Philip traced the origins of his family to the gods and he respected the ancient Homeric heroes. He saw himself as a knightly crusader who was out to punish the Persians for their intrusion into Macedonian and Greek affairs, but also at the heart of his ambitions was desire for plunder. His ego was fed by his growing military reputation, which also was based on the old Homeric virtues.

As the legitimate king of a long–established monarchy, Philip could never be labeled as a tyrant, since he was legitimized in the oriental sense. Following his victory at Chaeronea Philip presented his system for ruling the Greek states at the Council at Corinth in 337 BCE; the Greeks were expected to back Philip's planned invasion of Persia. The following year Philip sent two of his trusted commanders, along with 10,000 troops, into Asia to begin the process of liberating the Greek cities. Philip could move with lightening speed and was not concerned with an assembly or a lack of resources to fund his campaigns. He began to solidify his plans and to hire Greek mercenaries to fill his ranks. Although Philip was not bound by the traditions of the Greeks, he did share their love of the old religion and was obsessed by their knightly and other archaic traditions.

In 336 BCE, Alexander was proclaimed king and the commander of the army that Philip had organized and trained. Under Philip, Alexander expressed his bravado by leading the charge from the front ranks, which served to increase his popularity among Macedonian commanders. After the death of Philip in 335 BCE, when Alexander was in the north, the Thebans revolted, forcing him to return to Greece. The Thebans refused to submit to Alexander, testing his mettle and responding by destroying most of their city, killing six thousand defenders and enslaving another thirty thousand. Later he came to regret the devastation even though he had spared the Theban temples and the house that Pindar had once occupied. He now realized, through the destruction, that he must remain sensitive to Greek culture or he would lose the ability to incorporate the Greeks into his Macedonian leadership.

Alexander, like his father, united the Greeks behind his command by claiming that he would use his power to punish the Persians who had committed sacrilege against the Greek gods and temples. At this time, Alexander would prove himself to be more than the equal of his father by executing Philip's unfulfilled plan to conquer the Persians and to take their throne. "The superb army created by his father was still intact. Its core was the Companions, an élite cavalry force of perhaps 1,800 men whose leaders traditionally enjoyed a rough comradeship with the king" (Freeman 1996, p. 259). To this force Alexander would add the Greeks including their infantry, cavalry, and navy, which made the Macedonians the most powerful military force in Europe and Asia Minor.

Fourth Century Civism

The fourth century gave witness to the establishment of schools of higher learning to satisfy the growing demand for education. At the beginning of the fourth century there was an especially strong demand for schools of rhetoric, which allowed teachers of rhetoric to charge a hefty fee, and made oratory a reserve for young men from wealthy families. Schools of philosophy, on the other hand, tended to follow Socrates' example by teaching without charge although the students were expected to contribute to the communal lifestyle of these schools. The disciples of the philosophers ranged from the late teen years to the middle twenty years of age. These schools mainly were a fourth century phenomena and mainly were established in Athens, although there may have been many more schools than those reported in the historical record. "We know of Isokrates' school from about 390, Plato's Academy from about mid-380s and Aristotles' Lykeion from about 355 in Athens (to be joined later by Epicurus' Gardens in 306 and Zeno's Stoa in 301-200). There were others, less well attested, in Elis, Eretria, Megara and Cyrene" (Davies, 1993, p. 175). Additional schools probably were located in the outlying reaches of Greece, perhaps on the islands in the Aegean Sea, as well as in various cities of Asia Minor, Syracuse, and southern Italy, but not before the fourth century.

Elements of *civism* continued to evolve in the fourth century, especially as a side issue that became a concern of the intellectuals. Education remained an informal or private aspect of family life and generally speaking, there wasn't any form of state–sponsored education, although some aspects of universal education briefly appeared in some Greek cities. At the same time, some fourth century scholars began to view education as a means of influencing the civic culture of the state. "Education is the means by which the state ensures the authority and stability of its own particular constitution through the creation of a particular type of citizen or subject" (Too, 1995, p. 206).

Elements of *civism* could be detected in the intellectual debates over the acquisition of virtue, leadership, and the role of education in shaping the mindset of those who would participate in the affairs of the state. On a more practical level, *civism* during the fourth century was related to citizenship participation, which was expanded by the development of a broader bureaucracy. The fourth century bureaucracy was used as a means of keeping power from concentrating in the hands of the wealthy and powerful families. Positions requiring fiscal management were no longer chosen by lot, and education played a more important role in the affairs of the state.

The idea of educating students in the political arts first appeared in the *Protagoras*, Plato's dialogue in which Socrates and Protagoras discuss the question "Can virtue be taught?" The discussion between Socrates and Protagoras centers on issues related to the nature of virtue, or its unique qualities, and whether virtue is something that can be acquired from the father or from the teacher or whether it is inborn. Plato was convinced that most people did not possess virtue nor could they acquire it, therefore they could not be entrusted with political power, thereby making democracy the worst of political systems. Protagoras and Isocrates made the claim that they could teach virtue, especially for those who were seeking to become political leaders. Plato could not satisfactorily dismiss the claims of Protagoras and Isocrates, leaving the argument of whether or not virtue or *civism* could be taught in an instructional setting as an open question. The limitations of this problem did not stop the sophists of the fourth century from going about and offering instruction in the political arts. They, for example, offered instruction in rhetoric, grammar, the dialectic, and so forth as their response to the need to educate students in the political arts, which can be considered the beginning of formal instruction in *civism*.

Scholars who were interested in the political problems facing Greece and the condition of its degenerating culture led the way to these Athenian schools. As a consequence, new ideas emerged regarding the nature of the state, its citizenship and the role of education in creating a *civism* that could be used to shape the citizens outlook to be compatible with the nature of the state. "Greek education practices underwent changes between 450 and 350 BCE. By the fourth century formal schools with distinct curricula began to emerge and compete. There is a tendency to assume that the same was true of the fifth century. However, there is no evidence of distinct and competing 'schools' prior to the time of Plato" (Schiappa, 2003, p. 157).

Intellectual development made some of its greatest strides in the fourth century as scholars worked to investigate every aspect of human activity in search of principles to guide individuals seeking the good life. In addition, Aristotle would greatly advance the development of the sciences by investigating natural phenomenon, emphasizing the techniques and methodologies of inquiry, which could be applied to new logical forms of investigation.

Professional teachers (sophists), who began to appear in the fifth century, studied the techniques related to rhetoric, the political arts, and the application of dialectic to debate and argumentation; the investigations of the philosophers would begin the process of creating new specializations in sciences and mathematics based on natural phenomena. Specialization moved in many different directions to form biology, meteorology, animal biology, geology, and medicine. In addition: "Intellectual models were formulated to explain and simplify the phenomena, such as Eudoxos' theory of concentric spheres, developed to explain the stations and retrogradations of the planets, or Aristotle's concepts of telos ('end' or 'purpose') and *entelecheia* ('full realization of potential'), developed to explain the biological processes of growth and maturation" (Davies, 1993, p. 152).

The formulation of logical proofs began to appear in geometry, rhetoric, and history, which also advanced prose writing with new emphasis on biography, local history, and universal studies. As sophists and philosophers established their permanent schools to advance their studies (which gave rise to ethics, logic, metaphysics, rhetoric, grammar, political science, dialectics, as well as forms of deductive and inductive reasoning), they also advanced the status of the city–states where they were located. The new forms of written history came to require archives to hold and store historical records or the documentation of the writings of scholars. These documents included the reflections or memoirs of some of the important individuals, and were produced by some of their students. Socrates' most famous students, for example, wrote about their recollections of him, and some wrote on his defense at his trial and his execution. One of his students, Plato, established the most famous school in Athens, the Academy, while Xenophon did not organize a school nor did he acquire a large number of followers. He wrote important treatises, a novel, a history, as well as works on various issues related to his experiences as a military commander for the Spartans. Xenophon's writings are valuable in that they provided a balance to the views of Plato, especially his reflections of Socrates and his views on philosophical questions.

Historical writing also led to biographical writing, while philosophical writing also began to develop its own forms. The groundbreaking fifth century work of Herodotus and Thucydides became a model for the narratives of later historians of the fourth and third centuries. New forms of philosophical investigation began by Plato in his series of dialogues, which inspired other writers, including Xenophon, to advance narrative writing, although Plato also expressed some of Socrates' precautions related to all forms of written expressions. Plato, in the end, was willing to pen his treatises regarding reality, social justice, and notions about ideals, virtues and *areté* in regard to leadership. Aristotle carried the use of written forms even farther through his extensive observations and collections, which came to form the foundation of libraries that would become great edifices of research in the Hellenistic Age.

Written forms came to include the advancement of written law or statues known as *nomoi*. Law codes had been known in the Mediterranean world since the time of King Hammurabi of Babylonia (ca. 1955-1913 BCE). As the Greeks advanced their written forms, they also advanced the idea of written law, which could be posted in public places. Written law became important as a moral force in establishing standards of conduct within the polis. "The lack of a formal police force in the fourth-century Athens meant that the authority of the laws rested immediately on the ability of the populace to exert moral pressure upon individuals who broke the laws" (Ober, 1989, p. 300). The written law became the foundation upon which the principles of the democracy could be enforced within the popular courts. By submitting to the law and the judgments of the jury, a citizen, aristocrat, or commoner was presenting himself as a "good citizen", a *démotikos*, who was willing to serve the state in good faith. He was, in other words, demonstrating his democratic *civism*.

The Ideal Expressions of Civism

Part V
Political Art as Civism

In this sense, once teaching oratorical and intellectual skills for payment had become the norm, the long–term effect of this educational movement was deeply conservative, since it strengthened the hands of those who could afford to pay.

— J. K. Davies

The term *logos* had many meanings and applications and had been difficult to translate, but typically translated to mean "argument" or reasoned discourse. "*Logos* was a much–overworked word during the sixth, fifth, and fourth centuries BCE and its meaning must be derived from context" (Schiappa, 2003, pp. 91-92). This meaning has been extracted from the study of ancient linguistics by scholars whose range of understanding included speech, descriptions, arguments, oral forms of thinking and reasoning or logic, explanations of phenomena or natural processes, the formulations of principles, as well as claims of reality and truth.

The origins of *logos* also have a somewhat checkered history that has proved to be controversial and open to scholarly debate and disagreement. Generally speaking, *logoi* was accepted as a special area of instruction that was developed and promoted by a group of scholars that Plato called *sophists*. Demand for a more specialized learning grew throughout the fifth century until this need could sustain itinerary teachers, who made a living by going from place to place presenting their courses in local lecture halls or on market place street corners. The sophists made their living by teaching a form of public speaking and dialogue. Logos was a quick–study lessons in argumentation. Students were taught to use almost any means to sway an audience, which included memorizing passages from Homer and Hesiod, as well as the other poets. They studied history and the plays of the tragic playwrights to make a point. In addition, they were trained to use theatrics, gestures, satire, maxims, and vocal exclamations.

Fourth century rhetoric was related to *civism* because it could be used as an influence in creating, maintaining, or modifying the citizens' mind–set. Politically, *civism* became related to public speaking because of its *persuasive* powers in creating a reasoned form of evidence by argument. The educational attractiveness of rhetoric was found in the effect that a sample speech could have on an audience. Such a demonstration could have a stunning effect on youths who were interested in newly created public careers that were available to individuals who possessed the oral skills to argue before an assembly or a court.

This demand allowed some teachers to establish schools and to become very wealthy. Protagoras, for example, demanded and received ten thousand drachmas for his instruction. This demand could rise or fall according to prevailing conditions of the market place in Athens. "For a long time this was the standard practice, but prices began to fall rapidly and, in the following century, between 393 and 338, Isocrates was only asking a thousand drachmas, and lamenting the fact that 'blacklegs' were ready to carry on business at bargain rates of four hundred or even three hundred drachmas" (Marrou, 1956, p. 49). During the fifth and fourth centuries BCE, *persuasive speech* became so important that students were taught to argue effectively either side of an issue and become quite theatrical as they learned to play on the sympathies of the jury by arousing the emotional pitch of an audience to pity, anger, admiration, or disgust.

Twelve

Sophism and the New Political Art

Beyond elementary instruction in schools or by private tutors in reading and writing, music and dance, fighting and athletics, which was well established in the fifth century, lay, as we have seen, the need to acquire the more complex skills appropriate for participating in public life.
— J. K. Davies

The ability to speak in public and to carry on private discourse in democratic Athens was the equivalent to all the means of modern communications in the technical age of today. During the fifth century, it became the essential educational element for entering public service, as it was training in the political arts for the democratic setting. "The Sophists' skills would be useful only to agitators of the people in cities where there was a people allowed to assemble in order to be agitated" (McClelland, 1996. p. 15). If one had the ability to argue persuasively, that individual had the power to command the respect of an adoring city population — a power that could be used to control decisive votes on critical issues. This ability made the orators the political stars of the courts and assemblies. "Rhetoric teaches from the first that what matters is not what is the case, but what appears, what men can be persuaded of" (Guthrie, 1971, p. 179).

The "new education" of the fifth century provided for civic elements introduced by the study of logos, grammar, science, philosophy, and history, which was offered by the sophists. These elements were based on the needs of the democratic system and were different from aristocratic requirements. The democratic city–state required a greater level of participation in the affairs of the community; more important still, it required leaders who were skilled communicators in public speaking and in written communications. Democratic leaders were expected to address all sorts of public issues related to domestic and international affairs; consequently, the new forms of education required advanced studies in grammar, oratory, debate, and the application of logic to persuasive argumentation.

By the middle of the fifth century, a pattern of learning had developed in which the older boys would divide their time between the music school and the *palaestra* and then return home for an evening meal and bath and return to the music school for more instruction. At this time, the palaestra and the music school had reorganized to offer new courses of study and new specialties. The distinguishing feature of this "new education" was a greater emphasis on developing a refined artistic expression, which included physical movements, as well as dance, that were accompanied by the lyre or chorus. The music school combined music with reading, writing, and poetry. The lyre and the flute were used to give the spoken word expression; therefore boys were expected to learn to play a musical instrument. "In the earlier period, the pupils only learned instrumental music for the purpose of accompanying their own singing, and consequently were restricted to instruments like the lyre; but in these later times instruments like the flute, in which music was necessarily dissociated from words, were learned by free–born boys" (Boyd and King, 1995, p. 23).

The Origins of Sophist Learning

An advanced higher education became an important aspect of fifth century education for young men who were searching for new opportunities in the public affairs of the polis. The teachers of this higher education often taught specialized courses related to *logos*, which included grammar, poetry, and dialectics. These teachers were called *Sophistai*, which translated to mean "men full of intellect or wisdom". Plato may have coined the word "sophists" and made popular the term "rhêtorikê." "*Logos*, of course was a far more comprehensive term than the fourth–century term 'rhetoric'" (Schiappa, 2003, p. 54). The oldest definition for "sophism" is related to the word *sophia*, which meant wisdom, as well as *sophos* which meant expert or sage. Some of the sophists were considered clever, but only a few were considered wise. The Seven Sages of the ancient world were called sophists and Solon was one of these men. Teachers, in general, were called *sophistês,* as were the poets. "The term first appears in Pindar in the early fifth century and predates the appearance of the group of so–called 'Old Sophists' identified as such by Hermann Diels and Walther Kranz" (Schiappa, 1999, p. 50). The "Old Sophists" consisted of seven fifth century teachers that included Protagoras, Gorgias, Hippias, Prodicus, Antiphon, Critias, and Thasymachus.

In the fifth century and before, the term *sophist* generally applied to philosophers, medics, and persons with technical abilities, and in the fifth century the term became associated with prose writers as well, while modern scholars have come to question the usefulness of these labels. The Seven Sages issued maxims or profound statements, which deemed them wise men; they included Anaxagoras, the teacher of Pericles. Plato's list included: Thales, Pittacus, Bias, Solon, Chilon, Cleobulus, and Myson, and there were other lists containing different names. Some men acquired labels such as "philosopher" and "sophist" and some wise men like Socrates and Protagoras were considered philosophers and sophists, depending on who did the labeling. By the fifth century, the term "sophism" had acquired a more negative meaning associated with false reasoning. Analytical and administrative skills taught by some sophists often were aimed at formulating policy and maneuvering propositions through various obstacles and oppositions, which required cunning and persuasive strategies. "Unfortunately, however, many Sophists were guilty of that sleight of argument for which the term 'Sophistry' was coined" (Heater, 1990, p. 6). They appealed to public sentiment that required a general, but shallow knowledge of historical events. As a general rule, some knowledge was needed in the service of the vilification of one's political opponent in the democratic arena of public opinion.

In the age of Socrates, the term "sophist" was applied to a particular class of professional teachers, or men who taught for a fee. "The sophists regarded excellence in speaking (*eu kalōs legein*) as the key to success in civil life" (Too, 1995, p. 87). The fifth century sophists believed that they were in the tradition of the poets and rhapsodes, or reciters of epic poems. In general the sophists rejected the monism of Parmenides who advanced the idea of empirical findings as a common sense solution to difficult questions. At this time, Eleatic argument could be used to prove that nothing exists, and it influenced Protagoras and Gorgias, as well as Heraclitus. In response, Protagoras wrote a book on *Being,* and Gorgias wrote his *On Non–Being* and demonstrated his mastery of Eleatic argument by turning it around and using it against those who had invented it. The sophists tended to dismiss the idea of a reality behind appearances and the idea of the unity of *Being,* and as a result they developed phenomenalism, relativism and subjectivism.

The Sicilian School

The first teachers of public speech, according to the traditional story, appeared as early as 460 BCE and had its origins in Sicily. "Rhetoric indeed arose, not in Elis, nor even in Greece, but in Sicily. Aristotle attributed its rise to the sudden spate of proceedings for the recovery of goods that developed after the expulsion of the tyrants of the Theron dynasty at Agrigentum (471), and those of the Hieron dynasty at Syracuse (463), and the ensuing annulment of the confiscation which they had decreed" (Marrou, 1956, p. 53).

Persuasive speech came into being when truth could not be determined and there was no way to sort out opinion from fact; therefore, training in public speech was a way of seeing and had little to do with truth. Truth often existed in the perceptions of individuals, which were acquired from within the culture. The sophists learned to attack perceptions as a way to develop a new or different mind–set in order to create a new understanding that was to their advantage. "This innovation was to have far–reaching effects, for it made popular, probably for the first time, a pedagogic technique that belonged to the repertory of what later came to be called rhetoric" (Cole, T., 1991, p. 80).

As was previously stated above, according to the traditional story of the origins of sophism, the demand for language skills related to public speaking first arose in

Sicily. It began following a rebellion that toppled a tyrant in 466 BCE, which led to the establishment of a democracy. Corax and his student, Tisias, wrote a handbook that led to the invention of rhetoric based on the parts of forensic speech, as well as strategies of advancing arguments of probability. *Technai*, or the techniques, or art, of speech, allowed a new body of professional teachers to earn their living by teaching these skills to willing pupils. "Accordingly, three traditions of rhetorical theory are identifiable in the fifth and fourth centuries: technical, Sophistic, and philosophical" (Schiappa, 2003, p. 40).

Individualism, Relativism, and Skepticism

The goal of the fifth and fourth century sophists was to help their students become wise and respected citizens and gentlemen. Most sophists were foreign born and they traveled in search of new markets for their specialties. "They were foreigners, provincials whose genius had outgrown the confines of their own minor cities" (Guthrie, 1971, p. 40). Many came from the outlying regions of the Greek world where they were free to develop speculative thought without fear of government censure. They were a mixed lot of *pedagogues* who saw the possibility of a livelihood by meeting the demands of an expanding economic and political opportunity. Many were opportunists of questionable character who had acquired their knowledge by traveling around the Aegean world; many lived in the colonies, where it was becoming common practice to challenge the established norms of traditional society. This challenge was expressed in a growing individualism that accompanied spreading democratic reforms and the need for formal training in the political arts. Taking advantage of democratic political institutions (assemblies and jury courts), the sophists provided a pragmatic education that perfectly addressed the demands of the new democratic age.

Some sophists were interested in anthropology or the evolution of human beings as a product of nature. They also were interested in human society and the advance of civilization. In addition, some showed interest in science, and they addressed questions relating to cosmology, astronomy, earth and ocean sciences, or any other question that was of contemporary interest. They were not a united lot, but competed against each other for attention and fame; they were not a "school", although they shared a common philosophical outlook or an empiricism, which led to their skepticism about certain knowledge. They tended to believe that knowledge was fallible and reality was tentative or unstable. "Truth was individual and temporary, not universal and lasting, for the truth for any man was simply what he could be persuaded of, and it was possible to persuade anyone that black was white" (Ibid., p. 51). Despite their somewhat shady reputations, their influence helped to create the Age of Enlightenment in Greece, the Periclean Age. The sophists caused the philosophers to react to their *relativism* when they maintained that laws, customs and religious beliefs were conventions of the times or of a particular society, and were not aspects of a fixed or universal truth. The philosophers tended to reject *relativism* as "the measure of all things" in order to assert a fixed and unchanging knowledge that could be discovered rationally or metaphysically as the measure of truth and reality in the physical world.

The common thread shared by the sophists was to teach youth how to deal with one's own affairs and the business of the state, as opposed to the arguments of *Being* or in finding fixed truths that the philosophers cared about. For the sophists, there is no law or rule or all–embracing idea that is good for man or for society. The negative image of sophism was due, in part, to Plato's view that sophistry and rhetoric were almost one and the same thing. Plato also may have been concerned that the sophists used the term "philosophy" as one of their means to attract fee–paying students. "When the sophists engaged in intellectual pursuits that we might be tempted to call philosophical, it was only with an eye toward captivating their audiences and hence capturing more students" (Schiappa, 1999, p. 163). In other words, it was simply another way of making a living based on another form of chicanery.

The Shallowness of Sophist Instruction

The philosophers, as well as other literary figures, sometimes chastised the sophists because of the shallowness of their instruction; in addition, many felt that they lacked moral integrity. Aristophanes was most effective in his use of satire, which took direct aim at sophist methodology and their willingness to twist the truth to achieve desired ends. However other sophists were different, and instead of simply training their students to win arguments, they also included a component of moral training that urged their students to make carefully researched and honestly presented arguments, arguments that could stand up to cross–examination in a court of law. As time passed, however, rhetoric became more superficial.

Despite their detractors, the sophists as a group were responsible for many scholarly accomplishments that advanced Greek civilization. For example, they were responsible for inventing grammar, and they perfected the dialectic as a form of advanced logic. Reading texts containing narratives of events or incidents began to emerge in the fourth century. In addition, they developed techniques to clarify thought and reason as they pertained to the transmission of knowledge, and they advanced prose as literature.

The sophists are perceived as transitional figures in the change of Greek culture from its mythic–poetic tradition to its acceptance of a humanistic–rationalistic tradition. They were out to advance prose writing, or the *techné* of writing as opposed to the oral tradition. "The supposed difference between an oral and literate culture can be summarized as follows: An oral culture's thought and expression are additive rather than subordinate, aggregate rather than analytic, close to the human life world, empathetic and participatory rather than objectively distanced, and situational rather than abstract" (Schiappa, 2003, p. 28). The sophists often presented prepared lectures from texts, which made prose the focus of much of their work. "The Sophists engaged in giving lectures and writing texts, thereby providing prose as a competitor to poetry as a vehicle of wisdom and entertainment" (Ibid., p. 31).

Hence they became the "deconstructionists" of their day and they applied logic to an examination of both traditional and contemporary social and political problems or issues. "In Socrates' day, the Sophists were saying that law was irksome, intolerable to strong natures, setting undue limits to what those strong natures could achieve if they were allowed their natural sway" (McClelland, 1996, p. 14). As a consequence of their teachings, the sophists appeared to be attacking the traditions of society, including religion and the values that were used to promote moral conduct, and were accused of corrupting youth. On the other hand, the common interest of most of the sophists was to increase the reasoning power and language skills of their pupils, and an exceptional few even attempted to address the nature of the soul, as was the case with Protagoras.

Logos and/or Rhetoric

In the fourth century, logos became rhetoric to be used as an art form that was concerned with the development of analytical and administrative skills as well as oratorical skills. *Technai*, the art of *logos*, became a shared trait of sophistry that was typically taught or presented in handbooks or reading texts. "The reading texts that resulted were not simply a record for future use of some of the productive modes of argumentation that can emerge for such debates. It was a substitute for actual attendance at a debate staged between two great masters of dialect — a means of showing to the play–loving Athenians pedagogically serious eristics in action" (Cole, T., 1991, p. 116). Some of these texts contained narratives of incidents that had actually taken place, such as the mutilation of the *Herms* (good fortune statuary representing the god Hermes), and were used as the basis for shaping public opinion, becoming the basis for historical accounts; but in general, *technai* contained instruction in rhetorical argument and the correct usage of language (grammar).

It appears that all the sophists except one, Gorgias of Leontimi in Sicily, accepted logos, or the art of public speaking, as *areté* (the art of positive speech as a prerequisite to reach human excellence). Gorgias considered logos as a skill that had little to do with morals or virtues. It was a technique for affecting the psychological environment of a listening audience. Skilled *declamation* tended to follow *technai* patterns that began with an event to determine the empirical facts that could then be formulated into a set of general rules. "These declamations might be simply rhetorical exercises on mythical themes, designed to show how, with skill and effrontery, the most unpromising case could be defended" (Guthrie, 1971, p. 42). The sophists and their students practiced their art of persuasion by performing in small circles and in public lectures, and they performed in gymnasia and at recital halls, where people might be willing to pay an admission fee. A typical display might begin with an invited question from the audience, while others gave displays from prepared themes and texts.

Gorgias, who was accepted as an important founder of the techniques of *logos*, helped to lay the foundation for training in public speaking by developing set patterns or formulas for addressing large audiences. He left no detail to chance, as this was a meticulous art that rested on three great elements that included *antithesis*, *balance of clause,* and *final assonance,* or the three Gorgiac figures. This formula fixed rhetoric in place throughout most of the ancient world. The *art of logoi,* as practiced by most sophists, also included some aspects of poetry and grammar. In addition, there were other specialties such as mathematics, music, astronomy, and so forth. Hippia, for example, was a polymath, while some others specialized in training in memory or in the handicrafts.

Schiappa (2003) challenged the standard story by arguing that the term *rhetoric* came about because of Plato's need to address the differences between sophism and philosophy in the fourth century. Schiappa believed that Plato probably invented the term *rhetôrikê* as a means of challenge some of the more corruptive sophist speech methods of the orators. Rhetoric, as described by Plato, had become a searching after political success, creating the need for Plato to coin the word *rhetôrikê* as a distinguishing concept between speech methods associated with logos and those associated with the confusing and evasive techniques of political argumentation. "Plato opposed education aimed at producing such orators because he did not trust the training to produce proper statesmen. Hence, whether he originated the term or not, rhetôrikê was a useful label for Plato to distinguish Isocrates' (and others) training from his own" (Ibid., p. 46). Schiappa also argued that the term *rhetoric* first appears in Isocrates and also in Plato's dialogue *Gorgias*, which also credits Corax and Tisias with the term. According to some, the term actually may have come from Aristotle. Schiappa also insisted that by accepting Plato as the author of the term rhetoric and not the fifth–century sophists, he provided new insights regarding the purpose of rhetoric and what the sophists meant by teaching the political arts. Schiappa was concerned that the introduction of the term *rhetoric* has confused the nature of the sophist movement as it was expressed in the fourth century. *Logos*, in other words, was an intellectual approach taken by the sophists to advance prose over poetry, which opened the way for them to introduce or invent new and more specialized fields of study. The challenge to poetry also allowed the sophists to introduce prose into the educational setting, which allowed writing and written texts to become a powerful media for both instruction and entertainment.

By the fourth century, it was a common practice for the masters of rhetoric to provide their pupils with copies of model speeches, which contained the above three Gorgiac figures, which could be presented orally or in written form. The pupils departed with their written copies and studied them in great detail. These sample speeches were to serve as models for their own composition. In formulating a composition, the pupil was taught to deal with content, a branch of rhetoric called *invention,* or to deal with the issues, ideas, or circumstances that should be argued in the speech. Invention was the discovery of the ideas embedded in an issue. Once these ideas were revealed, the pupil put them in a persuasive argument according to the prescribed elements of the set speech.

Also by the fourth century, teachers of public speech commonly used writing skills as a form of advertisement or as a specimen of model writing that was to be routinely produced by prospective students. The written speech became a literary formula that was used to deliver a lecture and which had the power to persuade a public audience. Some of Athens' orators became the first pamphleteers and political propagandists. No aspiring leader could ignore this powerful means of confronting opponents, promoting new ideas, or bringing about social and political change. More important still, poetry, the main literary form of the ancient world, was about to be replaced by prose orations. Perhaps the greatest of the Athenian writers of prose orations was Isocrates whose style of writing and oration influenced his contemporaries and cast a long shadow over much of western education.

The Critics of the Sophists

As was stated earlier, philosophers and literary figures became the harshest critics of the sophists. Socrates piled scorn upon the sophists for their errors in logic and the use of rhetoric as a means to prove either side of a case. Most of all, he condemned them for their mercenary ways and claimed that his ignorance of grammatical construction was due to his inability to pay their high fees. Plato also condemned them for equating right with might and thereby rejecting morals, ethics, traditions, and important human virtues. Isocrates, also deemed a sophist, opened his *Against the Sophists* by charging them with greed, but then he proceeded to out–charge them with his exorbitant fees.

Perhaps the most devastating attack against the sophists came from Aristophanes (445-380 BCE) who used satire to destroy their reputation. He targeted their character and the nature of their instruction. He also expressed the growing opposition to their crass commercialism and moral relativism. In his play, *Clouds*, Aristophanes charged the sophist with a lack of intellectual substance and he also harpooned Socrates, whom he viewed as a sophist and a ridiculous character with his head in the clouds. *Clouds* was well known by 420 BCE and reflected the skepticism that was mounting against the sophists by Athenian citizens. According to Oswyn Murray (1986), Aristophanes was ". . . reflecting the prejudices of the ordinary Athenian, these men were all pretty similar in their skepticism and moral relativism, their love of money and pretentious intellectual claims: they made people question the basic values of society like the existence of the gods and the duty to obey the laws; some of them even seemed to encourage their pupils to think that the political constitution was a matter of indifference" (p. 229). He considered the best days for Athens as the days of the Persian War when men stood their ground and upheld their traditions, customs, and religion. For Aristophanes, a good citizen had courage for the demands of life and their only decision–making was a matter of simple choice between good and evil.

Aristophanes' play ridicules the sophists, but also contrasted the aristocratic or the traditional values of education with the "new education". He used these comparisons to shame the educational innovations, especially flute playing in the new schools. He considered the flute music as a corruption of its earlier pure form. The lyre, in its simple Dorian form, was considered manly and important to the development of moral character, while the flute was effeminate and corrupting to the soul. Aristophanes' character, Socrates, was portrayed as attempting to use dialectic tricks to prove that anything can be twisted into a desired outcome. Socrates, in other words, was unjustly treated as the goat of Aristophanes' facetiousness. While, Aristophanes' play stands out as a protest against the "new education", he also was concerned about the general decline in Athenian culture. According to Boyd and King (1995) Aristophanes made the following points: "(1) that there had been a relaxation of the strict discipline of earlier days which had made the boys less modest and well–behaved; (2) that there had been substituted for the traditional epic and lyric poems which had served the older generation the works of more recent and less worthy writers, and (3) that there had been introduced into the music various elaborations which had deprived it of its severe simplicity and lowered its educational value" (p. 22).

Despite the attacks of the critics, the sophist thinking had become a dominant feature of Athenian public life and it would go on to become a more important influence in the fourth century, when rhetoric came into its own. Public speaking in the democracy was a serious business in societies where an assembly or a jury held the power to make war, exile an opponent, or take a life. "As Plato's Sophist, Polos of Agrigentum, declares, skillful orators, like tyrants, can have anyone they dislike condemned to death, or to confiscation of their property, or to exile" (Marrou, 1956, p. 52). The demand for instruction in the political arts continued to gather momentum, but this instruction did not follow any standard other than the promise that their techniques worked.

Political Art as Civism

The sophists often were blamed for the disintegration of the traditional knowledge and values of Greek society, but these declines were symptomatic of the end of the Golden Age of Athens. In reality, sophism made contributions to Greek knowledge, it did not provide a system of knowledge. Individualism could not provide moral truths that could be used as a guide for groups of people living in a community; more seriously, the self–centered orientation of the sophists may have helped to destroy the citizen's sense of loyalty to the community, or his *civism*. As a result, democrats and oligarchs became embroiled in bitter social class warfare as they clashed over the spoils of the public treasury. The dole was becoming a way of life for the lower classes and the upper classes. No longer did citizens see value in the virtues of labor, or in honest trade, or in helping the less fortunate. Bribery became the common practice for procuring public office, and juries were open to bribery as the Athenian sense of justice began to disappear. At its most decadent level, murderers could be freed and the innocent could be executed. Once cultural decline began, its momentum increased until Athens became a museum of its glorious past. In the meantime, the Athenians would struggle on in an attempt to fend off their enemies until that effort also became futile. Alarmed at the prospects of the Athenian decline, a few thoughtful men began searching for a solution in the form of new ideologies that could redeem the ancient ethos, or a new *civism*.

Sophism was brought into place by the demands of democratic requirements for public office, but sophism was not grounded in a unified theoretical ideology, body of knowledge, or philosophical understanding. The sophists generally were not involved in the philosophical or the scientific movements of the age, but were involved in the educational and the social issues that characterized the fifth and fourth century's politics. As an educational movement, sophism was mainly a response to changes in culture and a growing demand for pragmatic instruction that would allow individuals to take advantage of current political and economic conditions. Although the sophists claimed that they were offering a form of leadership education, they generally failed to advance leadership principles or those ideals that could be used to prepare an individual to make decisions according to a prescribed set of values.

The sophists were successful in training an individual in persuasive argument or in the techniques of winning a case in court, but they could not provide future leaders with a program of personal development that allowed them to achieve a higher level of moral thinking that would advance their *civism*. In other words, while they promised training in "the political arts", they mainly failed to advance the type of moral training needed to shape good citizenship and they also failed to produce leaders capable of regenerating Athenian society. They lacked in the ability to help the individual citizens to advance to a higher level of civic understanding or to learn what was needed to revitalize, to reorganize, or to reform the state.

The sophists created pedagogical science and pragmatism and were the first to explore these possibilities They invented the science of *pedagogy* based on the notion that every person under their supervision could learn speaking and writing skills by studying and imitating ideal models. A great achievement of the sophists was the invention of the techniques of grammar, rhetoric and dialectic, and the technical rules that eventually standardized these forms. Perhaps the greatest claim of the sophists for western civilization was the idea of the creation of a science of education based on the proposition of specified aims or outcomes. They also claimed that they were teachers of a political art based on the idea that virtue could be taught as a means to shape the individual to fit into any *constitution* regardless of its nature. Stated differently, human nature, according to the sophists (i.e. Protagoras), is so pliant that it can be molded by educational means to any desired citizenship model. This form of *civism* would achieve its greatest influence in connection with the political "isms" of the twentieth century.

Thirteen

Protagoras and Civism

Protagoras has been called the first positivist, the first humanist, the forerunner of pragmatism, a skeptic, an existentialist, a phenomenalist, an early utilitarian, a subjective relativist, and an objective relativist.

— Edward Schiappa

Protagoras (c. 490 – 420 BCE) was born to a poor family in Abdera, an Ionian colony in the region of Thrace. In order to make a living, Protagoras was willing to work as a porter and at other humble occupations. Smith and Smith (1994) noted that: "A questionable source has it that Protagoras was educated by Democritus (famous for atomic theory and materialism) after the latter happened to see a device that the young porter had invented for carrying loads" (p. 11). Protagoras arrived in Athens in 450 BCE and was the first recognized professional marketplace sophist who offered instruction in specific skills for a fee or *misthos*; in addition, he may have set the pattern of traveling from town to town in search of students. Protagoras often would appear at public festivals or at the athletic games where crowds were sure to assemble, being attracted by his entertaining sideshow, where he demonstrated his ability to argue either side of an issue. One successful technique was for a sophist to draw a crowd and to demonstrate his skills through a sample lecture. When questioned about his offerings for students, the traveling teacher would claim that he focused on useful skills for the management of both household and public affairs. These useful skills included: "The ability to think clearly, speak persuasively, manage one's personal life satisfactorily, and enter prudently into public discourse . . . . Since each citizen was his own prosecutor or defender, the ability to reason clearly and speak persuasively could have profound importance for a person's property, life and liberty" (Smith and Smith, 1994, p. 12). These sophists were professional in that they may have originated the idea that the fee–agreement between teacher and student should be based on results. From the writings of Plato we learn that Protagoras was greatly admired by Plato, although he took issue with his philosophy, as well as his fee-based instructional system.

Grammar and Logic

The intense interest in the possibilities and limitations of language led to the beginning of grammatical studies (distinctions of gender, parts of speech and so forth), of which can be traced from Protagoras onwards. Moreover, Plato credited Protagoras with having developed a subjective point of view in philosophy that was grounded in four important processes: sensation, perception, understanding, and expression. Plato also credited Protagoras for his grammatical discoveries in connection with the three genders of nouns and for his use of tenses in verbs. "Protagoras, we are told, was the first to divide speech (logos) into four basic kinds: requests (or prayer), questions, answers, commands; or according to other authorities into seven: narrative, question, answer, command, report, request, summons" (Guthrie, 1971, p, 220). The contributions of Protagoras are those of a pioneer whose advancements would forever influence the study of grammar, although the greatest advancements in grammar would come in the fourth century. In the fifth century, Protagoras was searching for a "*logos* on *logos*," or a rational way to deal with persuasive discourse, rather than relying on advancements in grammar. Grammar advanced at a later time when writing began to replace many of the practices of the oral tradition. "Protagoras' insights concerning the parts of speech, the gender of words, and what are now called grammatical moods were not part of a *grammatiké* per se and should not be so 'reduced'. The first appearance of *grammatiké* to designate a specific verbal *techné* was in Plato in the fourth century" (Schiappa, 2003, p. 162).

Evidently, Protagoras used *techné* related to advancements in grammar to evaluate Homer and the other poets. "Aristotle reports that Protagoras was concerned with the proper gender of words, and in the *Poetics* claims that Protagoras criticized the opening of Homer's *Iliad* for using the mode of 'command' rather than 'request'" (Schiappa, 1999, p.78). Perhaps Protagoras' greatest philosophical achievement was associated with his early form of *positivist* thinking related to *relativism*. Protagoras may have been the first positivist philosopher, which allowed him to dismiss the notion of absolute *truth*. Aristotle credits Protagoras with making statements about making "weaker" *logos* the "stronger" *logos*, which related to his "two–*logoi*" hypothesis.

Things seemed to come in opposite pairs such as eyes, legs, up and down, etc. Protagoras asserted that for every "thing" there are two–*logoi* and one of the two was preferred. This "rule" set up the notion that the stronger *logoi* is preferred over the weaker *logoi*, or the less preferred (the "stronger" *logoi* being the one that is dominant in a particular culture). So, for example, if we take the *dissoi logoi* according to this statement: "gay marriage is Just" and "gay marriage is Unjust." The "stronger" *logoi* in American society is that gay marriage is Unjust since it holds sway in the laws of most of the states. What makes the "weaker" *logoi* the "stronger" *logoi* is *persuasion*. In other words, if the majority of American voters can be persuaded that gay marriage is Just, then the weaker *logoi* becomes the stronger. This is not an ethical distinction, but an empirical decision. The content or the subject matter is not considered relevant since all "things" have two-*logoi*. The origin of this distinction could be found in the discussions of the early philosophers who were attempting to deal with human perception of reality.

Consequently, Protagoras may have been one of the first sophists to demonstrate that it was logically possible to argue for or against the same proposition, which was related to the "two-*logoi*" proposition described above. "Two related views taught by sophists aroused special controversy: the idea that human institutions and values were only matters of convention, custom, or law (*nomos*) and not products of nature (*physis*), and the idea that, since truth was relative, speakers should be able to argue either side of a question with equal persuasiveness" (Martin, 1996, p. 143). However, Zeno of Elea and the Eleatic thinkers, Parmenides and Melissues, may have developed the origins of this persuasive strategy by attempting to prove, by argument, that a conclusion that nobody would accept could become acceptable. Zeno, who defended Parmenides, wrote a whole book consisting of argumentative strategies, based on opposites ("two–*logoi*" argumentation).

Protagoras extracted vital elements from these strategies and turned them into a systematized polemic method or debate technique, especially useful before a jury court. The process of this method was based on taking an opponent's conceded points and using them as a starting point to expand the argument in one's favor. This technique had the effect of confounding the opponent and collapsing his defenses. "Its historical importance cannot be over–estimated: the tradition inaugurated by Protagoras explains the predominantly dialectical tone that was henceforth to dominate, for better or for worse, the whole of Greek philosophy, science and culture" (Marrou, 1956, p. 51). This approach helped to reduce the art of practical debate into the sophists' cunning bag of tricks. Some of the philosophers also upset the traditional mind–set when they proposed new ideas about the laws of nature and the mechanics of the cosmos. Ionian intellectual rational thought in the sixth century, in other words, created further unsettling ideas in the fifth century related to the traditions of culture and religion as were expressed in the ideas of Protagoras. For example, Protagoras advanced prose writing as a challenge to the long–standing practice of the poets who had focused on a legendary *mythic–poetic* tradition, and he promoted the practice of *logos* through a *humanistic–rationalistic* tradition that would become the foundation of western humanism, making him a fifth century iconoclast. As was previously stated, he appears to have advanced the study of poetry by making it subject to critical analysis.

Prose in Preference to Poetry

Logos, as practiced by the sophists not only impacted philosophical thought among the Ionian intellectuals, but also had a direct impact on Greek culture by advancing prose writing over poetry. During the fifth century, prose writing gave rise to biographical forms, such as those developed by Plutarch, and also stimulated historical forms advanced by Herodotus and Thucydides. "In any case, the rise of prose writing permitted for the first time the treatment of poems and myth as objects of knowledge to be stored, manipulated, and rearranged for the purpose of analysis" (Schiappa, 2003. p. 53). This important cultural change had the effect of promoting writing over the oral tradition, which helped to stimulate written works as an important intellectual form.

Protagoras was one the first sophists to write in prose, which appeared as books of maxims for his students. By the fourth century the teaching of writing became a standard educational subject in most Greek schools and it began to change the practice of requiring students to memorize and recite poems to music. As books became more available in the fourth century, copy centers were created, which allowed individuals to collect books and created a need for libraries and archives, which became the workshops of scholars.

Protagoras' greatest and most controversial convention was his willingness to accept the above–mentioned processes, provided that they led the individual to knowledge and truth in the *relative* sense. The transformation of education based on this type of thinking laid the foundation for humanism based on the statement that "man is the measure of all things," which had the effect of turning the forces of tradition against the sophists. "A great deal of mischief has been done by trying to give this a metaphysical significance, turning its author into the fountain–head of phenomenalist empiricism, a forerunner of modern subjectivism" (Marrou, 1956, p. 51). Henceforth, there were no limits to bind human curiosity and there were no sacred realms that could not be investigated by humankind.

Justifying Democracy

Pericles included Protagoras within his circle of friends, and some writers credit him with providing a theoretical justification for democracy. "J. S. Morrison has claimed that Protagoras achieved such a position because of his ability to provide a theoretical justification for the practice of Periclean democracy" (Schiappa, 2003, p. 13). In 443 BCE Pericles sent Protagoras to establish a new colony at Thurii as a planned Panhellenic community. "His oratorical ability and his upright character so impressed the men of Athens that they chose him to devise a code of laws for a new colony to be founded in Thurii in southern Italy in 444 BC" (Martin, 1996, p. 142). The colony fell into strife and most of the Athenians returned to Athens. Pythagoras also got into religious trouble, which forced him to leave Athens after writing his treatise *On the Gods*. His *agnosticism* was established when he wrote: "Concerning the gods, I have no means of knowing whether they exist or not or of what sort they may be, because of the obscurity of the subject, and the brevity of human life." This work brought a lawsuit by Pythodorus who charged him with impiety. A jury found Protagoras guilty and ordered the burning of his written works. They sent him into exile for his role of appearing to have dismissed the gods, and his *agnosticism* was compounded by his *relativism* and caused many to find his ideas objectionable, if not sacrilege. "We may conclude that Protagoras adopted an extreme subjectivism according to which there was no reality behind and independent of appearances, no difference between appearing and being, and we are each the judge of our own impressions. What seems to me is for me, and no man is in a position to call another mistaken" (Guthrie, 1971, p, 186).

Civism as Relativism

There are scholars who contend that *On the Gods* should not be accepted on face value, as Protagoras' dismissal of the gods is only a fragment of a larger piece of work. They have speculated that he may have been following a sophist technique of raising a double discourse ("two–*logoi*") as a means of affirming a statement, principle or *truth*. In other words, Protagoras may have intended to affirm the existence of the gods, but was misunderstood according to the logic of his analysis; therefore, the statement that "man is the measure of all things" may be related to the issue of *Being* and *Non-being*. Protagoras might be saying that the individual must decide whether or not he believes in the gods. This reasoning may have caused Plato to oppose Protagoras' individualism and to assert: "God is the measure of all things," and also may have led him to argue the idea that our perceptions were not reliable measures of the *truth*. For Plato, Protagoras made the individual the arbiter of whether the gods exist, and this was unacceptable. Stated differently, Protagoras might have been asserting that each person must choose to become believers or non-believers, which would suggest that his *relativism* is in combination with his individualism.

In other words, religion is a matter of opinion and not truth; however, Protagoras also affirmed that if a person is a citizen of a city and if that city accepts the existence of a specific god, then that citizen is obligated to accept the existence of the god as an expression of his citizenship. Protagoras now was making it clear that he was not the enemy of social traditions or the customs of the city, but was its advocate. Political power, in other words, came from those influences that caused individual citizens to conform to the social and moral standards of the community and its constitution. "To this some may object that Protagoras accepts and exploits the *belief* in the existence of the gods more than the existence of the gods itself. But in fact, in his philosophy, this amounts to the same thing, since Protagoras suppressed the distinction between knowledge and opinion. What is true is collective adherence, which constitutes strong discourse. Such is truth, according to Protagoras" (Brunschwig, et. al., 2000, p. 727).

In relative terms, Protagoras asserts that the gods exist or do not exist according to the circumstances; therefore, the gods are valued for their cultural usefulness and not their absoluteness. In other words, the citizen living in a city that worships a deity is "required" to worship that deity. His rationale for this assertion was based on his belief that an established religion was useful and a denial of that religion was harmful. Acceptance of the established religion of the polis was a requirement for social unity and the harmony of the polis. More important still, he believed that citizens of a community or polis needed some form of religion or common belief to establish law so that justice could prevail. *Justice* allows a large number of people to live together in harmony, and this was the basis of political and social living, which was so essential to the survival of the human race. Therefore, citizenship was a reflection of the shared values of the community, and the leaders of the polis were required to emphasize those values that unified the community, including its religion.

Civism and Education

Protagoras maintained that he could make a student a better person, and he argued that a community was good, if it was based on *justice* and *reverence,* and that a good polis or community is capable of producing good citizens. The formula for his *civism* was based on the following principles: parents must provide an ethical education for their infants and young children; the primary school must teach moral education as well as grammar and poetry, musical and physical training; and the laws of the city must declare what was right and acceptable. Protagoras, in other words, may have been the first ancient Greek scholar to recognize that the state must play a role in the education of all students as a means of advancing a form of *civism* within the culture. *Civism* was to be based on the individuals' perceptions about the goodness of the state; therefore, the state should provide those persuasive elements that reinforced these perceptions as a necessary aspect of political power.

Protagoras prescribed a pattern of education in which the parents would be responsible for the initial stages of education. Parental instruction included such issues as: what is just and what is unjust, what is honorable and what is shameful, what is sacred and what is profane, and what is good behavior and what is bad behavior. In the next stage, the child would come under the influence of the tutor, who was to render instruction in reading, music, and good behavior within the public setting. In the third stage, the student would come under the influence of the epic poets and would be instructed in the study of noble conduct through heroic examples, to play the lyre and to sing the songs of the poets, and to advance in the graceful arts as a means of helping the student acquire a gentler nature. The teacher of gymnastics would be assigned the task of strengthening and developing the body to be in balance with the mind and to cause students to become courageous in the face of danger. The final course of study would focus on the laws of the state as a means of living in harmony with society.

In addition, Protagoras was interested in developing strong leadership traits to prepare his students for political strife, but also to prepare them to live as good citizens who could rule their own affairs and effectively express their political views in the democratic arena. Pericles also seemed to have adopted the idea that the state had a responsibility to advance the citizenship of the individual in order to achieve his vision of a great democratic society. "It was a purely practical aim: the 'wisdom' and 'valour' which Protagoras and his colleagues provided for their disciples were utilitarian and pragmatic, and they were judged by their concrete effectiveness" (Marrou, 1956, p. 50). In general, Protagoras claimed that his aim was to teach the *art of politics*. "The important thing was life, and in life, especially political life, knowledge of the truth was less important than the ability to make any particular audience . . . admit the probability of any proposition whatsoever" (Ibid., p. 51).

While serving as a lawgiver in Thurii, Protagoras may have proposed the formation of a state–operated educational system for the purpose of promoting citizenship, and he may have advanced a legal standard that would have required that students learn to read and write at public expense. "While serving as a 'lawgiver' in the colony of Thurii, Protagoras apparently proposed that sons of all citizens be taught to read and write at public expense" (Schiappa, 2003, p. 160). Education at public expense was a practice in some cities to provide war orphans with a basic education. Protagoras may have intended to extend this practice to all students as a means of providing a basic elementary education to the children of the lower classes as a reform that would advance the well being of the polis.

To elevate the rational cognitive skills of students of the upper classes, Protagoras would advance the Socratic method as a form of argumentation and declamation. Sophistic forms of education were a means of changing the mind–set of his students; it was logos acting on logos as a strategy of Gorgias, which may have been derived from Protagoras, his contemporary. For most Sophists, words (logos) were more than sounds that impacted mental images; words had the power to transform individuals and societies. Words (logos) had the power to change the mind–set of the hearer for the better; it had the power to create a new moral order.

Protagoras not only helped to justify Periclean democracy, but he also insisted that individuals possess a nature that could be educationally molded to meet the needs of the state and its political system. "Protagoras himself insisted that his doctrines were not hostile to democracy, especially because he argued that every person had an innate capability for 'excellence' and that human survival depended on the rule of law based on a sense of justice" (Martin, 1996, p. 143). *Areté*, in other words, was not innate and fixed, but was influenced by life's experiences, including the system of rule. Education was the best means for the state to control the development of citizenship; otherwise other influences and other forces within the culture would take over with unpredictable consequences. "It is virtually certain that Protagoras provided a theoretical justification for education and Periclean democracy. His Great Speech in Plato's Protagoras is generally regarded as a moderately reliable index of his actual defense, and in it one finds an argument for the teachability or *areté*—the underlying premise justifying education and Periclean democracy" (Schiappa, 2003, p. 170). Although it is not know to what extent the idea of education for *areté* was debated in Greek society, it had an impact on fifth century playwrights and was a debated concern among fourth century philosophers. This debate helped to lay the foundation for the future development of political and educational thought for centuries to come in western civilization.

Plato's *Protagoras*

Protagoras' *civism* can be detected in Plato's dialogue entitled *Protagoras*, in which his characters, Socrates and Protagoras, indulged in a *two–logoi* debate over issues related to human character and the nature of the political culture. Protagoras framed his argument in Greek mythology that suggested that the human race would have destroyed itself, without Intervention, because it lacked in the qualities needed to live peacefully in a community setting. In an earlier age the gods were in control of the affairs of humankind, but this age passed away and humankind was left to handle its own relationships. The plight of human beings was such that they were in danger of perishing because they lacked the qualities needed to establish a stable political community. Zeus stepped in to save humankind by sending the god Hermes from Olympus to teach the virtues of *justice* and *reverence* needed to allow human beings to live in harmony in the polis.

Protagoras used this story to suggest that citizens could learn *justice* and *reverence* from their societies through educational means. Education, in other words, was to be the means that could be used to help make individuals attain those virtues that made societies Good. Woodruff (2005) in his study of Athenian democracy argues that the foundation of democratic Greek societies was *justice* and *reverence*. "Justice involves balance; sometimes the balance comes through equality, sometimes through a fair division that is not equal, but proportional . . . (while) Reverence is a virtue that leaders need more than anyone, because it is an antidote to hubris" (p. 202). Woodruff reasons that *reverence* places limits on human arrogance, ambition and greed, and *justice* is taught in the administration of the law, crime and punishment. *Reverence* helps to make democratic leaders aware that they are ignorant of the future and as humans are likely to make mistakes. It reigns in those who claim to be better or more expert than all others to protect society or the state against bad decisions. In Athenian society, *reverence* and *justice* were learned by example within the community as well as through poetry and plays, which tended to focus on the follies of human nature.

Protagoras, according to Plato, accepted the idea that *justice* and *reverence* could be taught by example and that these virtues were <u>not</u> innate or a natural aspect of inherited human character. At issue is the question of whether virtue could be taught or whether it was an inherited quality that could not be taught. Socrates, in Plato's dialogue, takes the position that *justice* could not be taught nor could it be defined. Taking the opposite position, Protagoras argued that *language* could not be defined, but it could be taught. *Language* is learned by example, as are the civic virtues; however it must be accepted that not all students will learn what is intended, and some students will not learn at all. To compound the argument, Protagoras claimed that *justice* was whatever the community accepted as a part of their customs, traditions and laws, which made *justice* relative to local circumstances. Plato, on the other hand, argued that *justice* was a universal standard or a higher and fixed value. Plato also argued that *justice* is universal and not local and that it could not be defined in terms of customs, traditions, or by the law. According to Plato, the problem with *relativism,* as applied to *justice,* was his belief that injustices were built into all cultures and some individuals or groups would suffer as a result of cultural injustices. Plato also denied Protagoras' assertion that he was able to teach *areté* to make his students better persons. Plato's Socrates asserted this argument by claiming that it was not possible to teach *areté,* and he gave the example of the *good* father who raised the *bad* son. Protagoras insisted that he could use language in the form of *persuasive speech* (*logos*) to teach character and moral conduct as well as *reverence* and *justice.* In other words, he could teach *civism* through the acquisition of *virtue* and *persuasive speech.*

Civism and Virtue

Protagoras claimed that he could teach *areté* (excellence), or virtue in the form of good citizenship as important aspects of his *political art.* "That 'virtue' could be taught was the basis of the Sophist's claim to a livelihood, and its justification lay in the close connexion in the Greek mind between arête and the special skills or crafts (*technê*)" (Guthrie, 1971, p. 255). Consequently, most citizens share in having political virtues that are not innate abilities, but require teaching. Parents, schoolmasters and finally the laws of the polis were used to teach political arête in Ancient Greece. This instruction began in childhood and continued into adult life. *Areté* is only to be acquired by applying oneself diligently to it over a long period of time.

In addition, Protagoras argued that raw human nature *does* contain the possibility of moral advance, though its realization requires the right experiences and education. Moral virtue and political virtue need instruction and practice. "As to his own claims as a Sophist, given that virtue can be taught, and is continually being instilled in an infinite variety of ways simply by the experience of being brought up in a well–governed state, we must, he modestly concludes, be content if we can find someone rather better than the rest at advancing us along the road, and that is all I claim to be" (Guthrie, 1971, p, 68). The laws (*nomoi*) were to serve as the guide laid down to teach its citizens the limits of good conduct. Protagoras believed that man's nature brings him destruction while the laws are ordinances of 'nature', but he did not see law as a provision of nature. Man's weaknesses needed political organization to allow him to survive his nature. Nature gave man the intelligence needed to organize him politically. Intelligence was the link between *nomos* (law) and *physis* (nature), which is God–given to allow man to survive. When, or should the laws fail, tyrants emerged. Nature is disorderly and laws are needed as a common agreement that could be applied to all to give order and harmony to the civic community.

Civism, therefore, should be taught as a craft, or *technê.* The basis of *civism* is the ethical qualities of *justice* and *respect* for self and for others. The teaching of *civism* can be defined as prudence in individual conduct and the management of personal affairs as well as the affairs of the community. Protagoras' core argument was that *civism* is not a natural part of human nature, but had to be recognized and developed as a state responsibility. *Civism* in ancient Greece was an aspect of the persuasive skills and a necessary element in democratic debate, and these skills should be developed within some instructional setting. "Admonition and punishment are only appropriate in the absence of such good qualities as may be acquired through 'care, practice and teaching': they are not employed against natural deficiencies, which a man can do nothing to alter. All that the Sophists can claim is to carry the teaching a little farther and do it better, so that their own pupil will be superior to their fellow-citizens" (Guthrie, 1971, p. 256). Protagoras argued that youth could become good through appropriate study, and education and they must learn the techniques of *persuasion* as a defense against false logic. Stated differently, pupils must be taught to listen, to analyze, and to think before accepting a claim of truth, making a decision, or taking action.

Fourteen

Isocrates and Civism

For Isocrates logos politicos is the only legitimate language for a citizen and thus one to which all other discourses must be either subsumed or subordinated.

—Yun Lee Too

Born in Athens into a wealthy family, Isocrates (c. 436 – 338 BCE) received an extensive education that included important teachers such as Prodicus of Ceos, Gorgias of Leontini and several others. He also became a disciple of Socrates, who influenced his intellectual development and his moral and ethical outlook, and he was greatly affected by the Peloponnesian War, which destroyed his family fortune. The outlook of his teachers, who opposed both the democratic system of government and the Periclean Empire, complicated his attitudes. "Instead of regarding Isocrates as an anomaly for not participating in civic life, we need to recognize that he deliberately distances himself from a democratic Athens in which civic and political life is above all defined by public and oral performance of discourse" (Too, 1995, p. 112).

Isocrates, because of his discomfort with public speaking, would do his speaking through his writing. "By turning to written discourse, he was able to make the excuse that he was unable to speak well before an audience. Isocrates' characterization of the written text as *logos erēmos* emphatically reinforces his self–portraiture as an individual who refused to engage in public oratory and as someone who is disassociated from politics of the popular demagogue" (Ibid., p. 121). Isocrates was able to elevate writing to a form of new civic communication in which ideas about the civic culture of the community were shared and debated in written forms that included the dialogue. Through his written speeches, Isocrates hoped to claim a new status as the master of written political thought for all of Greece

Isocrates began his career by serving for a short time as a writer of court speeches or *logographos*; however, he soon turned to the teaching of oratory and began a career that lasted for nearly fifty–five years. His attempt to become a public speaker was hampered by his weak voice; in addition, he was ill at ease in front of a large audience, which forced him to write short works that he used to attract students. Later, as a successful teacher, he used his writing skills to influence the direction of Athenian politics and in the process became a pamphleteer. At the same time, Isocrates had disdained many subject areas, which included law court *eristics*, astrology, geometry and various forms of dialectics. He associated these areas with the sophists who participated in a form of eristic duels or disputations that sometimes used false proofs. He advanced a form of higher education based on a well–informed discussion of practical issues or problems that were important at the time. According to Isocrates, practical discussion could lead to practical actions, which often were the themes of his written speeches. He was not theoretical or dogmatic; instead, his goal was to teach men how to argue and to think, rather than to teach them what to think.

Isocrates used great care in preparing his students for their literary and civic work, and he took a personal interest in their lives and careers. He taught writing as an instrument for action and a means by which an author could lay out his ideas for circulation as a possible plan of action. Isocrates himself spent many hours, even years, in the construction of a speech before it was made public. Unlike other sophists, he developed a stable and a consistent course of study in which his pupils were required to develop the ability to speak well. His care in preparation rested on the notion that speech was *logos*, which had the power to influence the mind and to call it into action. Isocrates believed in the centrality of *logos* as the force of culture, as it helped to make humans more human and allowed them to become more civilized. He believed *logos* was the force that enabled humankind to be able to build cities, implant justice within the law, and create the technology that refined and advanced human society. Because of *logos*, humans can discuss social, economic, and political issues, and develop theories about the natural world; *logos*, the basis for abstract thought, was to serve as the driving force in education. At the same time, Isocrates recognized the power of myth and religion in the culture and was not above using aspects of religion in his own works. In his *Philippos* he was willing to use mythology to legitimize the claims of Philip, and used those claims to assert his right to the leadership of all of Greece.

The Isocratic School

In 391 BCE Isocrates established the most successful school of oratory and rhetoric in Athens. This school coincided with the establishment of Plato's Academy, which was founded around 380 or 390 BCE. Isocrates' early work, *On the Sophists*, also corresponded with Plato's dialogues, *Gorgias* and *Protagoras*. This work was designed to counter Plato's ideas regarding an education for solving the social and political problems facing Athens at this time. Isocrates attracted student from all parts of Greece who were interested in learning his system of rhetoric, which would have a profound influence on written and spoken language during the fourth century. Many of his pupils rose to positions of importance and Isocrates came to be considered a prophet of the Hellenistic Age, although some described him as a flatterer who used his skills to win the favors of powerful people. However unlike most Sophists of his day, Isocrates attempted to promote higher moral values and virtues as an element of his instruction. "Regarding education as the preparation for a useful life doing good in matters of public importance, he sought to develop an educational middle ground between the theoretical study of abstract ideas and training in rhetorical techniques for influencing others to one's own private advantage" (Martin, 2000, p. 186).

Consequently, Isocrates was able to transform rhetoric through his teaching of ethics, which encompassed his attempt to develop moral character. "Isocrates completely agreed (with Plato and Aristotle's views on a moral emphasis in education); his ideal *paideia* stressed not only the formal education of children but moral education which institutions would inculcate in the mature citizens" (Ober, 1989, p. 160). According to his approach, learning became a type of knowledge that was to enhance the nobility of the soul. "The things that Isocrates tried to foster in his disciples were—ability to make decisions, an intuitive grasp of the complexity of human affairs, and a perception of all the imponderable factors which help to direct one's 'opinion' and make it a just one" (Marrou, 1956, p. 90). According to Isocrates, one's actions were the result of a good way of thinking, which was expressed subtlety through thought produced by students as they addressed all types of public issues.

Models from antiquity were used for imitation, including those of Homer, which enabled Isocrates' students to confront the ideals that lay behind rhetoric. As a result, his students were able to produce written works that were easy to read and understand. In addition, Isocrates' pupils were required to debate issues for which they had prepared positions. Because his school never contained more than a handful of pupils, Isocrates was able personally to supervise their work, which was to prepare them to become men of politics and future leaders of the polis. Mainly, his pupils represented a select group of young men from wealthy families who would serve as an enlightened elite. He believed that if his students would work to limit some of the excesses of democracy, it would allow Greece to rise from the ashes of its ruin. If this meant a certain amount of demagoguery, it was acceptable in light of the present decadence. He encouraged his students to struggle against current political conditions, even if they had to live with the awareness that they were fighting a lost cause.

Throughout his life Isocrates remained cynical about the use of rhetoric as a means of self-advancement; but at the same time, he realized that in the proper setting rhetoric could be used to advance the public or community good. Isocrates' first great book, the *Panegyricus*, which brought him fame almost overnight, closely resembles Gorgias' *Olympicus*; and the fact that he deliberately chose to compete with such a celebrated author in treating the same theme — a call to the Greeks to achieve national unity — is, according to Greek usage, a proof that he considered himself Gorgias' pupil. To some extent his work might be considered an extension of the work of Gorgias in the advancement of the art of public speaking. Isocrates had made his living as a professional speechwriter and in every way, for at least a time, he was a Sophist. "For his part, Isocrates concedes that the contemporary logographers, or speech writers . . . are as contemptible as Plato makes them out to be" (Poulakos and Depew, 2004, p. 11).

Isocrates organized his school to make money because his father's property had been destroyed in the Peloponnesian War; consequently he brought on the charge of being a Sophist from the Platonic camp of supporters. But the real motivating force behind Isocrates was a desire for reform, and he considered rhetoric to be the foundation of a new educational movement that could be used to reconstruct the democratically corrupt Athenian society. He was unwilling to enter politics directly, but was willing bring change by training his students for political action that would unify the Greeks by bringing an end to the strife between the competing city–states and between conflicting social classes. For Isocrates, the solution to current troubles lay in creating equality among the Greek states by directing their attention to support for a new Panhellenism that emphasized a unifying national identity. According to this vision, the separate city–states would be dismantled and a superior state would be created with the power to end polis strife as a means of preventing the dissolution of Greece.

Plato Versus Isocrates

Isocrates became engaged in a generation long cultural war of ideas with Plato. Both parties would include the study of mathematics as an element of mental training, while Isocrates would use a form of verbal gymnastics as a means of preparation for a higher culture. "They both have a vision of civic education, puritanical and anti-democratic in one case, seductively aestheticist and at least controversially democratic in the other" (Ibid., p. 11). For Isocrates the art of debate, a form of dialectics, was a means of preparation for politics. For Plato dialectics was the special reserve for only the best minds, or for the training of philosophers. The sophists were, however, willing to teach dialectics and to apply it more generally within the public arena. Plato objected to this practice because it would be used to mislead or to pervert knowledge. Instead Plato would focus on finding a balance between training of *body* and *soul* in order to develop the "complete man". For Isocrates, it was rhetoric rather than philosophy that best addressed the conditions of the post–war Greek world, especially in connection with the political and the moral issues that came to occupy the times. It was Isocrates who came to intellectually represent a post–Periclean universal sophistic/rhetorical tradition, but he also laid claim to the philosophical movement that was emerging in the fourth century.

The Marginalization of Isocrates

The literature on Isocrates begs the question of whether or not Isocrates could lay legitimate claim to being a philosopher. Edward Schiappa (1999) takes up this issue in his analysis of Isocrates' intellectual focus. It is clear from this analysis that Isocrates claimed the mantle of philosopher and rejected the label of sophist. It is Schiappa's claim that for two millennia Isocrates had been marginalized in philosophy because of the charges of Plato and Aristotle. Schiappa argued "Furthermore, there is no prima facie reason to rejecting Isocrates' own words when trying to come to a historical understanding of his texts" (p. 168). Schiappa called upon his readers to focus on what Isocrates states about his own *philosophia*. Isocrates' most critical statement on the subject is found in his speech, *Against the Sophists*. "[T]hose who are willing to obey the instruction of this philosophy would be aided far more quickly toward equanimity (epiekea) than toward (rhêtoreia). Let no one think I am asserting that justice (*dikaiosynê*) can be taught; for I am absolutely sure that there is no art (technê) capable of implanting justice and good behavior (sôphrosynê) into those ill–informed by nature for excellence (*aretê*). But I still believe that education in composing political discourse (tôn logôn tôn politikôn) would give [students] the most encouragement and practice" (*Against the Sophists*, 13.21). In addition, Isocrates placed great value on producing students of good character above the value of producing good speakers. He also placed great value on training both the *body* and *soul*, with special emphasis on the development of the *psychê* as it relates to the human spirit or the soul. According to Isocrates, the province of *philosophia* is the training of the *psychê* (mind, spirit or soul), just as it is the province of the gymnasia to train the body.

As was previously stated, Plato considered rhetoric, as practiced by the Sophists, to be a danger to the culture. It perverted knowledge and the sophists used it to convince people to take sides in an issue without a moral consideration of its consequences. In his dialogues *Protagoras* and *Gorgias*, Plato makes the assertion that the dialectic is superior to rhetoric as an educational means, but also comes to realize the educational merit in rhetoric. The critics of the dialectic also complained that it was misused in sophistic argument and was without purpose: it is argument for the sake of argument and a trick of *persuasion*. Rhetoric, on the other hand, required years of instruction that could not be limited to a single school setting and was an appropriate means to train young men. In general, the sophists based their rhetorical instruction on three principles that included talent, study, and practice, which had made the approach to rhetoric mechanical and ineffective. Plato adopted rhetoric, but rejected its use or practice in the sophistic form; instead, he used it as a long–term means for shaping the soul by helping his students gain knowledge of the *Good*.

Isocrates rejected Plato's idea of a universal knowledge in favor of opinion and his models of excellence, which would be revealed through his rhetorical forms of instruction. Specifically, Isocrates did not believe that virtue could be taught, but he believed that Plato's approach to shaping the soul was too indirect. Isocrates wanted an education that could be related directly to the political culture. Plato, on the other hand, would not accept any form of education that did not address virtue and continued to complain that rhetoric often was void of ideal, ethical, and moral considerations. For Isocrates, Plato's metaphysical theorizing about Nature and Being was a form of intellectual vanity that served no practical purpose and it had the result of vexing the mind and the spirit.

The arguments between Plato and Isocrates was reduced to the idea that sophism, instruction in rhetoric, leads only to cosmetic changes in students, while philosophy leads to real changes in the soul of the student. In other words, sophism when mixed with rhetoric was a false art regardless of its claim to being a philosophy.

Plato's *Gorgias* advocated the idea that Plato promoted a separate way of life for the philosopher, while Isocrates advanced the idea that a true philosopher was involved with the affairs of the civic life of the polis and that there could be no separation between philosophy and the concerns of community living. Isocrates, like Plato and Aristotle, hoped to develop a philosophy that would train the students to live their lives according to a higher plane of existence by training the *psyché* to become noble and to serve as a means of contributing to the well–being of their community. Plato's view of the philosopher as living a separate life from the affairs of the state may seem a strange notion to the modern reader, but given the political conditions of his time they make perfect sense in light of his views on democracy.

The Orations of Isocrates

Twenty–one of Isocrates' written orations continue to exist and bear witness to the care that he took in the preparation of his work. All his speeches are highly polished and some may have taken years to complete; all were designed to make a political impact on the affairs of the Athenian polis. In other words, his speeches were not produced for the sole purpose of providing models for his students. He became a truly prestigious teacher and author who loved Athens, and in return, became an adored public figure. He was one of the first individuals to organize his instruction into a graded sequence of studies that focused on specified aims. His pamphlet entitled *Against the Sophists* attacked sophist practices, which according to his caustic view was aimed at developing mindless dolts into strutting intellectual pundits. Isocrates' aim, on the other hand, was to create a higher form of teaching in which the goal of instruction was to produce students of a higher moral character. He based this on his belief that a good mind was a reflection of a good soul.

At the same time, Isocrates could be considered a sophist and he, more than anyone else, contributed to the advancement of this educational movement, but his contribution was an attempt to elevate the movement and to make it respectable so that it could serve as a legitimate alternative to philosophy. "This conflict between Plato and Isocrates developed the systematic theories of logic and of rhetoric which we find in Aristotle; it also developed a polarity between philosophy and rhetoric as two forms of mental activity suited to the adult mind, which was to dominate culture for the rest of the ancient world" (Murray, 1986, p. 230).

Isocrates was like the sophists, but there were subtle and important differences. "Like them (the sophists), he charged fees to the students who flocked to his school from all parts of the civilized world, though not, it is said, to the Athenian youths; and his methods of instruction, apart from the greater elaboration made necessary by a course extending over four years, do not seem to have differed substantially from theirs" (Boyd and King, 1995, p. 25). He differed from the sophists, by advocating the inclusion of politics, ethics, and history in the training of future leaders and citizens, which allowed him to advance the development of their citizenship. "Ethical and political studies were intimately related and referred to the practical application of the codes of right conduct toward the gods, parents, children, friends, enemies, and society" (Gutek, 1972, pp. 44-45).

Isocrates also has been deemed the "Father of Humanism", and there is little doubt that he claimed the title of Supreme Master of the Oratorical Tradition as was practiced in fourth century Athens. His school established a pattern for higher education that would be copied or followed in Rome and in Europe. This genre was destined to become the most important feature of classical education, even in the face of the dialectical tradition that was taking place among the sophists and in the critical philosophy of Socrates, Plato and Aristotle. According to Murray (1986): "He also offered an education in general culture, and numbers of competent speakers and literary figures are said to have studied under him; but his theories lacked any incentive to serious thought" (p. 230). Plato's views may have colored Murray's perception, which depicts Isocrates as scholar "on the make", or "a wheeler-dealer charlatan".

In addition, Isocrates actually provided future moralists with the means for examining ideas and gaining the moral high ground in any argument. Isocrates' philology became a powerful means to turn youth into worldly men, and he helped the educated Greeks to advance to a more civilized station and status within the ancient world. In later centuries, Isocrates' influence would be carried on the wings of Hellenistic dispersion. "It is important to realize that, while Isocrates gives Athenian Greek a privileged status, he does not grant to anyone speaking or teaching Greek at Athens the prerogative of determining Greek identity. He arrogates this privilege to himself, as the city's preeminent writer of *logos politicos*" (Too, 1995, pp. 147-148).

Panhellenism as Political Ideology

Isocrates was the first Athenian scholar to look beyond the fragmented Greek city–state and to anticipate the rise of a unified state. Throughout his life, he was concerned with Panhellenic unity, as a means for ending the constant warfare that existed between the Greek cities. In addition, he was seeking an issue that could be used to advance rhetoric as the foundation of a moral crusade. In other words, he needed to reinvent rhetoric in a new ethical or moral form that could be used to provoke a righteous political action. Panhellenic unity was this form, and through it, he hoped to unify all of Greece. Earlier his teacher Gorgias had advanced Panhellenism in his *Olympicus*. "For Isocrates, the state of affairs in Greece had become so unstable that only a radical remedy would do: Panhellenism—political harmony among the Greek states—put into action not by Greeks but under the leadership of Philip II, king of Macedonia" (Martin, 2000, p. 187).

In *Panegyricus*, Isocrates hoped to reduce class antagonisms through the shaping of a new unity between Greek cultures by developing a new national identity. Isocrates also recognized that the excesses of democracy had to be controlled to bring about a greater political unity. His remedy was to reform the democracy by reviving the political power of the Areopagus, which would be used to rebalance distribution of power between the lower and the upper classes. In his speech *Areopagitcus*, Isocrates complains about the power of the majority, or the masses, over the propertied minority. This speech was completed around 355 BCE after the loss of the Social War, which destroyed the second empire.

Isocrates was convinced that Panhellenism was the key to end the hatred and corruption that had come to characterize the relationships between the Greek city–states. Realistically, however, there was little basis to build a permanent unity according to Panhellenism. City–state citizenship was so well engrained in the fabric of Greek culture that little could be done to shift the mind–set to a broader citizenship that would be needed for Greek unity. Greece, at this time, was simply incapable of achieving unity by dissolving the independent city–state into a single state. Refusing to concede defeat, Isocrates was ready to offer education as the means to advance a new universal spirit among the Greeks. He believed that by changing the culture based on an education of *logos*, a united Greece would emerge as it had in the past to once again defeat the Persians and change the world. Isocrates' vision was to make Athens the figurehead of intellectual development and the lighthouse for the advancement of a higher universal civilization that would spread beyond Greece.

At the advanced age of ninety, Isocrates was searching for a strong unifying leader, who could exercise a patriotic hegemony over the Greek city–states for the purpose of defeating the threatening and surrounding barbarians. "In a recitation written for the Olympic Games of 380 he had argued that the only way to bring unity to the fragmented Greek world was to launch a national crusade under one leader against Persia" (Freeman, 1996, p. 257). His influence may have helped lead Philip of Macedonia to the idea of invading and conquering Persia. Isocrates lived long enough to witness the invasion and conquest of Greece by Philip and he also witnessed the rise of powerful monarchies. But despite his vision, the death of democratic Athens came as a great sorrow. "A late Greek tradition says that when the news came (of the Athenian defeat at Chaeronea) he forgot about Philip and unity, and thought only of his native city humiliated, the days of her glory ended; and that at the age of ninety–eight, having at last lived long enough, he starved himself to death" (Durant, 1939, p. 488).

Isocrates' views on learning would give shape and form to all future educational movements that claimed *excellence* as their credo and ultimate mission. Higher education, aimed at refining the intellect, was to advance our ability to communicate so that misunderstandings could be limited and ideas could be shared. His concern for *logos* was to advance the quality of life within the human community regardless of the state or the culture, which characterized Isocrates' higher form of humanity.

Rhetoric, Philosophy and Civism

Elements of Isocrates' views on good citizenship were contained within his approach to rhetoric and the training of the mind and spirit of his students. "A hallmark of Isocratean civic education is that it recast philosophy as rhetoric precisely in order to introduce an element of reflective, aesthetic deliberation into the discussion of rhetorical training and practice" (Poulakos and Depew, 2004, p. 2). Isocrates argued that good speech and good prudent action were at the core of the educational process. His aim was to develop leaders, as well as monarchs, who would rule as selfless servants of their citizens. At the same time, Isocrates hoped to promote forms of collective deliberations in dialogue and debate. He persists in the notion that rhetoric was a form of deliberative philosophy that could be used to shape the individual to a higher level of excellence (or *areté*). In their best applications, polished speeches were to express virtuous metaphors that emphasized the principles of good government and citizenship. "Isocrates regarded the beautifully written speech, disseminated by the powerful technology of writing, as having immense potential to transform all aspects of the existing landscape of civic education and political life" (Poulakos and Depew, 2004, p. 5). A well–trained orator should be capable of providing an aesthetic depiction of an event or an issue as a display of his eloquence, as well as his dexterity, and a well–developed and polished speech in written form should be an aesthetic production that would appeal to a greater audience of citizen readers. "The style Isocrates developed as his students took over was believed by critics to be more appropriate to written than spoken discourse" (Cole, T., 1991, pp. 119-120). Moreover, Isocrates demanded that rhetoric reflect deliberative choices that were logical and based on sound reasoning; consequently, he was different from the sophists of his day who were mainly concerned about winning arguments.

Isocrates considered himself to be a philosopher with a distinct moral message that was expressed in his system of education in which debate was used to advance worthwhile causes. "Isocrates used the open form of educational contest and debate in *Against the Sophists*, as in the introduction of *Helen*, to disarticulate his perceived association with sophistical civic education, to contest the relevance of current eristic practice to the affairs of the city, and to claim for his own rhetorical practices, against the Academics, the title of 'true' philosophy" (Poulakos and Depew, 2004, p. 6). His *Antidosis*, written in 353 BCE, reflects a situation in which the wealthy Isocrates was required to pay the cost of building or equipping a trireme. As was previously stated, he went to court over this issue to plead his case, and lost. In his apology he defended the reasons for his actions and also laid out his system of education. It was his claim that he had used rhetoric as his means to train orators who would devote their lives to the service of their fellow citizens and their polis. "By blending forms of oratory, he carved out a deliberate practice that attached moral choices to political questions and addressed ethical concerns as they could be realized concretely in contingent action" (Ibid., p. 7). This trial and his experiences with the politics made him angry and forced him to address the excesses of democracy. He soon became an advocate of his Panhellenic outlook and in 346 BCE he published his *Philippus*, where he called on Philip II to enforce a concord between the Greek states and to attack the Persians. "*To Philip*, *Helen*, and *Antidosis* suggest that in Isocrates there generally lies a powerful articulated civic ideology beneath a 'panhellenic' veneer" (Too, 1995, p. 132).

The Battle Over Civism

The course of *civism* in the fifth century flowed in channels that had been carved out by the rigors of polis living, its childrearing practices, its religious festivals and customs, its kinship traditions, and the need for political leadership. In the fourth century, it was taking its future form in the formal schools of philosophy and rhetoric. Isocrates' idea that the beauty of the spoken word had power and influence could be seen in the assembly and in the courts as the best expression of ancient *civism*. Isocrates' *civism* came to represent an opposite pole from Plato in the debate over how to reform and save Athens from its decline and destruction. Both sides of this debate offered educational solutions that were miles apart, but not totally opposed to each other. "In slipping between these poles, Isocrates can serve as a stimulus for contemporary thinking about how we can conceive and devise a program of education that is sufficiently realistic to account for the sprawl of democratic practices and that is also sufficiently idealistic to promote civic virtue" (Poulakos and Depew, 2004, p. 18). Both Isocrates and Plato had battled over an education for leadership and both had much to say; this was the focus of their *civism*. "Isocrates in his old age defended the profession, which he equated with his own philosophic ideal, an ideal much closer to Protagoras than to Plato" (Guthrie, 1971, p. 36). *Civism* had, by this time, acquired a substantial intellectual foundation that could be used to erect a new edifice that would emerge in nation–state Europe in the ages to come.

In searching for the ancient origins of *civism*, Dr. Yum Lee Too (1995) suggested that Isocrates is an important original source for the growing awareness of the idea of *civism*, and she cited two works by Isocrates, *Concerning the Chariot–team* and *Busiris*. In these works pedagogy became a means for shaping citizenship. She stated that: "In a number of his works Isocrates constructs a history which authorises the pedagogue as a political figure. If *Concerning the Chariot–team* commemorates the Alcmeonids as civic teachers, the *Busiris* provides a historical perspective on how the figure of a teacher gained a political identity" (Too, 1995, pp. 209-210). Dr. Too credits the Egyptians as being the source of Greek philosophy and the origin of their political thinking in *Busiris*. *Busiris* is described as an Egyptian ruler who based his rule on knowledge and wisdom, and under his influence, philosophy emerged as the means for training the soul of the responsible citizen. To accomplish his political aims, *Busiris* required that young men study a scientific curriculum containing such subjects as astronomy, mathematics, and geometry. According to Dr. Too, section 28 of *Busiris* described the role of Pythagoras in bringing about an education–centered philosophy to Greece. "The most interesting detail in Isocrates' Egyptian history comes, however, at section 28, where he recounts the impact of this pedagogical culture upon Greece. He related how Pythagoras of Samos journeyed to Busiris' Egypt. Here Pythagoras becomes a student of the land's religion, and he later returned to Greece to introduce the study of philosophy there" (Ibid., p. 210). This most ancient form of *civism*, according to this history, was a product of Egyptian religion. "Isocrates states that Busiris passes laws demanding that his subjects worship animals for two related reasons, first to gauge how his citizens will conduct themselves with regard to commands more important than these and second to accustom them to obeying the commands of their leaders (26-7). This section of the narrative thus redefines Pythagorean wisdom as a technique of political control, substantiating the view that Pythagorean silence is a political discourse" (Too, 1995, p. 210). Dr. Too suggests that Isocrates described his discovery of *civism* as the means whereby the teacher had become a political figure, with his main task in society being to teach a form of political mind control. Teaching, according to this interpretation, had taken on its primary role as the agent of a form of socio–political instruction. According to this role, the teacher has become the citizenship development agent of the state.

In addition to *Busiris*, Dr. Too finds elements of Ancient Greek *civism* in several of the letters written by Isocrates. For example, in his letter to Archidamus III, which may be of doubtful authenticity, Isocrates appears to have presented the idea that it was a city's responsibility to educate its citizens for citizenship. She writes: "His *Archidamus* invokes this ideal of civic pedagogy at the close of *Archidamus*" (Ibid., p. 212). In this letter Isocrates appears to be performing the role of civic educator as a means of strengthening the civic culture and its related constitution. However, Isocrates' strongest case for *civism*, according to Too, came in his *Areopagiticus* in which Isocrates called on the Athenians to return to a constitution that was under the control of the aristocrats. According to Isocrates, the Areopagus performed the task of educating its citizens in moderation as a part of polis living. Too wrote: "At *Areopagiticus* 20 the speaker declares that the pristine democracies of Solon and Cleisthenes 'educated (*epaidene*)' their citizens to be better and more moderate by punishing those who took advantage of the democratic ethos, for instance misinterpreting 'democracy' (*dêmokratis*)' as 'intemperance (*akolasian*)' and 'freedom (*eleutherian*)' as 'lawlessness (*paranomian*)'" (Ibid., pp. 212–213). Isocrates, in other words, saw the city as the civic school, and the *paideia of civism* was the task of inscribing the laws of the city into the minds and hearts of its citizens.

In *Concerning the Chariot–team*, Isocrates saw the role of education, as a means of creating an identity that was based on the societal values. Too wrote: "Education perpetuates what is good in the city, making relationships, above all those of teacher and student, which enable the skills and qualities of outstanding older citizens, such as Pericles, to be passed to and recreated in their protégés" (Ibid., p. 221). Consequently, Dr. Too credits Isocrates as being one of first civic educators to recognize the role of the state as the primary agent of education whose primary mission was its responsibly for *civism*.

Fifteen

Demosthenes and Civism

Demosthenes has been presented as the last Greek statesman, standing above the grave of Hellas and delivering her funeral oration.
—Werner Jaeger

Demosthenes (384 – 322 BCE) was the son of a Greek sword-maker and his mother was the daughter of Gylon, a man who had been forced to flee Greece after being accused of treason. At the age of seven, Demosthenes was under the protection of his father's two brothers and his father's best friend who served as his trustees in charge of a substantial inheritance. Demosthenes fell victim to embezzlement and was deprived of a chance for a more advanced education. Despite his problems, however, Demosthenes pursued the study of rhetoric. Following his preliminary training, Demosthenes attempted to speak in public, seeking a career in the courts and possibly the Assembly. At the age of twenty in 363 BCE, he successfully used the courts to recover his stolen property and he used a part of his recovered wealth in the service of the city. He then began to seek a career related to what might today be called a legal career. Like Isocrates, he became a *logographos,* or speechwriter, and his occupation opened the way for him to become an assistant to the public prosecutors. This role placed him in a position to take an open stand for or against public issues and to propose new public policies.

As a youth, Demosthenes suffered from poor health caused by a weak constitution. His halting speech and the quality of his voice was irritating because of his whining tone and his annoying manner of expression. Nevertheless, Demosthenes was determined to overcome these handicaps to realize his ambition to become a skilled orator. He dropped out of public life and began to train himself to become a public speaker, turned to Isaeus who served as his tutor. He did not apply to Isocrates because of his poor financial circumstances, and Isaeus had pedagogical strengths that were different from those of Isocrates. Some accounts suggest that he attended

Plato's school as part of his agenda to learn some of the skills of eloquence, while others have credited Ctesibius with helping him learn the secrets of the Isocratic method of public speaking.

In his early attempts at public oratory, Demosthenes demonstrated a lack of natural talent and his audiences derided his strange style of speaking. Audiences sometimes hurled insults at him, and in one attempt to speak before the Assembly, the audience refused to give him a hearing, and he left in a state of humiliation. Legend holds that Satyrus, one of Athens' great actors, followed Demosthenes from the Assembly. Satyrus attempted to console Demosthenes and to advise him and he directed him to study the great works of Euripides and Sophocles by memorizing several passages of their works. Once Demosthenes learned some passages, Satyrus tutored him in their correct emphasis and pronunciations. Demosthenes now realized the importance of diction along with facial and body gestures and he also learned that pleasant enunciation should be a part of a proper delivery. Inspired by Satyrus, Demosthenes built an underground studio in a cave where he could practice his speaking skills, along with the full gestures of a melodramatic actor.

According to Plutarch, Demosthenes shaved half of his head to keep himself in isolation in dedication to his task. He attempted to cure speech impediments by speaking aloud with pebbles in his mouth and he ran about the countryside until breathless in an attempt to overcome his weak voice by reciting memorized speeches as he ran. In front of a large full–body mirror, he coordinated his gestures with his speech. After growing back his hair, he attended the public speeches of Athenian orators and made a painstaking analysis of the presentation and construction of each work. Following this analysis, Demosthenes would make more corrections to each speech This practice allowed him to reorganized the weaknesses of the work and to convert it into a more effective speech.

He refused to speak unless or until he had thoroughly prepared himself by taking painstaking care in the reconstruction of a more refined and elegant oration. As a result of these efforts, he perfected his speaking voice and gestures to such an extent that he was able to gain the attention and the devotion of his audiences. "On the rostrum he contorted his figure, whirled round and round, laid his hand upon his forehead as in reflection, and often raised his voice to a scream" (Durant, 1939, p. 483). Through these means, Demosthenes became the greatest practicing orator of the fourth century, and as a consequence, his fame gave him wealth and made him an important Athenian politician. Demosthenes' political power was not due to his military exploits, his wealth, his philosophy, or his writing, but mainly was due to his power of *persuasion*.

The decline of Athens was punctuated by the fall of the second naval league at a time when Isocrates was calling for a savior in his speech *On the Peace*. According to the Isocratic formula, Athens was to abandon its empire and turn to Philip as a means of addressing a growing Persian threat. By this time the democracy had degenerated into a quagmire of class conflicts in which the institutions of state had fallen into the hands of unscrupulous politicians when the shrinking upper classes were giving up on the democratic constitution. A new voice was heard in opposition to these politicians in a desperate attempt to save the Greeks from new forms of military despotism.

In his speeches, Demosthenes chastised the Athenians for their self–indulgences: he charged the leading politicians with making the citizens of Athens into slaves of the mob, and he also charged that the offices of government had been turned over to ambitious and self–serving rogue politicians and generals. According to Demosthenes' charges, the citizens of Athens especially had become too generous with grants of citizenship. The decline in the value of citizenship had the effect of weakening the cultural unity of the people. "The people are accused of being too generous with grants of citizenship of giving over their mass power into the hands of a few evil men, of ignoring their own laws, of trusting rhetoric instead of depending on their collective wisdom" (Ober, 1989, p. 320). Decades of decline had caused idealistic young men to look for new leaders that would promise them a brighter political future and they began to follow Demosthenes and believing in his vision for a revised Athenian state.

Rhetoric as Civism

For Demosthenes, rhetoric was a powerful means of *persuasion* that could be used to direct public perceptions in favor or in opposition to domestic and foreign relationships. Demosthenes' approach to rhetoric was to draft and polish an oration until he deemed it persuasive enough to bring about a desired outcome. His early political endeavors led to the development of three orations, which included *Against Androtion*, *Against Timcrates*, and *Against Leptines*. These were well–planned political attacks against the politicians, whom he blamed for leading Athens into the disastrous affair known as the Social War. These politicians were members of the same party that had controlled Athens at the time of its fiasco that had ended the second Athenian Empire. Demosthenes made current political leaders a target of his anger, in part because he recognized their vulnerability, which motivated him to attempt to remove these leaders from office as an act of deliverance.

Because of the chaos in Athens, Demosthenes hoped to establish a more aggressive foreign policy for Athens to deal with its external threats, which caused him to write a series of orations that included *For the Megalopolitans, For the Liberty of the Rhodians*, and *Against Aristocrates*. In *For the Liberty of the Rhodians*, Demosthenes focused on problems with the Rhodians who had seceded from the Athenian league. The citizens of Rhodes were now subject to the aggressions of the king of Caria who was threatening to take away their freedom. The citizens of Rhodes appealed to Athens for help, but the Athenians were angry about the withdrawal of Rhodes from its alliance. Consequently, the Athenians refused to help. Demosthenes attacked this decision as narrow minded, but nevertheless was defeated in this attempt at reconciliation. The Rhodians were then forced to join an alliance that opposed Athens, causing the loss of Rhodes along with several other small states to the Athenian alliance. In *Against Aristocrates*, Demosthenes focused on the growing threat to its security in northern Greece and the possible loss of the Dardanelles. Athens had controlled the Dardanelles as a means of securing its commerce and grain supply; however, the Thracians were threatening to take control of the area as a result of a power struggle between two brothers. Demosthenes planned to take advantage of the feuding brothers to maintain control of this critical waterway, but Philip had entered the picture and revealed his aggressive tendencies. This threat was so great to Demosthenes that he launched into violent attacks against the corrupt democratic political system in Athens.

In a related speech, *On Armanents,* Demosthenes argued that the Athenian people had grown soft and were seeking ways to live off the state, instead of relying on their own sense of self–reliance. He therefore called for a new type of education that would change citizenship attitudes, or a new *civism* that would strengthen the will to stand against isolationists at home as a means of defending against foreign threats. He also called for a new order of politician who would lead the people by telling them the truth and by preparing them for the hardships that lay ahead in the upcoming struggles.

Because of growing external threats, Demosthenes attempted to advance his foreign policy that was aimed at holding Philip at bay. According to his reasoning, the Athenians must set out to create the conditions for forming new alliances to keep Philip out of Greece. To accomplish his goal, Demosthenes had to reinvigorate the declining Athenian state, but these were acts of desperation that would prove to be too little, too late, as Philip would return to Greece and destroy all opposition.

Demosthenes' written speeches expressed his political criticism of the behavior of the Athenian politicians in the Peloponnesian War, and throughout much of his public political career, he used these speeches to warn the Greeks of the dangers of the growing military strength of the Macedonians. In 351 BCE he directly attacked Philip as the enemy of the Athenians. Demosthenes realized that Philip was determined to become the leader of all Greece by subjecting it to his rule. "In the 350s Philip achieved a great coup by convincing the most powerful leaders in Thessaly, the prosperous region of central Greece just over the mountains south of Macedonia, to elect him hegemonial commander of their confederacy, thereby investing him with legitimacy as a leader of Greeks" (Martin, 2000, p. 189).

Perception and Persuasion in the *Philippic* Speeches

Demosthenes responded with a series of carefully crafted speeches known as the *Philippics*. These speeches represented Demosthenes' attempt to persuade the Athenians of their impending dangers. The democrats of Athens embraced these speeches, thinking that Demosthenes was defending the democracy, although his goal was not in support of democracy, but to begin a resistance movement against Macedonia.

In the *First Philippic* he urged the Greeks to fight a more vigorous war for Amphipolis, but his pleadings were ignored, forcing Demosthenes to go on the offensive. At this time, the Athenians were more concerned with their own Social Wars than with Philip's encroachment, causing Demosthenes to chastise the citizens for being distracted, lazy and full of indolence. The *Three Olynthiacs* followed the *First Philippic* in 349 BCE. These speeches warned the Greeks that they were about to lose their freedom if they did not render aid to Olynthus against Philip. In 346 BCE, Demosthenes issued his speech *On the Peace*, in which he urged the Athenians to end the Phocian War (the Sacred War), which had opened the way for Philip to force the Greeks to accept his leadership. In this speech, he advised the Athenians not to resist Philip because he now occupied Phocis and Thermopylae. In writing this speech, Demosthenes realized that the peace with Philip was to be a temporary arrangement. Meanwhile, Demosthenes' political nemesis, Aeschines, worked to fulfill Isocrates' solution for the troubles of Greece and would make Philip the master of Greece. The peace gave Demosthenes a limited opportunity to attempt to convince the leaders of Athens to make peace among the other Greek cities in preparation for war with the Macedonians. To accomplish his goal, Demosthenes would advance the cause of his version of Panhellenism in opposition to Isocrates' Panhellenism. Demosthenes' Panhellenism was aimed at uniting all the Greek city–states into a new powerful force that could withstand the aggressions of the Macedonians.

The *Second Philippic*, which was delivered in 344 BCE, warned the Greeks that they were wasting their time in attempting to negotiate peace with Philip. In 343 BCE Demosthenes issued his speech, *On the False Legation,* in which he accused his rival, Aeschines, of taking Macedonian money to advance his cause. By 342 BCE, Philip was directly intervening in Greek affairs, which caused Demosthenes to travel about Peloponnese in his attempt to create a new Hellenic alliance and to prepare the Greeks to go to war against Philip. This effort proved to be an uphill battle because of bad feelings between the Spartans, Thebans, and Athenians. The war with Philip had not yet become a bloody affair, which allowed Philip to make political inroads within the Peloponnesian states, as these states were seeking revenge for the Athenian support for the Phocians. These conditions made it nearly impossible to form a Panhellenic alliance, but after years of work Demosthenes managed to create such an alliance.

In 341 BCE, Demosthenes delivered the *Third Philippic* speech in which he argued that the actions of Diopeithes against Cardia were justified since Philip had already started a war with the Greeks. He warned that the Greeks should ignore a Macedonian letter proposing peace and he emphasized the need for the Athenians to lead the Greeks who opposed Philip. His speeches *On the Chersonese* and his *Third Philippic* reflected Demosthenes' attempt to calm the fears of the Greeks and to fan the flames of patriotism in the cause of resistance.

Demosthenes reminded the Greeks of their glorious past and the worthiness of the cause in which Athens was to serve as the leader of the civilized world. In this sense, Demosthenes the orator became Demosthenes the civic educator, and his message was one of patriotism and survival. Following the advice of Isocrates, Philip attempted to counter Demosthenes efforts by presenting himself as a Greek whose sole mission was aimed at creating a united Panhellenic front to punish the Persians for their sacrilege in destroying the sacred temples of Greece and for their transgressions into Greek affairs. Demosthenes knew that Philip was not as he presented himself and he attempted to spoil Philip's plan by stating: ". . . not only (is Philip) no Greek, nor related to the Greeks, but not even a barbarian from any place that can be named with honors, but a pestilent knave from Macedonia, whence it was never yet possible to buy a decent slave" (*Third Philippic*, p. 31).

In his *Fourth Philippic*, Demosthenes demanded that the Persians be allowed to join the war against Philip after the Macedonians had seized the Athenian cornfleet. At this time, Demosthenes was placed in full charge of the war, and his greatest diplomatic success came in the formation of an alliance with Thebes who would fight on the side of Athens at Chaeronea in 338 BCE. In addition, Demosthenes attempted to bring about better relations between the rich and the poor classes of Athens by ending the hostilities that had been created by long standing class conflicts. In his final appeal before the war, Demosthenes attempted to win over the Persians who were indifferent to the fate of the Greeks. His message was full of good reasoning in hopes of causing the "Great King" to realize that he too was in danger should Philip defeat the Greeks.

The *Philippics* suggested that Demosthenes was a crafty and cleaver strategist in developing public perceptions through persuasive argument, which was demonstrated by his ability in unifying the Greek states to resist Philip. As a result of these efforts, the Greek states were able to resist and maintain their independence until 338 BCE. In addition, Demosthenes was able to forge a mutual defense pact among the Greek states. His greatest achievement was to entice the Thebans into his confederation, and it was Demosthenes' rhetoric that rekindled the fires of war by appealing to Theban honor. This diplomatic success was so great that it forced Philip to petition for peace rather than to face a united front of Greek states. Unfortunately, however, Demosthenes lost some of his credibility when he betrayed his own rhetoric by setting forth to do battle with Philip and disgracing himself by fleeing the battlefield. When the combined forces of Athens and Thebes were defeated in 338 BCE at the battle of Chaeronea, Philip declared himself "Commander of the Greeks". Demosthenes' enemies now were able to indict him, but the people of Athens continued to hold him in high regard. They assigned him the honor of making the funeral oration over the remains of those slain at Chaeronea. Despite this honor, however, Demosthenes had lost his courage and refused to continue speaking against Philip and he withdrew from politics until after the death of Philip.

Demosthenes used his secret knowledge of the death of Philip by calling on the Greeks to stand against the Macedonians to secure their freedom. Because the Athenians did not know that Philip was dead it appeared that Demosthenes was able to foretell the future. Once the official news of Philip's death had reached Athens, the people gave sacrifice in the temples, and some demanded that Demosthenes be presented with a golden crown. In 330 BCE Aeschines brought charges against Demosthenes for his part in divining Philip's death. But Demosthenes responded with his own defense, which lead to his acquittal.

Following the death of Philip in 336 BCE, Demosthenes set about to form a Greek league capable of maintaining its independence. The Thebans slew the occupying Macedonians and Athens made ready to join them in a common defense. Demosthenes became the ruler of the popular Assembly and was able to organize the Athenians in a defensive effort. At the same time, the Persians were preparing their military for war against the Macedonians. The Greeks faced Alexander who had assumed the throne and was moving to consolidate his grip on Macedonian power. Alexander led his forces into Greece causing the courage of the Athenians to evaporate and the Thebans to desert the battlefield; as a result, the people of Athens sent ambassadors to Alexander to sue for peace. By this time, Demosthenes had lost his nerve and he had fled to Cithaeron. In his anger, Alexander sent for a group of Athenian politicians, which included Demosthenes. Demosthenes was able to escape when Demades, a leading Athenian statesman, agreed to go to Alexander and to plead for his life and for reconciliation with Athens.

In 335 BCE the Thebans organized an insurrection and Demosthenes attempted to inflame a revolt, but this time the Athenians were not willing to follow his lead. The only remaining hope for Greek freedom was a Persian defeat of Alexander. This hope was dashed in 331 BCE when Alexander at Gaugamela defeated the Persians. The insurrection against the Macedonians ended in failure and the leader of the revolt, Agis, was killed. The Spartans and the Thebans were vanquished and they were no longer of military importance.

While Demosthenes was abroad, representatives from Athens came to him in an attempt to convince him to return to Athens. In the course of their conversation, Demosthenes revealed his distain for politics; but despite this distain, he was once again returned to Athens. His return was prompted by the death of Alexander in 323 BCE. Upon his arrival, Demosthenes attempted to convince the Assembly to dismiss the Macedonian garrison in order to restore Athenian freedom. This attempt collapsed into total defeat when Antipater took control of the Macedonian government, forcing Demosthenes again to flee the city. He was now under the sentence of death according to a vote of the Assembly and a decree of Demades.

Antipater pursued Demosthenes and several other Athenian orators, and several leading politicians were executed. Demosthenes hid in the temple of Neptune in Calauria, where Antipater's envoy located him. Archias spoke to him sweetly to convince him to leave the temple and to go to Antipater, who was sure to pardon him. Plutarch reported that Demosthenes responded in the following manner: "O Archias, I am as little affected by your promises now as I used formerly to be by your acting." Archias, now in a fit of anger, threatened Demosthenes and caused him to say, "Now you speak like a genuine Macedonian oracle; before you were but acting a part." At this point, Demosthenes entered the temple to write his farewell letter to his family, but instead took a reed containing poison, and he fell dead before the statue of Neptune. Upon hearing of his death, the citizens of Athens dedicated a brass statue in honor of his service to Athens.

The Legacy of Demosthenes

Demosthenes had opposed Isocrates and the general direction of the Athenian leaders, who were ready and even eager to capitulate their freedom to Philip. Trained as a fourth–century rhetor, Demosthenes came to exemplify the idea of combining the skills of rhetoric with the virtues of citizenship. During the course of his training, Demosthenes had acquired the skills and the civic values needed to look to the future and to map out a plan of action designed to save the Greeks from their impending doom. In essence he became a new kind of politician who was able to rule through the force of his reason as was outlined in his speeches. His amazing counter–intuitive insight was powerful enough to almost reverse the impending course of events. Demosthenes convinced the Greeks to take to the battlefield to oppose the greatest military force of this age, a military machine that eventually would conquer the entire eastern Mediterranean world. What was most unique about his forethought was that he was able to formulate, in opposition to Isocrates, a new vision of Panhellenism that would preserve the role of Athens as the intellectual and cultural leader of the civilized world. Demosthenes was even willing to preserve the democracy that he opposed because of its excesses, if that would preserve the freedom of the Greeks. He recognized that the time of an independent polis was passing away and that new accommodations were needed; however, no rhetorical force on the face of the earth could overcome the hostility that the Greeks had brought against each other as a result of their constant state of polis warfare.

As the fate of the Greeks became more evident, Demosthenes became concerned about his legacy and how he and the Greeks would be remembered. He had been corrupted and had been charged with cowardice conduct on the battlefield. His defense was a speech *On the Crown,* a masterpiece in which he looked to the judgment of history. This speech presented Demosthenes as he would be remembered, a lonely heroic figure fighting for his ideals and ready to meet his fate without shame, but in the awareness that he had fought the impending darkness of the on–coming age. Forced into exile to await the arrival of the agents of Antipater, Demosthenes stood in the knowledge that this was the end of a glorious age. More important still, he stood in the knowledge that the Greeks were willing to take on the risks that their heritage demanded of them. To the end, the *civism* of Demosthenes took the form of a heroic speaker and political leader who was willing to take a stand for the good of the state regardless of its personal consequences.

The Ideal Expressions of Civism

Part VI
Philosophy, Ideology, and Civism

As far as Socrates is concerned, it is the many's custom of deciding on moral issues on the basis of their unreliable opinions that generate the need for measurement in ethics in the first place.
—Thanassis Samaras

Religion, in the fourth century BCE, no longer completely satisfied the Athenian curiosity about life and death matters. During the fifth and fourth centuries, Greek intellectuals glorified reason over superstition, and inquiry became the honored method of investigation. With the rise of an educated leadership, there was an awareness of the importance of basing decisions on a body of knowledge. The sources of this body of knowledge were derived, in part, from the philosophers who were more likely to investigate all aspects of the meaning of physical nature, as well as the meaning of human existence. Humanist thinkers, in particular, were dedicated to the application of human reason to understanding the dilemmas of life. In this quest, they attempted to discover fixed patterns or universal truths that could be formulated into principles that might be used to regulate human behavior.

The fourth century was an age of complexity, which was influenced by philosophers who resided in schools of advanced learning in Athens. By this time, Plato and Aristotle had developed an intellectual tradition aimed at developing new theories related to virtue, knowledge, and the natural sciences. In particular "Socrates, Plato, Aristotle, and Isocrates, each in their own way, sought to discover these universal truths and to make them known to their fellow men so that they might follow them and thereby live the good life" (Gutek, 1972, p. 19). They contributed to understandings of the relationship between the individual and society. "Classical civilization was not to be restricted to one type of culture or one type of education; it was torn between two rival forms: one form was philosophical and its protagonist was Plato; the other form was oratorical and its protagonist was Isocrates" (Marrou, 1956, p. 61). In competition with schools of philosophy, there were the schools of rhetoric which created an ongoing and sometimes bitter rivalry, especially between the two leading fourth century school protagonists, Isocrates and Plato. This competition led to a series of dialogues and speeches that fought over issues related to philosophy, knowledge, virtue, moral conduct, and the role of the individual in civic participation in the affairs of the state.

In the process of debating the issues of their age, the philosophers explored ideas pertaining to the ways and means of educating individuals to meet the expectations of living in different political settings and according to different constitutions. These issues led Plato to write several important works that addressed the nature of the state and the type of education that should be used to advance leadership and citizenship. Aristotle and his students, on the other hand, were led to examine the constitutions of many different cities as a means of sorting them into categories of best and worst governments. In the process, Aristotle was forced to grapple with the issues of leadership and citizenship that suggested new forms of *civism* that were correlated to the constitutions of states.

To the philosophers of the fourth centuries BCE, Athenian culture appeared to be caught between an idealized past and a new social order that appeared as a result of the formation of the Athenian Empire. This new democratic order was failing to provide a satisfactory social and political ideology that could be used to harmonize and unify a growing and diverse cosmopolitan population. An awareness of this problem led the fourth century intellectuals to contemplate new theories for the reconstruction of society. Their concern was to find a political ideology that would reconcile self–interest with the greater demands of a stable collective society.

Sixteen

Socratic Civism

Now, if good action depends to this extent on knowledge, it follows that virtue is teachable, and ought to be taught; and that the only way of escape from the uncertainty created by the sophistic discussions was to carry these discussions further and find out by personal learning what were the ultimate grounds of action in which consisted its goodness or badness.
— Boyd and King

Socrates (c. 469 – 399 BCE) was born in poverty to humble parents. To many, he was considered ugly, or aesthetically unpleasing, because of his bulging eyes and coarse facial features. He stood out in the marketplace with his bare feet and his well–worn cloak. He was known for his ability to drink great quantities of wine at symposium, and as a soldier, he was courageous and had the stamina to endure almost any hardship, including marching barefoot through the snow. In his youth he had attempted to follow in his father's footsteps as a stonemason or sculptor. He married an ill–tempered woman, Xanthippe, and found value in living with her, as it taught him how to get along with almost anyone regardless of personality. Evidently, he quit the stonemason's trade to become a full–time self–appointed gadfly who worked incessantly to goad the lazy Athenian citizens into becoming more self-aware and self–critical.

Because his mother had served as a midwife, he often used terms connected with labor and birth as metaphors in his conversations. Socrates, examined individuals in the same manner that a doctor would examine a patient, and once the diagnosis was determined, he would prescribe a cure. He was a doctor of the human soul, which he viewed as being in a constant state of danger. "Here we can penetrate to the very heart of his view of his duty and mission: he felt that it was educational, and that the work of education was the service of God" (Jaeger, 1943, vol. II, p. 39). What mattered to Socrates was the soul or the effects of our actions on the soul.

A Civism of Self-Knowledge

Foremost in his teaching was Socrates' faith in the human capacity for self-knowledge and self–control or a *civism* that came about as a process of introspection. For Socrates, morality was the expression of human nature once that it had been shaped by knowledge and harmonized within the natural order of the universe. He believed that each individual must become the master of himself by searching the depth of his own soul. For Socrates, what mattered was the inner world of the individual, which resided in the cultivated soul. Socrates believed that the soul was a self–constructed inner being, which was shaped by the purposeful will of the individual and was related to his virtue, character, and moral living. In other words, the individual was responsible for the goodness of his own soul. By seeking or striving to become more godlike, the individual could slowly perfect his soul. Socrates might accept the idea that the soul was reflected in human attitudes and behaviors, virtuous or not, which might suggest that the soul also was reflected in citizenship behaviors.

Dana Villa (2001) explored Socratic Citizenship in regard to its unconventional notions about the relationship between the individual and the state. According to this author, Socrates was the first western intellect to relate citizenship to the virtues of the "good man" and not a standard of citizenship engrained in the culture. "Socrates can be said to put intellectual doubts at the heart of moral reflection; he makes such doubt the duty of any conscientious citizens" (p. xii). Citizenship, in other words, came to rest on the notion of the integrity of the individual and not social norms. Socrates, according to Villa, was the creator of moral individualism, which espoused a changed relationship between the individual and the ruling authorities. "By making the avoidance of injustice the moral center of 'care for one's soul' (or self), Socrates transforms both the meaning and the practice of citizenship, pushing it beyond the boundaries of the 'official' public realm" (Ibid., p. 1).

Unlike Plato, Socrates did not delve into idyllic notions related to the creation of a utopia, although he was concerned with the notion of the perfectibility of the soul. Mainly, he was concerned with the problems of everyday life and the ability of the individual to rise above his circumstances to become a better person. In addition, Socrates was concerned about the quality of justice in society. "Socrates' life had been devoted to combating the idea that justice should be equated with power to work one's will" (Martin, 2000, p. 168). He wanted to know why some individuals were moral, while many others were not. For Socrates, justice, goodness, and beauty were the essence of human existence and were immutable qualities that had little or nothing to do with the nature of the state. In other words, these qualities were eternal and fixed forever and had little or nothing to do with culture. He was constantly searching for a good man as a means of identifying those qualities that made him good. In the end, his students declared that the only "good man" in Athens was Socrates. According to his students, Socrates lived on a higher plane of existence and was capable of seeing deeper into the human *psyche* than any of his contemporaries.

What is known about Socrates comes from a variety of individuals who, during their lifetime, had interacted with him, including his students and contemporary intellectuals. He did not write down his ideas, but preferred common conversation to the preservation of his ideas. Socrates did not view himself as anything more than a common citizen of Athens. He did not teach in lecture–halls or classrooms, but was often found in gymnasia where he spent his days in conversation with young men interested in sports, physical training, and intellectual discussion. "Socrates . . . was an ordinary Athenian citizen belonging to no philosophical school; he may have had an early interest in cosmology, but if so, he abandoned it" (Annas, 1986, p. 237).

A Rejection of Individualism

According to Aristophanes, Socrates and his students met regularly in the same place, but most writers describe him as teaching anywhere and any time that he found willing listeners. He did not teach a common doctrine and his students were a mixed lot of individuals from various backgrounds. He opposed the sophists' individualistic philosophy and their views on society. Socrates believed that the philosophy of individualism led to claims of unjustified rights and allowed the individual to oppose the laws and customs of his community, ultimately leading to *skepticism*, as opposed to the moral principles and virtues of the *Good*. As was previously stated, he emphasized the universality of virtue in which each individual possesses a self–constructed soul, which is developed in accord with the higher virtues. "Temperance, justice, wisdom, are not merely what the individual man chooses to consider them, but are the essential ideas that underlie certain lines of conduct, for which the ordinary person can find the warrant in his own experience when that experience is properly examined" (Boyd and King, 1995, pp. 27–28). Socrates also believed that every citizen must reside within the confines of the polis or state and accept its limitations and its requirements and that no person was above the law. Because of the devotion of his students, several Socratic schools of philosophy emerged upon his death based on his concern with ideas and issues related to the human soul.

Although Socrates took exception to the social views of the sophists, he adopted the dialectic method of probing into issues that had been used by earlier teachers and may have been invented by Protagoras (Smith and Smith, 1994, pp. 13-14). While his philosophy was a somewhat vague and unsystematic study of virtue, he was committed to turning over every stone of human conduct to see what truth lay beneath it. He mainly found misconception and ignorance. Socrates passed his form of dialectic on to Plato and Aristotle who transformed it into a more complete form and the foundation for their system of *logic*. Socrates also was acquainted with Anaxagoras, the Ionian philosopher who was a member of an exclusive intellectual circle created by Pericles. Anaxagoras' student, Archelaus of Miletus, had served as a teacher to Socrates for a short period of time. In addition, Socrates also may have been influenced by Archelaus' teachings on morals, which may have caused him to turn toward a concern for ethics.

Even though Socrates rebelled against the teachings and views and virtues of the sophists, he also resembled them in certain ways. He was full of crafty dodges and used many tricks and sly maneuvers to shift meanings and definitions. Gorgias would most likely say that to ask for a definition was wrong. In the use of definitions, "Gorgias would no doubt have claimed that Socrates was trying to extend a method appropriate to natural science beyond its proper sphere" (Guthrie, 1971, p. 254). Socrates shielded himself against his own techniques by claiming that he knew nothing and that his questions were designed only to gain knowledge. "Essentially, he seems to have argued that just behavior, or virtue, was identical to knowledge and that true knowledge of justice would inevitably lead people to choose good over evil and therefore to have truly happy lives, regardless of their material success ... Moral knowledge was all one needed for the good life, as Socrates defined it" (Martin, 2000, p. 170). He never claimed to be a wise man nor a philosopher, but simply a man on a quest for answers to questions. Despite his seemingly sophistic behaviors, he differed from them in four important ways. "In four points he differed from the Sophists: he despised rhetoric, he wished to strengthen morality, he did not profess to teach anything more than the art of examining ideas, and he refused to take pay for his instruction—though he appears to have accepted occasional help from his rich friends" (Durant, 1939, pp. 368-369).

According to Murray (1986): "Plato also sets up an antithesis between these figures, the so-called 'sophists', and Socrates the Athenian: they profess knowledge of all sorts, he professes ignorance; they parade skill in public speaking, he can only ask questions, and rejects the elegant prepared answer; they offer to teach, to make men better; he merely offers to confirm man's ignorance; they charge high fees, his teaching is free" (p. 229). Socrates felt that the sophists were doing a disservice to Athenian youth by confusing the skillful use of oratory and persuasion with the idea of human *excellence* (*areté*) or the higher virtues associated with human abilities. He countered their techniques of oratory with reason: "The man who is excellent as a human being is one whose actions are governed by reason" (Gutek, 1972, p. 34). Excellence in living and citizenship, in other words, is duty and responsibility as governed by reason, which also suggests his thinking on *civism*.

Socrates and *Logos*

Although Socrates is known to have despised sophistic logos, as it is so closely associated with the traveling marketplace teachers, Plato attempted to take the art of *logoi* away from the sophists, as it contained philosophic merit with respect to the soul. Words are a window to the soul and they give expression to its inner landscape and to the state of its development. *Logoi*, it was believed, could serve as an instrument to cure a damaged *soul* or contained the means to create a healthier soul. "The rhetorical art was also known as 'the art of logoi', and the wide meaning of this word made possible very different conceptions of the art of which it was the subject. Plato's aim was to get it out of the hands of superficial persuaders and special pleaders, and show that, properly applied and based on knowledge of the truth, it was coextensive with philosophy" (Guthrie, 1971, p. 177).

Plato argued that the real master of *logoi* was Socrates, even though he would never claim to be a speechmaker. He was, instead, a physician of the soul and he found the techniques of *logoi* useful in connection with his investigations. Thus his demand for definitions was a starting point in his discussions, which were aimed at revealing the inner truth. "He was convinced that if one understood a thing one could 'give a logos of it', and his demand for definitions was a demand that people should prove that they understood the essence of courage, justice or whatever else under discussion by finding a verbal formula which would cover all cases of it" (Ibid., p. 178).

Socrates on Politics

In addition to his dislike of the sophists, Socrates also disliked the extremes in belief systems. In politics, for example he held that such political systems as democracy or oligarchy were sources of corruption to the minds of men. "In politics, he does not support democracy; in religion he has offended by challenging traditional myth and claiming access to his own personal divine voice (the *daimonion*, which simply tell him not to do certain things); in his friendships he has been tainted by close contact with Critias (the man who became the leader of the Thirty Tyrants), and also Alcibiades (the man who betrayed Athens to both the Spartans and the Persians). These may have been the young men he accused of corrupting" (Woodruff, 2005, pp. 109-110). He also believed religion to be a corruption of the many and politics to be a corruption of the few, nor was Socrates a respecter of wealth and social status.

As was previously stated, Socrates died as a martyr in defense of his beliefs and he refused to retract his statements or to defend himself against charges of corrupting Athenian youth. Prior to his execution, he was charged with impiety, but in actual practice, he paid respect to the state religion and even attended official ceremonies, never being accused of uttering an impious word. More important still, he was willing to sincerely accept the notion that the designs found in nature could not have occurred spontaneously; accordingly, the world must be the product of an intelligent reasoning source. He applied his criticism and his skepticism to the accepted explanations that man claimed for truth and knowledge. Socrates was convinced that erroneous explanations related to religion and politics were used to blunt further investigation into reality. But even in the face of questionable myths and traditions, Socrates was willing to accept some explanations to preserve the unity and the morality of the fabric of society. By searching for truth, he hoped to reveal new insights and new knowledge as a guide for living the good life.

Overtime, Socrates' interest turned from the examination of facts and origins related to the study of human values to helping human beings to achieve higher ends. Socrates believed that philosophy, the logical and rational pursuit of ideas according to Socrates, was the best means to study ethics, politics, and logic; therefore, the study of philosophy was the best means of creating a rational way of life. In addition, the study of philosophy led the individual to study his relationship to the *Good*, which could lead to good thoughts and good actions that were so essential to the acquisition of his *happiness*. Socrates considered education as a form of philosophical discussion, as well as a means to help individuals seek after the Good in order to advance the secular moral development of society. Philosophical discussion, in other words, was a way of promoting or developing the Good. Or stated in question form: "Can philosophy as a form of education provide the means to end class–warfare and political polarization that works to teardown the unity of the community until it reaches the point of social and cultural disintegration and decline?" Stated more succinctly: "Can philosophy be used to promote social harmony in order to create the Good polis and can the good polis produce the good citizen?"

Socrates on Trial

Recalling that Socrates was a well–known figure throughout Athens and by luck of the draw he was a member of the Assembly that tried the eight generals who were charged with dereliction of duty in the sea-battle at Arginusae (406 BCE). As a member of the presiding *Prytany* (controlling assembly officers) on that day, Socrates refused to allow a motion for a vote on the execution of the generals. He was over–ruled and the generals were sentenced to death; later the assembly repented of their hasty action and executed those who had forced the death penalty. The trial (406 BCE) was an aspect of the political struggle–taking place between those seeking more democratic power and oligarchs who were attempting to hold onto power. The Spartans had blockaded Athens and starved its population and after the defeat of the Athenians, a ruling Spartan *junta* was put in power and many fled the city. Socrates refused to go, but also refused to serve the Thirty Tyrants. Democracy was restored in 403 BCE and recriminations were brought against many of its citizens, which was a period of settling old scores. Socrates was put on trial in 399 BCE and charged with impiety and corrupting the morals of youth and was sentenced to death as a political act of revenge by the democrats.

Socrates was accused of teaching "a generation of young Athenians the ideals, metaphysics (view of ultimate reality), and values that were friendly to aristocracy" (Smith and Smith, 1994, p. 16). The despised oligarchic leaders were delighted in Socrates' humorous quips regarding the follies of the democrats and democracy. Critias, an associate of Socrates and a contemporary sophist, was a member of the right wing of the Thirty Tyrants. He wrote an incriminating play depicting the gods as the creation of politicians to force humans into decency, which was contrary to the realities of human nature. He also was a conservative revolutionary and terrorist. As a consequence, Critias had implicated Socrates as an agitator and troublemaker. Critias also was charged in the mutilation of the *herms* that took place in 415 BCE, which also involved Alcibiades. In response, the new democratic leaders charged that, just prior to the oligarchy revolution, Athenian youths were too busy listening to the declamations of Socrates to attend to their responsibilities and had become disrespectful of religion, the city's political leaders, and their parents. Socrates, in the words of his accusers, had become a corrupting influence on youth and was guilty of destroying the traditional values of Athenian society.

These charges against Socrates came at a time when Athenian society was suspicious of the influence of intellectuals on wealthy youth, who in turn had separated themselves from the common citizens and had turned to the business of tearing down (deconstructing) some of the symbols and traditional values of society. Socrates, it might be said, was unfairly considered an anarchist of his age. According to Finley (1973): "Pestilence, oligarchic coups, mutilation of the herms — that is what came of these new intellectuals and their wealthy pupils, intellectually divorced from the mass of the citizenry as never before, men who did not hesitate to tear down traditional values, traditional morals and religion" (p. 133). In reality, Socrates was encouraging the youth of his day " . . . to think more carefully but also to obey their parents, and he had patriotically recommended obedience to the existing laws of the state while seeking to improve some of its institutions" (Smith, S. 1979, p. 16). The tragedy, if it can be called a tragedy, occurred because of closely held values that Socrates would not relinquish. "Socrates, however, replied to the prosecutors' proposal of the death penalty with the brash claim that he deserved a reward rather than a punishment, until his friends at the trial in horror prevailed upon him to propose a fine as his penalty" (Martin, 2000, p. 172).

The jury, however, whipped up by demagogic emotion, decided on the death penalty. The question remains: Was Socrates guiltless of the charge of corruption? In his 1889 book, *The Trial of Socrates*, Sorel described the accusers' charges against Socrates, which included the damage that the Socratic philosophy had committed upon youth; but more serious was the damage being caused to the unity of the city–state and its traditional beliefs and values. In his review of Sorel's work, Vernon (1987) concluded that Sorel's attempts to make the case that Socrates had " . . . cast potentially ruinous doubt on the unquestioning loyalties and faithfulness to routine upon which classical citizenship depended . . . ." (pp. 149-150).

From the perspective of Socrates, Athens was sliding into a period of crisis that had dire effects on society. "By the end of the war many Athenians were no longer asking what they could do for the polis but rather what it could do for them" (Riesenberg, 1992, pp. 23-24). The city no longer was able to support the poor and the social environment was poisoned by a new competitive scramble for self–preservation, as well as by growing class antagonisms.

It may have been true that Socrates, to some extent, had unintentionally damaged Athenian morals through the promotion of his form of introspection and intellectual ethics. By appearing to have rejected the traditional values of Athenian culture, Socrates fell into the hands of his enemies. At seventy–one years of age Socrates capitulated to the passions of the mob, which became one of the greatest ironies of western history. If in fact, he had fueled the flames of youthful rebellion, it was an unintended consequence of this desire to free the individual from the chains of culture that were based, in part, on ignorance. In addition, Socrates valued rational thinking as a source of greater good for the polis than was its traditional demand for social conformity. In death Socrates became a martyr in the cause of reason. The philosopher's work with youth on citizenship focused on the advancement of rational thinking as the basis for human conduct, as the old traditions would no longer suffice in the face of a divided and self-serving society. Socrates' reputation as philosopher, martyr, and person of purest ethics is associated with his refusal to escape his circumstances.

Despite the pleas of his friends, Socrates refused to depart when the opportunity arose. "In the first place he said that it would be undignified; in the second, it would nullify all the teachings of a lifetime; in the third, it would be a crime against the state--and Socrates was unwilling to buy his freedom at the cost of breaking laws" (Cole, 1950, p. 14). At the end of his life, Socrates became a living example to others of his devotion to his ethics, ideals and virtues. He refused to compromise on the importance that reason must play in the lives of the average citizen, but also in his respect for the law. "He is willing to die rather than to undermine the law" (Woodruff, 2005, p. 110). The execution of Socrates set into motion a great flurry of writing in his defense that had the effect of advancing philosophical thought in the fourth century and helping to frame the great debate that would take place among future scholars.

Socratic Knowledge

Socrates began his search for knowledge and truth with the works of Protagoras, and out of it drew the conclusion that "man" or "humankind" is not an individualistic *me*, but an aggregate *we*; that humankind possesses and shares a body of common knowledge (the shared experiences of living) about the truth that is held in common by all men of intelligence, and that "man" is the measure of all things only so long as he is capable of applying this shared knowledge. After disavowing much of the self-centered individualism that dominated sophistic thinking related to education, he emphasized an education that encouraged individual thinking, but in harmony with community agreement and universal virtues. His emphasis, in other words, called for correct individual thinking and an understanding of "right mindedness".

His credo was to "know thyself," which he intended to use as a means of focus in education based on the development of virtues and personal morality. For Socrates, *knowledge* consisted of a shared or universal validity, which should be applied to whether something is true, or not. Universal validity is not a particular conclusion of a single person who claims to represent the *truth*. According to Socrates, the truth was the shared and accepted knowledge that is the same for everyone regardless of time and space. "He differed from the sophists, then, in emphasizing in man not his mere peculiarities, as tested by his sensations, impulses, and feelings, but rather his rational, and so universal self" (Graves, 1929, p. 180). By stripping away the clutter of perception based on opinion and ignorance, each individual could be taught the processes of reaching or finding the *Truth*. Stated differently, to find the truth, each person needed to learn *how* to think logically by learning how to become skilled in the processes of *reasoning*.

In general, Socrates believed that the sophists had mistakenly adopted a process of pouring information into the pupils' minds rather than teaching them *how* to think and thereby shaping their perceptions about reality. This wrong–headed *pedagogy* could lead pupils to claim that they possessed knowledge, but this was misguided knowledge that was false, or incomplete, or based on misconception. The true pedagogy was one that stripped away the ready–made answers and opinions in order to get down to the bedrock of the truth and to build upon it through a process of dialectic analysis, as well as its related elements such as observation, exploration, and investigation.

Virtue as Civism

Like the sophists, Socrates was an educational innovator and was willing to teach his students to advance the betterment of their fellow citizens to improve the social environment of their city–state. He had an acute sense of the importance of an inner life or introspection, in which each individual was to search for knowledge and truth as the most worthwhile way of living. His mission, therefore, was to question established truth and to prod men to thinking about what they already had accepted without question. Although Socrates favored training the mind and the body, he also taught the rule of *moderation* in all things, including physical exercise. Aristotle, taking his cue from Socrates, called on individuals to look for a moderate balance or middle ground in conduct and in thinking about political systems that he called the "golden mean" or rule of reason. According to Aristotles' principle, extremes of any sort were to be avoided; but at the same time, individuals were encouraged to perfect their minds and their bodies guided by the rule of *moderation*.

Scientifically, Socrates was interested in unraveling the mysteries of life and he encouraged youth to examine the nature of physical objects—the mystery of the nature of the world and *Being*. For Socrates, unraveling the mystery of things and their nature was the essence of education, but *virtue* was the ultimate aim of education and it impacted the inner life of the soul. "This great effort Socrates now re–directed, preserving its strict integrity, from things to man: it is by Truth and not by any power–technique that he will lead his pupil . . . to spiritual perfection, to 'virtue': the ultimate aim of human education is achieved by submitting to the demands of the Absolute" (Marrou, 1956, p. 58). The outcome of his thinking on education led to the doctrine in which *virtue* equaled *knowledge*. "By this he did not mean that the mere knowledge of what goodness is is enough to make a man do what is good; but rather that unless there is such knowledge of the object aimed at, no action that the ignorant man performs deserves to be regarded as good" (Boyd and King, 1995, p. 28). Good action depended on good or correct knowledge; therefore, it appears that *virtue* could be taught. Virtue, in other words, was the core of Socratic education.

Virtue was the screen that should be used to direct our thoughts and actions, as well as our social and political relationships. "Not only did he establish the intimate connection between right action and right thoughts, but he tried to show how it was possible to think right thoughts" (Ibid., p. 28). Virtue, in other words, equals what I am calling Socratic *civism*.

A Methodology of Knowing

To accomplish rational thinking in his students, Socrates established the Socratic method of teaching that we have been calling the dialectic. This approach was designed to help the individual resolve or correct misconceptions and other errors in their *perceptions* about reality. These misconceptions were rampant with politically organized and controlled civic cultures that were designed to control human behavior. "According to Aristotle the contributions made by Socrates to human knowledge were two—the 'universal definition' and the 'dialectical argument.' The former phrase means that Socrates tried to establish definitions of justice, right, nobility, and so on that would be true under all conditions. The 'dialectic argument' is the question–and–answer technique that comprises the Socratic method" (Cole, 1950, p. 20).

The dialectic required citizens to establish a definition of the phenomena to be discussed, but first they had to discard all preconceived notions about the issue or topic. Next, the citizen had to provide a statement about his understandings or beliefs about the issues, questions, and problems. Once established, the teacher followed with questions aimed at clarifying the citizen's understanding. Through these means, Socrates hoped that the citizen could come to realize that his beliefs contained contradictions and inconsistencies. As was previously stated, some of the Socratic dialectical terms included medical or midwife phrases or nomenclature. "In thus developing the logical implications of a person's position, whether they led out to truth or error, he used a procedure that he called maieutic ('midwifery'). In this, by means of questions, he caused the individual to see that the opinion he had first expressed was but a single phase of the universal truth, which he had thus helped him to develop or 'give birth to'" (Graves, 1929, p. 182). Socrates' passion for logical thinking caused him to realize that *pedagogy*, the art of teaching, required a great deal of clarification to get rid of word clutter, misunderstandings, and strongly held misperceptions.

Socrates' goal was to reconcile the individual's understanding with that of the social group or "universal man". Through this reconciliation, the teacher would instruct his pupils in the proper way of living in society according to certain universal truths. Because citizens often did not possess adequate and in-depth knowledge of a topic, the Socratic method also was used to expose their level of understanding or misunderstanding, and as a way of exciting pupil interest in knowing more about an issue or topic. The ultimate goal of Socrates' instruction was to help his students focus on *excellence* (*aretê*) as a standard for every aspect of their lives, regardless of occupation or circumstances.

Socrates remains a somewhat enigmatic figure, both loved and hated by many; his impact on the intellectual traditions of the western mind proved enormous, but to his students he was an idolized hero. "To one of his students, Xenophon, he was a model of all the virtues; to another, Plato, he was a great teacher and a martyr; to a contemporary comedian, Aristophanes, he was a dangerous, advanced thinker and Sophist; to Aristotle" a generation later "he appeared a gifted and great but a sometimes mistaken philosopher; to Diogenes Laërtius, the Walter Winchell of antiquity, he was a subject for amusing stories and anecdotes" (Cole, 1950, p. 8). In his search for knowledge and truth, Socrates spent his days in daily conversation with individuals that he encountered in the marketplace or in the gymnasium. He never tired of prodding and poking into every corner of the human *psyche* to discover the hidden world of the soul.

Socrates was especially fascinated with human behavior in all its expressions of good and evil and realized that human beings were capable of a wide range of emotions that could be noble, salacious, generous, ravenous, self–sacrificing, cowardice, and/or courageous. For him, the issue was not that human beings were capable of expressing a wide range of emotions and behaviors, but why some individuals seemed to articulate a more consistent level of morality, while others were controlled by immediate circumstances. Because he believed that God was interested in "the best" (*excellence or aretê*), he became interested in discovering those forces that were at work in some individuals to cause them to communicate *excellence* in moral behavior. One might say that philosophy for Socrates was a quest for *excellence* seasoned by *moderation* for the advancement of the mind–set of the individual, or the development of his *civism*.

Socrates' search for an ideal inner life of the soul came to be represented by his search for the good man. His many encounters with foreigners had caused Socrates to conclude that all individuals share certain common values that are of a permanent and unchanging nature. He believed that a good person was the same regardless of cultural or state differences (which is contrary to Plato and Aristotle), although he too recognized that the nature of the state could influence the development of virtue. As far as we know, he never asked an individual to define his sense of identity in terms of his citizenship, nor did he directly probe into the nature of good citizenship. Socrates recognized that the survival of a community depended on the attainment of a certain level of goodness, which was an inner goodness that influenced the social state of humankind.

It appears that Socrates believed that most individuals were sleepwalking through life and were unaware of the forces that had helped to shape and control their behavior. He also believed that a citizen of a city–state could not contribute to advancing the quality of life of the state unless he was able to attain a certain level of self–awareness. Socrates maintained that goodness in human conduct is the result of self–reflection because it produces a higher degree of wisdom in the individual. The goodness, in good citizen, is something that the individual does reflectively and is something that is done because of his intrinsic valued, which is self–rewarding. Citizenship is something that is developed through an awareness of social relationships and social norms; it is something that becomes useful and enjoyable to the individual since it produces a certain level of happiness and happiness also is related to one's self–identity, which is related to one's soul.

According to Socrates, knowledge should be used to construct a bulwark against all those forces, or that political power, that would corrupt moral character and to keep it steadfastly aimed at a higher ideal of life and civilization. Therefore, Socratic *civism* should be used as a force to reform a wayward state, a state that is out of harmony with the general good of society. Reform is a constant state of reconstruction that requires the services of good citizens with correct or an inner knowledge of the Good. For Socrates the individual must be taught the art of measurement and the techniques of scientific prediction of an outcome to answer the questions: "What are the consequences of my thoughts and my actions on my soul, on my fellow human beings, and on my society or state?"

SEVENTEEN

Platonic Civism

The greatest man of his age, the thinker who saw the difficulty involved in building up society and the state more clearly than any other was Plato; and Plato in his old age took up that challenge.
— Werner Jaeger

Plato (c. 427 – 347 BCE) was born into an influential aristocratic family and may have been related to Solon on his father's side, while his mother's relatives included Charmides and Critias, who were powerful political oligarchs. Named Aristocles, his nickname became Plato(n), which meant broad–shoulders in reference to his athletic appearance. He excelled in both physical sports and intellectual pursuits and also was recognized for his courage in battle. Because of the wealth of his family, Plato was given the benefit of a good education. Plato met Socrates at the age of twenty–one and he became interested in studying philosophy, which completely changed the direction of his life. Although Plato became a follower of Socrates, he maintained his own intellectual independence.

Plato's philosophy was influenced by the humiliations that the Athenians had suffered during the Peloponnesian War, especially the occupation of the Acropolis by the Spartans, as well as the internal power struggle between Athenian oligarchs and the democrats. In 404 BCE, Plato witnessed rebellion against the Thirty Tyrants, which led to the death of Critias and Charmides. At this time, Plato's stepfather, Pyrilampes, stood against his mother's relatives in support of democratic rule. Plato's hostility towards democratic rule came in 399 BCE, when the Athenian democrats returned to power and executed Socrates. Plato blamed the policies of Pericles for much of the mischief caused in Athens. "He said that Pericles' establishment of pay for service in public office, the linchpin of broad citizen participation in democracy, had made the Athenians 'lazy, cowardly, gabby, and greedy'" (Martin, 2000, p. 178).

Plato, as young man, departed Athens and sojourned around the Mediterranean where he continued his studies. Through his travels he came into contact with a variety of philosophic perspectives that he had not encountered in Athens. Prior to meeting Socrates, he had encountered Cratylus. After returning to Athens and meeting Socrates, Plato's philosophical horizons were broadened to include issues related to morality, and as a result, he attempted to clarify the eternal virtues including the *Just*, the *Good*, and the *Beautiful*.

In 387 BCE, Plato traveled to Italy where he studied with the Pythagoreans, who included Archytas at Taras and Timaeus at Locri. The Pythagoreans influenced Plato's views on the importance of numbers, the nature of the soul, and societal rule by philosophers. In addition, he recognized the proper education of philosophers, as it related to music, astronomy and other subjects. Plato now looked to mathematics as a means to train and discipline the mind for rational thinking regarding issues, questions and problems. *Dualism* also became a means that Plato would use to shape the mind and body of his students, which caused him to rely on music and gymnastics in a balanced program of physical and mental training.

In 386 BCE Plato moved from Italy to Sicily for the purpose of viewing Mt. Etna and while he was in Sicily, he met the tyrant Dionysius II. As a result of this meeting, he applied to educate the sons of selected individuals of the princely elite. At this time, Plato's goal was to train potential leaders in the manner of a philosopher–king, which eventually would be outlined in the *Republic*. Plato reasoned that the sons of kings and tyrants were next in line to rule, and he believed that they should become educated to rule in better ways by instilling those virtues needed to become wise and just rulers.

In general, Plato's efforts were less than successful, which was demonstrated when Dionysius II attempted to claim credit for some of Plato's ideas and when he turned out to be a cruel ruler. Plato, despite his best efforts, made powerful political enemies in the court of Dionysius and was forced to flee back to Athens. Later he reportedly returned to the court of Dionysius only to fail again and to return to Athens to remain at the Academy. Some accounts claim that Plato was sold into slavery on his first trip to Sicily and may have been ransomed to his friends who brought him home to Athens in 386 BCE. Plato may have attempted to raise the money to repay the ransom, which was generously refused. Plato then may have used these funds to purchase a grove on the outskirts of Athens where the Academy was to be located. This grove had belonged to the hero of the Trojan War, Academus and was located in an out of the way place where regular funeral games had been played.

Following in the footsteps of the Pythagorean school of Crotona, Plato organized his version of a school for higher philosophical learning. Some versions of this story claimed that Dionysius II contributed to the financing of the school. Like the Pythagoreans, Plato organized a brotherhood that operated as a continuous *symposium*. The Academy has been referred to as an "ancient university," but unlike a modern university, it operated as an informal philosophical school. "The Academy was not a school or college in the modern sense, but rather an informal association of people, who were interested in studying philosophy, mathematics, and theoretical astronomy with Plato as their guide" (Martin, 2000, p. 179).

The Reconstruction of Greek Society

The work of the great philosophers was, in part, the result of the disintegration of Greek society and the search for alternative choices for its reorganization. According to Plato, the central problem was the nature of the state, so he advanced the philosophical creed that "virtue is knowledge" as the basis for organizing a new type of state. He was particularly interested in providing a leadership based on a rational order for the state that also would provide the foundation for a more just society. Plato's approach was to organize society on a hierarchical division of the population that was to be led by individuals of the greatest merit. These individuals would be provided with leadership training that would set them apart from the temptations to misuse power. Such a system would require both the selection and the training of individuals who demonstrated both the temperament and the rational ability to serve as guardians of the state.

In Plato's *Republic*, temperance, virtue, and rationality is the basis of the new political order in which Plato laid down the groundwork for philosophy as a discipline in the preparation of reflective thinkers. Plato's dialogues also addressed the evolution of his educational thinking, which appeared in his final work on *The Laws*. "In *The Republic* Plato does not discuss how the state educational system is to be organized. He explains that problem later, in *The Laws*. Here he is exclusively concerned with the content of education; in trying to work out the fundamental lines along which it is to run, he is finally led to discuss how we can see and recognize the highest standard" (Jaeger, 1943, vol. II, p. 210). Plato's purpose in *The Republic* was to describe the best means for preparing the guardian class for political leadership, and the training of the guardians was the most significant educational institution within his idealized state. The selection of the guardians was to be based upon the notion that almost every person should be considered for leadership, and then this large population was to be winnowed down to a select few who would receive decades of special training related to the development of their *bodies* and souls. Guardians were to be those individuals who knew what justice was and who perpetuated it in their private and public affairs. More important still, the guardians would be educated in the science of right choices as related to the acquisition of knowledge in the metaphysical sense. Education was to teach leaders to rule justly and its citizens to obey the just rules of the state. Plato rejected sophist education of the type described by Protagoras, Gorgias, and Isocrates because it was aimed at self-interest, which would not suffice as a model for the ideal state. He also believed that sophist education led to the misuse of power and to personal and public corruption.

In accordance with Plato's plan, the population would be divided into three classes that were classified by the metals copper, silver and gold. Copper consisted of artisans and farmers whose chief attribute was physical strength, and this class tended to be ruled by their appetites. Silver consisted of soldiers whose chief attribute was courage, and this class tended to be ruled by their passions. Gold consisted of individuals whose chief attribute tended to be their intellectual capacities and their natural capacity was to gain wisdom (*knowledge*). In addition to the metaphor of the metals, Plato went on to use the metaphor of the human body to describe the divisions of the society.

The Ideal State

Plato's vision of his Ideal State, as reflected in the *Republic*, was to be constructed into a pyramid in which each of the three occupational classes was expected to attend to its own affairs. The magistrates (guardians/gold) were selected to rule and make decisions and render judgments, the soldiers (protectors/silver) were to be trained for the defense of the state, and the industrial classes (artisans/copper) were to produce goods for the well being of the entire population. Individuals, regardless of gender, were to be assigned to a role in society according to their appropriate category and ability and this assignment would create equilibrium, which was required for *justice* to prevail.

As previously stated, Plato hoped to create a society whose supreme core and controlling virtue was *justice*. Plato's goal was to create a collective virtue based on civic justice that would help to guide and shape individual development. "The State, in fact, is the soul of man 'writ large,' and it is only in so far as the child enters into its spirit through taking part in civic life and studying the literature, science, and philosophy which are its highest expressions, that he can grow into the fullness of the proper life of man" (Boyd and King, 1995, p. 35).

Justice in the ideal state according to *The Republic* would boil down to the notion that those with the capacity to become philosophers should go through years of training until they reached a level of rational thinking. A rational level of thinking would allow guardians to rule the state unselfishly and in accordance with the virtues of *justice* and *temperance*. Also in the *Republic*, Plato's Socrates used state regulations to guide the child's education in support of the state's constitution. "Education is the basis of political authority in the Ideal State. A 'correct pedagogy (*orthê paideia*)' creates compliant citizens (416c) and trains the state's future leaders to assume their positions of authority" (Too, 1995, p. 208).

As Plato evolved his philosophical theories regarding the Ideal State, he also evolved his thinking on educational theory. His final thoughts on education for the Ideal state were delineated in *The Laws*. The transformations of Plato's philosophical positions, his philosophical and educational journey, ranged over his dialogues to provide a continuous line in the development of his thoughts. Plato's thoughts on citizenship education were summarized by Jaeger (1943) in his analysis of Plato's works, when he acknowledged that Plato had come to realize that education is a function and a responsibility of the state, and that the state was responsible for mentally shaping its youth for citizenship. In *The Laws*, Plato gave a fuller, but different, expression to his notions of education through a state run public education system. Plato, at this point in his thinking, came to realize the difficulties in creating and empowering the pyramid state and its idealized philosopher–king. In *The Laws* he modified his political and educational theories once he realized that the "best state" would require compromises and a greater degree of participation. For example, in place of *truth* he was now willing to accept informed "true" *opinion* as his standard for knowledge, and he was willing to acknowledge that common citizens could acquire a measure of virtue.

Plato's Dialogues

While at the Academy, Plato wrote at least 36 dialogues of which the *Republic, The Statesman* and *The Laws* were cited as his most important works. Generally, it was accepted that the *dialogues* were written at different times and were not connected to any pattern, plan, or system. Some scholars, however, have insisted that Plato's dialogues are a systematic and unified series related to his philosophical development. These scholars divided the dialogues into three categories based on Plato's teaching career at the Academy and consisting of his early, middle and late works. The early dialogues included works in which Socrates was presented as a central figure that explored the ideas of others through a cross–examination exercise, and these dialogues included such works as *Hippias Major, Hippias Minor,* and several other works. The middle dialogues included works in which Socrates was a central figure but the cross–examination was dropped, and these dialogues included the *Republic, Phaedo and Symposium,* as well as several others. The later dialogues included works in which Socrates retreated to the sidelines and Plato examined the ideas of others, as well as some of his own ideas which were presented in a rather technical way, and these dialogues included *Parmenides, Sophists, Statesman, The Laws,* and several others. In the *Republic* Plato was not willing to settle for anything short of a philosopher–king, but in his later dialogues he modified his views, which also pointed to his last work, *The Laws.* By this time, Plato had abandoned his strict dogma on the unity of *virtue* and now was willing to compromise his views on the political reality of his times.

    The dialogue allowed Plato to advance his philosophical ideas in ways that were both dramatic and free of the defects of sophistic techniques. "Misinterpretation is something techne not only allows but actually invites — by leaving entirely to the student the choice of which one among the various arguments it presents to use and when" (Cole, T., 1991, p. 123). He provided a setting in which an exchange of ideas could take place within a specific framework and between scholars with strong ideologies or philosophic perspectives and perceptions. Each speaker advanced the issue, question, or argument in opposition to his opponent. Consequently, Plato advanced philosophical forms in which claims and counter–claims could be tested in a manner that allowed observers to decide the issue based on its merits. The dialogue, in other words, was designed as a counter–measure in the form of argumentation that had been used against the misapplication of *knowledge*. Plato was convinced that rhetoric, in the sophistic form, did not do any good for the soul, as it lacked *areté*, but instead equipped a person to win an argument by any means of *persuasion*.

Rhetoric and Philosophy

Plato was also convinced that rhetoric or logos could be applied to the study of philosophy, and he introduced it into the Academy in order to meet the demand for a more formal type of education. It would serve as a complement to the course in dialectics as an additive to the process of philosophical discourse. Rhetoric or logos in philosophic form was stripped of its sophistry, which allowed the philosopher to harness argumentation as a mission in the search for knowledge and to advance virtue. Although, some of Plato's most important dialogues dealt with educational concerns, their intended purpose was aimed at persuasion in the attainment of the Ideal State.

Turning to dialectics in dialogue form also emphasized that Plato was reluctant to place himself in the public spotlight. To avoid notoriety he chose to transform the dialectic into a dialogue form of discourse. This form allowed Plato the means to explore new social arrangements and to challenge various controversial ideas, including his rejection of democracy. In other words, through the dialogue Plato was able to detach himself from the social issues that he wished to explore without becoming controversial. Plato also used this freedom to dissect the ideas of others without directly attacking them, and it also provided Plato an opportunity to independently accept or reject the results of his own rational or analytical thinking.

The "Good" in Civism

Plato's main philosophical concern was to advance the establishment of *justice* as the standards of *civism* in the Good Society, and an important goal of his philosophical analysis was to help citizens and others to understand the nature of *justice* and it's relation to *happiness*. "Happiness is the motive for justice: happiness now, not happiness in some state of future bliss after death, and not happiness defined out of existence as something else" (McClelland, 1996, p. 22). Plato also suggested that injustices, or the lack of *happiness*, arose from a wealth of complexities. These complexities included the formation of new occupations, which appeared to change the social relationships between citizens. "The increase of lawyers and doctors in a state is an evil symptom: one points to lack of a sense of justice on the part of citizens, the other to luxury, intemperance, and resultant increase of disease" (Woody, 1949, p. 434). Corruption lay at the root of human unhappiness, as it often led to actions that were destructive. According to Plato, war was the result of competition between evil states, and the evil states were a reflection of corrupt governments. In addition, some governments manifested this corruption because of hidden goals, or because of political structures that masked the reality of politics and the hidden desires of controlling groups. While these states often claimed to practice a form of *justice*, they were in reality concealing their love of wealth or a greed for power that masked their hidden purposes. "It (injustice) arises from immoderate pursuit of wealth on the part of the oligarchic rules of the state, for 'the love of wealth and the spirit of moderation' cannot exist together in citizens of the same state" (Woody, 1949, p. 434).

Political Corruption

Plato went on to comment on the corruption of unfit leaders and he described them as individuals who were unwilling to abide by a simple way of life and who held avaricious appetites for wealth and power. Corruption gave evidence of unfitness and the consequences when an unfit leadership befell the polis. According to Plato, the solution to the problem of corruption was to train worthy individuals to become lawgivers and rulers who would live in a manner that removed them from the temptations of material corruption. "But since those who are not satisfied with the simpler life have proved themselves incompetent and dangerous rulers, it is desirable to set up certain restraints and controls in a reconstituted society, so that each and every sort of work will be done by those who are best fitted by nature and perfected by training; and in particular it is necessary to place the guidance and the protection of the state in the hands of those who are pre–eminently qualified to serve its ends, and are by nature and training least inclined to use it for their personal gain" (Woody, 1949, p. 434). The philosopher–king, according to Plato, was to be educated to serve as a completely good person who was trained to possess perfect knowledge. Knowledge would serve as the qualification for those selected to serve as philosopher-kings, and their preparation for leadership would depend on a form of right moral training or right philosophy. This education was the necessary stepping–stone on the way to the acquisition of knowledge of the idea of the Good. But education alone was not adequate by itself to produce a philosopher–king. The acquisition of pure *knowledge*, the ultimate goal of education, was seen as the only means of finding the Supreme Good, which was recognition of Gods eternal truths and laws. Philosopher–kings were individuals with the capacity for knowledge and goodness, which could be advanced or refined with an appropriate education.

Plato's *Republic* and Civism

Written in about 375 BCE, many consider *The Republic* to represent Plato's best system of rule based on an assemblage of elements from various forms of city–state systems, which included democracies, oligarchies, and tyrannies. This dialogue took the form of a conversation between Socrates and those whom he encountered and it ended in a Socratic discourse. In this dialogue, Plato explored the question of who was best qualified to rule and the ways of selecting those individuals. He also described a method of shaping the leadership class from which a philosopher–king was selected. "Plato's specifications for education should be the training of the mind and the character rather than simply the acquisition of information and practical skills" (Martin, 2000, p. 181). Through his main character, Socrates, Plato examined justice through a dialectic process. Justice, according to Plato, also was the means that citizens used to identify their special interests and to integrate these interests into the interests of the community.

According to Plato, Callipolis was a city in open conflict with hostile surrounding cities, and was in danger of being destroyed, and it appeared that its only defense was to create a more powerful army. The city's population consisted of three classes that included Guardians, Auxiliaries (professional soldiers), and the third class made up of workers and artisans, or Producers. The Guardians were few in number, but they consisted of the most competent citizens of the city and were responsible for the welfare of the city. The Guardians were given a special education that was designed to produce leaders who were capable of making the city strong and brave. According to Plato's plan, the Guardians were to be trained in four important virtues that included: *wisdom*, *bravery*, *temperance*, and *justice* so that they could come into possession of full knowledge. The philosopher–king was an individual who was selected from among the Guardians because of a special capacity for mastering his emotions and for a capacity for the exercise of justice, which suggested that he was in possession of a well–balanced soul.

Democracy was not an option for the *Republic,* as Plato insisted that the average citizen was not capable of holding political power. Plato drew on the Phoenician myth regarding the three metals for his classes. According to this myth, all citizens were born of the Earth and so all were brothers, but they were different as some contained gold, some silver, some iron, brass, or copper. The gold class was made up of individuals who were able to rule, the silver was made up of individuals who defended, and the iron was made up of individuals who were the farmers or workers, and so forth. At the same time, some silver parents possessed a certain amount of gold and were capable of producing children who could be elevated to the Guardians, but none of the worker parents possessed gold in their soul so that they could not produce children capable of being elevated beyond their current status. As a consequence of these class distinctions, the premise of the *Republic* was based on a social gradation, or pyramid. It was designed to create a meritocracy, or excellence in rule for the city of Callipolis. In addition, Plato's ideal state was based on the idea of eugenics, or paired breeding to produce the best leaders. "The fact that the ideal state breaks down exactly when its heredity principle is compromised conclusively proves that Plato regards this principle, and not merit independent of class, as the bedrock of his social order" (Samaras, 2002, p. 51). Like the Spartans, Plato would rid the Guardians of its weak or unfit offspring.

Despite eugenics and the differences between the three classes, Plato maintained that the fundamental foundation of his Ideal State was based on kinship relationships, or a common ancestry of all citizens. But the government was to be under the control of a natural oligarchy that directed the state. At the same time, Plato restricted private ownership in order to curtail greed and corruption so that power was not determined by property qualifications. Callipolis, in other words, was a refined Sparta without the extremes or the Spartan unbalanced occupation with war and their lack of arts and intellectual pursuits. "Plato's remark that those who in the ideal state were 'free men, friends and providers' become in timocracy 'serfs and servants' suggest that the willing acquiescence of the third class in the *Republic* becomes enforced submission on the Spartan model" (Ibid., p. 56). Plato did not rule out force against the Producers (third class), and he contemplated the various techniques of coercion that could be employed.

For Plato, democratic freedom was the same as a license that led to unlimited moral decadence or anarchy. Also, according to Plato, true freedom was when "the best" ruled over "the worst" in society—freedom, as license, was deemed a form of slavery to desires and emotions and was the worst part of the soul. Plato believed that physical labor had the effect of distorting the soul, which made it irrational; thus freedom for the lower classes was out of the question, as they were slaves to their passions. The Guardians were the only ones who could grasp *Forms*, especially the *forms of the Good*; therefore, the Guardians had permanent command of their souls, allowing them to formulate their actions based on ethical knowledge. Plato's ideal city was the eternal and unchanging world of the *Forms,* and it existed on a higher plain than any earthly city — it was the city of God — and only philosophers could begin to establish such a worthy city.

In the Republic Plato would remove everyone over the age of ten and he would regulate wealth and poverty and advance the notion of the common possession of goods. He would limit the size and the borders of the state and also limit innovation in music and gymnastic education, as well as changes in children's games. The children were not to know about change, as it was not a part of Plato's metaphysics. The citizens of the Republic were deprived of history and the notion of time in an attempt to divest them of their memories of the older cities of humankind. Plato especially rejected the idea of change in education. Learning was hard labor and a lifetime struggle to free oneself from ignorance. It was a means of acquiring knowledge of the Good, and corruption of the Guardians was avoided by placing them into a state of isolation from almost all–human intercourse.

According to Plato's metaphysics, the primary world or the world beyond the physical world, was related to the physical world in that the metaphysical world provided the physical world with ideal truths, or knowledge that was just beyond the pale of human experience. Plato, in other words, based his perception of knowledge and truth on his understanding of the metaphysical realm. This realm, which the human mind might approach from philosophical studies, contained specific objects in various modified forms. The metaphysical observer, therefore, might be able to envision the perfect or the ideal that consisted of a pure and unchanging nature. By ascending to the realm of the ideal, the observer could obtain a glimpse of pure reality. These individuals with these exceptional intellectual capacities were educated to serve as philosopher–kings, as they had acquired a depth of knowledge by entering this ideal realm, which qualified them to rule with justice and truth.

Plato was so determined that the ruling class operate outside of self–interest in order to avoid corruption, that he insisted that they must be freed from all pursuits that threatened to cause them moral contamination. Once free of such contamination, the Guardians were unencumbered to focus their efforts on the betterment of the community. To achieve this aim, Plato relied on some aspects of the "old" education and some aspects of Spartan education. These elements consisted mainly of music and gymnastics, the twin pillars related to body and soul, which he used as his means for shaping the body and the soul of the Guardians. In addition, Plato used a discriminatory means or a censorship approach in the teaching of subject matter; for example, the censorship of literature was aimed at making sure that the Guardians were not exposed to illusions. He also developed elements of character education in which a cult of heroes served as his ideals.

Plato also came to oppose the poets, as he had found them guilty of creating myths and lies, and he believed that poetry presented a false picture of reality. But despite his severe condemnation of poetry, Plato's dialogues contain many examples of the things that he condemned. "Plato's own work bore witness against him: are not his dialogues models of magnificent poetry, shunning no artistic device, and even using myths to instill conviction by a kind of quasi-magical incantation" (Marrou, 1956, p. 72)? In addition to literature, Plato censored music by focusing on patriotic and religious themes based on rhythms of the simple Dorian chants. Plato believed that musical innovation was a threat to the status quo of the Ideal State and that it reflected changing morals that were corrupting. "Music also comes under censorship because 'any musical innovation is full of danger to the State, and ought to be prevented', for 'when modes of music change,' the state changes with them" (Woody, 1949, p. 435).

Plato's second pillar of his leadership education was gymnastics, which also was employed to shape the body and the soul. He believed that regimented simple exercises should be used to inspire a modest lifestyle; therefore, Plato proposed that exercise and games be censored to keep them pure and robust. Dance would not be allowed because it was deemed a corrupting influence on the soul. Plato was convinced that every lesson should dwell on those virtues that were selected to improve the soul. In addition, Plato hoped to use gymnastics as a way to re–associate exercise with moral discipline, but despite Plato's reliance on the "old" types of education, he also broke with the past by introducing some new elements. He proposed, for example, that gymnastics include instruction in hygiene, which focused on the daily care of the body through proper nutrition. He also emphasized the establishment of the habits of an orderly daily life based on the principle: "everything in moderation".

In addition to music and gymnastics, Plato placed great value on the teaching of mathematics as a means of disciplining the mind. He included mathematical processes and exercises similar to those that Pythagoreans had taught for the development of models, such as the circle. The purpose of these exercises also was employed for the discovery of universal virtues such as temperance, justice, and wisdom. Plato, in other words, wished to use mathematics as a means of dealing with concrete problems found in commerce, the art of war, agriculture, and navigation, as well as in daily life. Mathematics, according to Plato, also appealed to the soul, as did music, and helped to awaken the mind by exercising its flexibility, speed and liveliness, as well as aiding the mind's ability to memorize and to advance the skills of problem solving. He argued that through mathematics the soul was awakened to the true light of day, which allowed it to contemplate real (or metaphysical) objects, knowledge and the truth. His interest in mathematics extended to advancing its development as an important aspect of research in the Academy. "Plato was anxious to include in his teaching the results of the most recent scientific discovery, and so he completed it by adding cubic geometry, which had just been discovered by the great mathematician Theaetetus and which indeed the Academy, through Eudoxus, was to help to develop" (Marrou, 1956, p. 75). But in the *Republic*, mathematics was considered an important means of taking those destined to become philosopher–kings to the highest levels of the philosophical development.

Plato also believed that truth could be pursued through a dialectic approach, his third pillar of Guardian education. Plato believed that dialectics could be used to dismiss the sophist's claim of relative truth. Plato argued that because truth was fixed for all times and across all cultures, it transcended relativism. The dialectic process was designed to separate the truth from faulty thinking and it became Plato's epistemology. This approach was based on the understanding that knowledge came to man through ideas, generalized images that could be used as a means to make order out of the chaos. These images were, at best, imperfect perceptions that came to the human mind from the senses of touch, sight, hearing, taste, and smell. However, since perceptions were flawed, they needed to be tested to determine their validity. In other words, the dialectic was a thoughtful process whereby knowledge of fixed forms could be accurately determined through a process of critical analysis. The education of the Guardian was designed to reject all forms of indoctrination including the detection and rejection of false perceptions, which placed learning on the dialectic level or method of instruction. "Far from instilling into his disciples the finished results of his own efforts, Plato's Socrates likes to set them to work to find out for themselves both the difficulty of the given question and then, after a progressive clarification of the issues, the means of surmounting it" (Marrou, 1956, p. 67).

According to Plato's educational prescription for the Guardians, the development of reason began according to a series of educational stages that covered a range according to their difficulty. "The less difficult subjects of literature, mathematics, music and gymnastics are followed by the most difficult subject of all, dialectic, or training in philosophy" (McClelland, 1996, p. 32). Plato's education began with prenatal care for the health and physical fitness of expectant mothers. Children too young to walk were expected to participate in motion exercises, while toddlers were expected to mildly exercise developing limbs. In part, the goal of early exercise was to help the child to develop a sense of harmony of mind and body, as well as to establish good habits. Regimented habits were established early and were used to develop a routine of disciplined conduct. Once selected, these students were trained in the virtues of a just society and they were taught to focus the "eye of the soul" on the real world, and to ignore the false or misleading impressions of the sensuous side of the soul. This training was based on rigorous exercises in speculative analysis of the dialectic.

To enhance the Guardians' speculative skills, Plato developed an advanced course of study that was to begin at about the age of twenty and was designed to include two parts. The first part would continue for about ten years and would include the study of mathematics, music and astronomy. During these years the pupil would be evaluated according to the quality of their moral and intellectual development. More important still, was their ability to deal with abstract thought as applied to addressing the ideal. The second part of the course began at about the age of thirty and included only a select few who had proven their ability to learn and apply the dialectic to complex abstract ideas. Only the best of pupils were selected for these studies, which were based on the mathematical sciences and included arithmetic, geometry, astronomy, and the mathematics of music, or harmonics. Those who had distinguished themselves in mind, body, and moral character would spend five years in philosophic studies, which included advanced dialectics, or the science of the Good. At about the age of thirty-five, some of the select would perform the duties of philosopher–king and would address the problems and concerns of society. Those not selected would serve as auxiliaries or reserves to be called upon in times of crisis. At fifty years of age, the most select individuals would retire to a life of reflection by contemplating the study of excellence and a consideration of real (metaphysical) existence.

The culminating end of formal instruction was the successful application of the dialectic to the issues and problems confronting society. "Recognizing that what a seeker after truth, like Socrates, aimed at was not victory in debate or the elucidation of some particular truth, but the discovery of the all–comprehending truth which he called the good, that is the presupposition of any search for truth whatever, he called this science of the good (which is just the science of the whole truth) dialectic" (Boyd and King, 1995, p. 35). Although Plato's educational design for *The Republic* might seem to be uncomplicated, the theory behind its features was based on a well–thought out complex of pedagogical principles. For example, to establish the Ideal State, the individual had to be convinced to forgo his pleasures for the sake of the general Good.

Perhaps Plato's most radical innovation was to include women in Guardian education. He recommended music and gymnastics for girls, and made no gender distinctions regarding who should serve as Guardians of the state and share in the toils of warfare. "The innovation respecting women's education was not entirely theoretical, is suggested by the report that a number of distinguished women were in the Pythagorean community, and two women attended Plato's school" (Woody, 1949, p. 438). He justified the education of women on the principle that the Ideal State should consist of every adult; therefore, women, as well as men, should be educationally prepared to defend the city. Women Guardians would be selected and educated in the same manner as men, since they were expected to perform the same duties and the same tasks as men. The most gifted would be educated as Guardians, while the majority would serve as soldiers, or Producers. Women as the protector, or soldier class, were trained in archery skills, the javelin throw, marching in ranks, camping, and in field maneuvers. According to Plato, family Guardian life was based on a communal form of living and state nurseries would be created to rear the children of Guardian women, thereby freeing their mothers to perform their specialized duties.

The Laws

The setting of *The Laws* was the island of Crete and the imaginary colony of Magnesia. This dialogue consisted of three–way conversations between a Spartan by the name of Cleinias, a Cretan by the name of Megillus, and an Athenian stranger. Most of the elements of philosophy were presented through the Athenian stranger. The social structure of Magnesia was based on four social classes, which were determined by property standards. In general, Magnesia was more egalitarian than was the *Republic*, as land and property ownership determined the social rank and political participation in the affairs of the state. The government was based on a mixed political system, which included a college of twelve censors with impeachment powers, a hereditary and elected priesthood, a night council of 360, and a magistrate of education, as well as a cadre of salaried teachers and an array of lesser bureaucrats.

The relationship between the four classes was different from the *Republic*, based on the idea that citizens were required to sustain themselves and could not rely on the labor of others. The key political characteristic of the city was the relationship between the classes and the extent of class owned property. This city was modeled on an agrarian society of the type that had existed in the time of Solon. The constitution of the city consisted of a compromise between political systems, and all higher government offices were determined by election. The elected magistrates were required to obey the law and the all–powerful nocturnal council was charged with the protection of the law. The law and obedience to the law was the central focus of this dialogue, including its state–run education system.

Economic conflict was avoided by a set of laws that were designed to restrict excessive wealth as a means to limit poverty, which suggested a communal or collective social system. In addition, political experimentation was restricted in favor of an orthodoxy that stressed political stability. The land was divided into 5,040 lots, distributed to each qualified citizen, and was organized into twelve regions. Citizens were forbidden to work as artisans, but some form of labor was recommended as a means of commerce. Physical exertion was used as a means to limit passions and to promote good health. In addition, there was a humane form of slavery, which was considered a necessity. The slave body consisted of non–Greeks as: "It will work best if the slaves are of different stock; they should be treated well, not just for their own sake, but more because of the master's self-interest, for 'man is a troublesome animal'" (Woody, 1949, p. 440). The most distinguishing characteristic of this dialogue was its emphasis on education and the power of its superintendent to dictate educational policy. Therefore, *The Laws* contained some of Plato's most important educational ideas aimed at creating a social order based on a combination of law and education.

Although Plato did not live to see this dialogue in its final form, he nevertheless considered it the completion of a philosophical journey. Despite its existence in antiquity, it appears that this dialogue attracted few readers. By this time, Plato had given up on the idea of educating undefiled experts who could run society; instead, he turned to the law as a primary means of curbing greed and corruption. According to Plato, the ability to create, or formulate, just laws was one of man's highest achievements. To insure high civic standards, each youth who was qualified for citizenship was to receive a state sponsored education. The first two books, as well as the Seventh Book of *The Laws* specifically addressed the issues of education and this emphasis suggested that Plato was addressing the real political and educational problems of contemporary Greek cities, rather than metaphysical problems. "Plato hoped that, instead of ordinary politicians, whether democrats or oligarchs, the people who know truth and can promote the common good would rule because their rule would be in everyone's real interest" (Martin, 2000, p. 182).

The most powerful state bureaucrat was the magistrate of education who was empowered to direct a state system of education toward shaping citizens to be compatible with the city's constitution. But at the same time, Plato's education continued to rely on a proper understanding of man's relationship to the cosmos and his relationship to God. In other words, all education must be dedicated to the service of God, the source of the Good. Plato's education and *civism* was different in *The Laws* and this difference was due to changes in Plato's views regarding the nature of man, human politics, and the reality of the less perfect state. In *The Laws*, Plato had realigned his views regarding the written law, which he now accepted as a realistic reflection of human experience in history.

In both the *Republic* and *The Laws*, Plato was concerned with the issue of character education, but with some important differences. In *The Laws* character education was broader and required a more inclusive educational system so that the souls of children and youth could be purged of their irrational tendencies. Character education (*civism*) in *The Laws* was the basis of the development of those virtues that could impact the development of the soul, but virtue in *The Laws* was dependent on a "right education". This meant that the most important means for impacting moral conduct was education, especially in support of the law.

The law, as the source of state power, was used to impose moral rules by controlling corrupting influences within the city, and the law became the domain of those who accepted it as truth. Magnesia was located on an island so that it would be free of outside influences, which allowed the state to be walled–off from the rest of the world. Magnesia, in other words, was turned inward, and its laws advanced its conception of politics. Plato had turned back to the reforms of Solon for his model constitution, although he continued to assert the importance of knowledge as the source of political authority and *truth*. He now was required to modify his standard for knowledge and truth to "an acceptable lower standard" in recognition of imperfectability of this world, and he recognized that an alternative political system was required in light of the realities of the human condition. Therefore, the citizens of Magnesia were given a limited voice in their government, and Plato conceded that educational means were capable of producing a moderate state.

Plato now adopted an historical perspective that looked back to the lawgivers, Solon and Draco, and to the "ancestral constitution" based on a land owning aristocracy. These important changes had the effect of making education the key element in political development. History, as Plato's source of knowledge, shifted the search for wisdom into avenues of human experience. "With the wisdom of the Ideal Ruler absent, ancient law and the exhortation of history becomes the materials of the prudent — though not wise in the strict sense — politician" (Samaras, 2002, p. 126). However, history could not produce knowledge or truth in the metaphysical sense, as its focus was social, economic, and political change. Change suggested that the nature of politics was relative, and this shift also suggested that truth was relative, which affected political decision–making and all aspects of Plato's philosophical constructions. While Plato continued to maintain that virtue was fixed and unchanging, the citizens of his new republic had to contend with the relative appearance of virtue, knowledge, and truth.

In this unstable world, Plato attempted to replace the philosopher–king with a scientific *statesman* who possessed powerful analytical skills. This leader was capable of understanding the forces of history, and also was capable of making the right political choices that were needed to educate citizens and to reconcile political differences in order to resolve political conflicts and to maintain civic harmony. Plato's statesman was expected to serve as the leader of the citizens for the purpose of bringing about the reconciliation of class and social differences through educational and persuasive means. "Moreover, it is obvious that the Scientific Ruler (*statesman*) will need to possess a complete, unified virtue if he is to succeed in the task of even partially reconciling the conflicting virtues of the common citizens" (Ibid., p. 184).

Plato was now forced to consider the culture of the community, as knowledge remained his top priority; and so, for Plato, historical knowledge was used to produce a measure of moderation, which could be used as a standard for governing the state. Law was the best solution that Plato could devise under the conditions of relative knowledge; therefore, strict adherence to the law became a fundamental requirement of citizenship. This requirement was based, in part, on the principle that bad constitutions and bad states ignore the law, while good constitutions and good states enforce the law. Respect for the law became the primary virtue of this second best state. In addition, the statesman, to establish true opinion as the best substitute for metaphysical knowledge and truth, used rhetorical persuasion. Plato conceded that, even though the rational skills of the common people were limited, these citizens could be convinced to follow a correct political pathway through a combination of leadership, persuasion, and appropriate education in support of the law.

In *The Laws*, Plato's idealism was now being replaced by a rigid "no nonsense–realism" that could enforce proper civic behavior. At this stage in Plato's life, he appeared to have come to distrust human nature because of its natural tendency to do evil. He also developed something akin to the early Christian's notion of original sin. Ironically, if Plato had lived in such a state, he may have become its first sacrificial victim, as this centralized state had no place for a non–conformist intellectual idealist like Plato. It is more reasonable to think that Plato would have found a kinder refuge in a liberal state that tolerated freethinking philosophers in a democratic state similar to the one in Athens that he despised.

Also in *The Laws*, Plato accepted the idea that the moral and civic level of the citizens' perception could be controlled through educational means, thus the need for a system of universal public education. The magistrate of education was responsible for the supervision of teachers on the basis of their comprehension of the laws that regulated education. The purpose of education was to train children in the virtues as expressed in the laws. State education was based on a system of unchanging values that was compatible with the values of the political system (*civism*).

After receiving a state education, most citizens were expected to learn to reconcile their social and political difference. Unitary thinking was the goal of state education, which justified the employment of a powerful magistrate who had the power to impose a standardized curriculum to ensure the compliant moral development of children. From his educational prescription, it appeared that Plato had come to fear freedom of thought to the point that he now turned from the philosopher to the state policeman who was willing to censor all elements of education. State censorship was used as a means of purifying literature, science, and the arts and to prevent the children from being contaminated by the pleasures and vices of social corruption. Those who resisted this form of education could be jailed or killed, as Spartan discipline had replaced Ionian morality. At the same time, Plato did not completely deny self–choice, but the primary purpose of education was to train students to be virtuous and to obey the laws. It was especially important that citizens accept their roles and responsibilities to cooperate with other citizens in the common aims of the state.

Plato had demanded censorship of the arts and the poets in connection with his state education; the poets were not allowed to teach young children and there was no innovation in poetry. The poets that were included in state schools were required to teach the values of the just life, which equaled a model for the happy life. The law was to be included in poetic form as works appropriate for educational purposes. In general, poetry was forbidden in *The Laws* except for song and dance, and then there were strong religious overtures connected with instruction. Tradition in the arts was the rule in education and respected older men were empowered to judge musical contests that displayed student work. The content of all artistic and musical works was to be according to traditional themes and designed to promote moral conduct. Mathematics was introduced to discipline the mind, to exercise the intellect, and it was to be presented according to a scale of difficulty.

Plato's civism in The Laws was closely associated with his need to address the concerns of the real world and with providing a universal education for the children of its citizens. "The Laws succinctly pronounce that it is the city's responsibility to nurture the citizen's child" (Too, 1995, p. 212). In The Laws, citizenship was associated with the four classes, but the first, or the wealthiest class mainly served as its government. This class possessed the leisure time needed to serve as city-wardens and to participate in bureaucratic work. At the same time, all of the classes had a voice by selecting government representatives who were chosen from the highest classes. The powerful nocturnal council consisted of the two highest classes and their participation was mandatory. The third class was allowed to vote on the council members, even though they did not serve on the council. The fourth class was allowed to vote for members of the two higher classes, but because they had no leisure and they did not actively serve in the government.

In addition to a limited or restricted government, Plato also restricted individual liberty and perceptions about truth as a means to enforce his type of social conformity, and he used his educational system and his laws to shape citizenship behavior. As an expression of his belief that the state must do all that it can to help encourage individuals to be virtuous, Plato had turned to a mild form of citizenship coercion through the power of the state. The state, in other words, had the authority to force individuals toward the formation of correct perceptions about reality and virtue, but this influence was not absolute. Plato also recognized that vice and corruption could not be eradicated by strictness in education, by censorship, or by an authoritarian threat of punishment. States failed because of the weakness of their constitutions in combination with weakness of their laws, but also because of engrained cultural flaws related to moral decadence. The weakness of the citizenship body, in other words, determined the fate of states, and in some cases, education contributed to this weakness.

Plato's Civism, taught in connection with public education is a reflection of the struggle that takes place within each city, state, and society and it often represents the constant conflict between emotion and reason that is a part of human nature. "First of all, by accepting human free will, Plato indicates that opinions of the citizens and the virtue that these citizens acquire are not merely the result of indoctrination, but are also due to the capacities of the citizens themselves" (Samaras, 2002, p. 324). Plato's education in *The Republic* and in *The Laws* was aimed at teaching virtue and was designed to create a desire within the individual to strive to become Good, or to overcome innate natural tendencies to be manipulated and controlled. In addition, Plato's education was aimed at developing a state of harmony through educational means, which was designed to confront human natural tendencies to be directed and controlled by selfish motives. Early on, Plato had concluded that the Athenians had failed because they lacked in those virtues needed to create civil harmony, and this failure had caused them to loose their sense of moderation, which allowed their base, animalistic, tendencies to rule in place of their god–like reason.

Eighteen

Aristotelian Civism

While Plato was always concerned with what could be discovered beyond physical reality, Aristotle was fascinated by what could actually be seen in the real world, especially what could be learnt from observation.

—Charles Freeman

Aristotle (c. 384 – 322 BCE) was born in Stageirus (Stagira) Chalcidice (Macedonia) from a long line of physicians who had served the Macedonian court. The name Aristotle suggested a bright future and resulted from combining the Greek words *ariston* meaning "best" with *telos* meaning "end". Because his parents died young, Aristotle was not trained as a physician; instead, he fell under the care of his guardian, Proxenus, who sent him to study in Athens at Plato's Academy. He arrived at the age of seventeen and remained for twenty years. During this time, Aristotle became Plato's teaching assistant and was his most brilliant student. He may have expected to succeed Plato as the head of the Academy, but contrary to this expectation, the leadership of the Academy would fall to Speusippus, Plato's nephew. Demosthenes warned the Athenians against the Macedonians, and this growing unrest forced Aristotle to leave the city following the death of Plato in 347 BCE.

Aristotle and his friend Xenocrates departed Athens and traveled to the Asia Minor kingdom of Hermias, which was an independent Anatolian kingdom. The capital was at Atarneus, a port city near the coast of Mysia. Hermias was a petty tyrant who, under the influence of local Platonist philosophers, modified his government into a milder form of rule. His kingdom expanded and came to include Assos, where he provided a place for philosophers to gather and teach. Aristotle and Xenocrates found this city suitable for their residence where Aristotle met his wife Pythias, niece (or possibly the daughter) of Hermias. Also at Assos Aristotle attempted to transform Hermias to rule as a philosopher–king. "He (Hermias) even had the courage to put their ideas into practice, and found the resulting conciliatory policy perfectly satisfactory from a practical point of view" (Guthrie, 1981, p. 31).

After three years, Aristotle crossed over to Mytilene, located on the island of Lesbos, to reside at the home of his friend Theophrastus where he completed some scientific observations and collections. In 343 BCE Aristotle traveled to Pella where he learned that Hermias had been killed after being captured by the Persians.

In 343 BCE, Aristotle became the tutor of the 14-year–old Macedonian prince, Alexander. "Of course the greatest ruler of his day had to have the greatest philosopher of his day as tutor, and of course the greatest philosopher of his day had to have the greatest pupil" (McClelland, 1996, p. 53). Alexander absorbed Aristotle's keen interest in distant cultures and in the flora and fauna of the surrounding regions, which gave him an awareness of ecological systems. Following his tutoring assignment with Alexander, Aristotle was assigned the task of rebuilding Stageirus, his hometown, which had been devastated by war. His tasks included the re–population of the city and the drafting a legal code for the new civic order. He also established a school in the town of Mieza. Aristotle remained in Macedonia until the assassination of Philip and then moved back to Athens to organize a new school of higher education dedicated to his study of philosophy and science. "The uncompromising ideal of the philosopher – king had yielded in his mind to something more practical, and united with his conviction of the superiority of the Hellenic race to all others, and his belief that it could rule the world if only it achieved political unity" (Guthrie, 1981, p. 36). Tragedy followed Aristotle back to Athens when Pythais died leaving him with a daughter. Aristotle acquired Herpyllis, a slave, who relieved him of his domestic responsibilities and also provided him a son named after his father, Nicomachus. Following the death of Aristotle, Nicomachus was reported to have edited Aristotle's book on ethics, which became known as *Nicomachean Ethics*.

Aristotle sent his nephew Callisthenes to accompany Alexander on his conquest of Persia to serve as a trained historian; however, he fell into disfavor with Alexander and was charged with insubordination and died in prison. Aristotle was aware that Callisthenes was prone to provoke trouble. "His own verdict on his nephew was that the boy was certainly a powerful talker, but had no sense" (Ibid., p. 38). Before the death of Callisthenes, Alexander had attempted to keep detailed accounts of his sojourn and he also attempted to advance his scientific knowledge by collecting biological specimens, which were sent to the Lyceum for study. This event may have had the effect of causing an estrangement between Aristotle and Alexander.

The final 20 years of Aristotle's life were happy and productive years and he continued to have the support of the Macedonians, who subsidized his work; however, with the death of Alexander, Aristotle's world was shattered. He was unpopular with those who controlled the Academy and with those who taught in Isocrates' school. The Athenians used the death of Alexander to drive Aristotle into exile and they passed a death sentence upon him. In 322 BCE, Aristotle fled Athens for the city of Chalcis, a Macedonian citadel in Euboea. Chalcis was the home city of his mother and the founding city of Stagirus. In that same year Demosthenes took his own life and Aristotle died of a digestive illness.

Aristotle's greatest strength may be that he did *not* hesitate to tackle big questions; questions for which he was not afraid to seek answers in his quest for knowledge and truth. As a result of his intense curiosity and drive, he is regarded as perhaps the greatest scholar of antiquity and his work continues to influence modern philosophers and scientists. Without Aristotle, the orientation of western intellectual thought might have remained shrouded in superstition and without a clear understanding of the nature of the physical reality; with Aristotle, western intellectual thought arrived at a place where it could focus on all aspects of matter and the mechanics of the physical world. For scientists, the political reality came into focus on the complexities of cosmopolitan living and the importance of the civic culture. For educators, Aristotle's message is obvious and clear: the primary task of the schools is to focus on the cultivation of citizenship, morality, and reason.

He was interested in almost everything natural and he had a great deal to say about the role of nature in man's purpose on earth. He never came to worship nature, but within its boundaries he found its rhythms and rules, as well as a purpose that equaled Plato's heavenly forces. "Aristotle seems to be suggesting that there is an underlying purpose to nature, that of the self–fulfillment of every living being through the correct use of the attributes it possesses" (Freeman, 1996, pp. 236-237). He allowed his ideas to ripen before committing them to pen and paper; unfortunately, he was not able to complete all of the treatises that he had explored. Aristotle's greatest accomplishments were his works on politics, logic, rhetoric, metaphysics, ethics, as well as his related work in science and his lists of written works which included more than 170 items. From the beginning of his teaching he was aware of the need to develop a consistent and integrated system of thought, as well as the need to verify his conclusions through experimentation and observation. Knowledge of the type Aristotle sought was aimed at a precision of study based on observations, and science was his passion that he used to guide his search for *truth*.

Aristotle believed that the state represented man's highest good, but that some systems of government were better than some others. Like Plato, Aristotle was critical of democracy; however, he was more moderate than Plato in his criticism of democracy and his studies suggested that he was convinced that every type of government had its good and bad forms. Democracy, when ruled by the poor, was a bad form, as it had its own elements of injustice. "The rule of the poor was regarded by elite writers (philosophers) as unjust, since they saw this situation as giving unfair advantage to mere numbers over quality and virtue" (Ober, 1989, p. 193). Aristotle dismissed all of the bad *forms* of the tyrannies, oligarchies and democracies as perverse forms of government. He also had concluded that all such bad *forms* of democracy represented lawlessness akin to anarchy. "The goal of democracy, he said, was living exactly as one likes, which could never be a valid principle for organizing the best government" (Martin, 2000, p. 185). Aristotle also argued that it was impossible for every citizen to participate in the decision–making process of the polis. Democracy, while it appeared attractive on the surface, could not provide for the law. A mass audience or even a committee of well–intentioned legislators could not construct

The Lyceum

Aristotle's Lyceum, located at the site of an old gymnasium, was situated in the precinct of Apollo Lykeios and had been a gathering place of sophists and rhetors and served as one of Socrates' old haunts. Aristotle patterned the Lyceum after the Academy, which was dedicated as a cult to the muses; also like the Academy, the Lyceum followed the practices of *symposia* and a shared communal lifestyle. The school complex consisted of associated buildings, which included a large building that served as a dining room for shared meals.

Aristotle established the Lyceum in 334 BCE, where he taught for the next twelve years. The Lyceum also was known as *Peripatos* or *Peripaetic School* and was named for its colonnaded walkways and Aristotle's habit of walking about with his students in contemplative discussion. According to his routine, he lectured on advanced studies in the morning, which was followed by discussions in the afternoon. Aristotle's pedagogy consisted of two types of instruction: *exoteric* and *acroatic*. Exoteric was presented in *rhetoric* form in which Aristotle lectured on specific topics, and his *acroatic* was presented in a dialectical form, which consisted of investigation followed by discussion. For advanced students, the early morning was spent in (*aroatic*) dialectical discussion of various subjects, while the evening was spent in *exoteric* lecture followed by discussion and socializing. Aristotle's extensive book collection provided resources for his instruction and his studies. Aristotle's books and resources also were divided into two sections consisting of the *aroatic* dialectical discussion sources and resources for his *exoteric* exercises in applied rhetoric. In addition, Aristotle produced great collections of notebooks that also served as resources for further research. These notebooks consisted of his scientific observations and included his political science collection on the Greek city–states, which described the various political systems of Greece and also contributed to his *Constitution of Athens*.

Over time the library, became such an extensive collection of books and natural specimens that Aristotle was required to invent a cataloguing system to manage it. "Strabo called him (Aristotle) the first known collector of books, and if this can hardly be literally true, it probably means that he was the first to establish a library in the full sense of a properly arranged collection in its own special building" (Guthrie, 1981, p. 40). Aristotle trained Demetrius of Phalerum to maintain his system and he managed the library for about ten years. After Aristotle was exiled from Athens, Demetrius was forced to take refuge in Alexandria in Egypt, where he became the advisor to Ptolemy Soter. Demetrius became famous after he used his influence with Ptolemy to help build the ancient world's oldest and greatest state library. The other Hellenistic monarchs also built competing libraries, but none as grand as the one built in Alexandria.

Aristotle's instruction focused on various topics pertaining to rhetoric, politics, ethics, poetry, and natural studies. "The curriculum at the Lyceum contained biology, theology, metaphysics, astronomy, mathematics, botany, meteorology, ethics, rhetoric and poetics as well as politics, so that Aristotle has a much better claim than Plato to being the founder of the first real university" (McClelland, 1996, p. 52). In addition, while at the Lyceum, Aristotle concentrated his studies on the philosophy of nature by focusing on *form* and *matter* in an attempt to explain the nature of things in the natural world. Aristotle wrote extensively on scientific subjects that ranged from the cosmos to the place of human beings within the natural order.

Aristotelian Science

Aristotle's scientific investigations led to many written works, which included his *Organon* (or Instrument) in which he laid down the foundations for the application of *logic* or scientific thought in the form of *deductive reasoning*. Aristotle desired to explore the secrets of nature, which led him to conclude that almost any problem could be resolved by constructing a definition and by classifying the subject according to similar items. He also formulated hypotheses as a means of seeking truth and used data collection as a means of accepting or rejecting a hypothesis. He applied the same logical processes to an investigation of societies and reviewed a wide range of sources to confirm his findings about them. *Syllogism* became the basis for Aristotle's philosophy of logic, as well as his system of *deductive reasoning*.

The *Organon*, which was circulated after Aristotle's death, became the standard text for the study of logic in the western world. "Logic was regarded by him not as a separate science, but as introductory to all sciences; and, for this reason, his philosophy and science were universal in nature, and he may be considered the father of the whole progressive search for truth" (Graves, 1929, p. 212). This desire to think clearly required defining and describing the specifications of the object of his interest, which led him to the process of classifying genus, or classes, of specimens by making distinctions between their various members. Aristotle's logic also grew out of his concern for sophistic teaching. He responded to their form of argumentation by attempting to work out a system of logic for addressing or identifying precise arguments as opposed to their form of rhetoric, or persuasive argumentation. "He strives always for the appropriate level of generality which will illuminate without over–simplifying" (Annas, 1986, p. 248).

To advance his work Aristotle developed a set of ten categories that served as a system, which allowed him to categorize almost any living subject. This system, however, seldom answered the question that he was investigating. In spite of this condition, he was scientifically correct to think that through observation, one could learn the nature of most things in the physical world. In addition, Aristotle was interested in the ways that *form* was related to *function*, which also contributed his *teleological* thinking.

In his *Metaphysics* he presented the development of his philosophy as a search for and an understanding of natural phenomena. In his *Physics* he provided a description of *types of explanations* that a natural philosophy should provide by answering the question "why". The question "why" was approached from the point of view of acceptable and valid argument. "According to Aristotle, four different categories of explanations exist that are not reducible to a single, unified whole: *form* (defining characteristics), *matter* (constituent elements), origin of movement (similar to what we commonly mean by "cause"), and *telos* (end, aim or goal)" (Martin, 2000, pp. 182-183). These four categories then served as a way to describe objects, whether organic or inorganic. They consisted of the forces or causes, which included *material, efficient, formal* and *final*. Aristotle used these principles to construct a set of questions that he would ask when making observations about an object or physical phenomena.

According to Aristotle's scientific philosophy, nature contained the means to accomplish a built-in design that expressed its purpose, or *teleology*. According to this theory, an organism was expressed through the processes of growth and development, or an unfolding that was directed by nature to complete its intended "end". Although there has been some disputed debate over the extent to which Aristotle actually believed in a teleological explanation, it appears from his written work that he did accept this idea. Nature, according to Aristotle, was an efficient and purposeful force and its "ends" were predetermined and fulfilled under natural circumstances. His idea of "ends" also extended to the inorganic. "Whether Aristotle invokes teleological explanations to relate one species to another is highly uncertain, as is the question whether such explanations apply to the nonliving. The *Physics* also contains valuable discussions of place, time, and the nature of change" (Nussbaum, 2000, p. 54).

Also according to a teleological perspective, living organisms could only be understood by observing them in their natural surroundings; therefore, all that was necessary to reveal the secrets of nature was a form of field study, or a study of the subject in its natural surroundings. Aristotle also was seeking to answer questions related to the force in nature that gave an object its essential characteristics, its *form* and its *function*. Therefore it was necessary to study surroundings, settings or the environment to understand the *form* and the *function* of a subject. In other words, nature (surroundings) not only provided the subject with its *form* and *function*, but also its "end" purpose. "When looking at living animals he was fascinated by the problem of why they had the physical attributes they did. Why does a duck have webbed feet? Aristotle argued that is was because it had a role, that of being a duck, and the webbed feet were essential to fulfilling this role" (Freeman, 1996, pp. 236-237).

Aristotle's teleological understandings also extended to his sociology, which was based on his belief that human beings were striving toward an end goal as a designed purpose. "Thus the highest good for any living organism is to be discovered in the full flowering of its nature; and that involves the realization of all its endowments, of which, Aristotle adds, the most distinctive for man is reasoning, for it is this which distinguishes him from plants and animals" (Winn and Jacks, 1967, p. 10). Therefore, to understand organisms, one must come to an understanding of the nature of the organism's goal or mission. The mission of a giraffe was to feed off of high trees of the forest or jungle, while man's mission was to create the perfected *polis*. "Aristotle seems to be suggesting that there is an underlying purpose to nature, that of the self–fulfillment of every living being through the correct use of the attributes it possesses" (Freeman, 1996, pp. 236-237).

According to Aristotle, the human mission was to control irrational appetites related to the *soul* and the *body*. "The aim of education is to dissuade people from this inclination (greed) which has its worst effects when it is directed at acquiring money or honor" (Martin, 2000, p. 185). The divine human purpose was only attainable by creating surroundings or an environment that was ideal for assisting human beings in the achievement of those ends for which they had been designed to achieve in the ideal political polis.

Politics, Ethics and Civism

Plato's interest in political matters and his search for an ideal state, may have led Aristotle to begin a massive project aimed at analyzing the political systems of the Greek city–states and their constitutions. Before the project ended, Aristotle and his students had collected over 158 separate political case studies in which he described the operation of polis governments according to their variations. This work eventually led Aristotle to write *Politics* in which he laid down a theoretical foundation for an ideal polis based on mixed constitutions. According to Aristotle, everything in his ideal state was to be regulated by law, in which a core responsibility of his polis government was to educate its citizens. Citizenship in this state was based on a type of collective body of thought in which the best men of equal status were to elect a rotating kingship.

In addition to *Politics*, Aristotle wrote a companion work that is known as *Nicomachean Ethics*. Originally, *Ethics* may have been a part of *Politics*, but was separated from it at a later time. In this work, Aristotle set out to examine the problem of morality as an influence on the behavior of citizens and as an important aspect of their rational thinking. *Civism* enters into Aristotle's thinking as he, like Plato, was forced by their political reasoning to advance the shaping of the citizen's civic values. "Like Plato, Aristotle writes in the conviction that the formulation of the individual child's êthos or character has a direct and significant bearing on the preservation of the whole state's êthos" (Too, 1995, p. 209). Mainly, however, *Ethics* was Aristotle's attempt to deal with questions regarding the good life in which the state government worked to make its citizens happy, which was related to his notion of the influence of social and political settings. Aristotle's ideal state was a state in which individuals could seek after their collective and individual happiness, or the "end" meaning of their purpose for existing, based on their natural activities.

Also, *happiness* required that men know their particular strengths and apply them according to a standard of excellence (*aretê*). The *happiness* described by Aristotle was only available under the best societies, cities that were dominated by their best people. More important still, *happiness* relied on *virtue* and the practice of wisdom, which required that individuals rationally evaluate their *goodness* (conduct) according to a standard as measured by a *golden mean*. Recalling Aristotle's work related to his evaluations of state constitutions, the golden mean was the midpoint or mid–range between the extremes in every political system. Human behavior also required such a measure, as it related to self-control or moderation. Reason on the other hand consisted of two kinds or types, which consisted of a practical (or an applied type) and a theoretical (or an abstract type).

Studied together or separately, both Aristotle's *Politics* and his *Ethics* reveal some interesting insights on his thinking about citizenship and the nature of a *civism* that could be used to advance an ideal citizenship. Aristotle's treatise on *Politics* had its origin in the ideological disputes between Plato and Isocrates. "This conflict between Plato and Isocrates developed the systematic theories of logic and of rhetoric which we find in Aristotle; it also developed a polarity between philosophy and rhetoric as two forms of mental activity suited to the adult mind, which was to dominate culture for the rest of the ancient world" (Murray, 1986, p. 230). Aristotle's contribution to politics was, in part, based upon his effort to place political philosophy above rhetoric in the education of youth; therefore, he attempted to create an empirical approach to the study of human behavior.

Aristotle called ethics and politics a philosophy of life, which could be used as a guide to happiness. In his work, *Ethics,* he established the form of the good life, which was best realized in the good state, and in his work, *Politic*s, he dealt with the principles that were used to form a good state. Education in these works was subsumed under political art, which was to organize and direct it. Political art, in other words, determined the system of instruction that was to be used in the instruction of young citizens. At the same time, the state must be well run so that the individual could develop his own potential to its maximum level of possibility. The aim of the good state and the aim of education were the same. The city must call forth the best virtue related to justice and intelligence, and the state is responsible for training its youth socially and politically in ethics. "Ethical training is the indispensable foundation for political life, or rather for citizenship" (Guthrie, 1981, p. 333). For Aristotle, ethics was the doctrine of virtue, which was the pathway to happiness through reason. Therefore, social and political well–being required moral training (*civism*) in the *virtues* and, according to Aristotle's *civism*, a good person rejects self–gratification and does not indulge his appetites, and he keeps his distant from those who seek honors.

Politics was written around 330 BCE as a system of rule based on an equal citizenship of elites that may have reflected something akin to the Macedonian aristocracy, and may have been directed at justifying the reign of Philip and Alexander. "It was the rise of Macedon under Philip and Alexander which put an end to the free and independent *polis*, and Aristotle himself may have come under suspicion as some kind of Macedonian agent, as the philosophical wing of semi-barbarian military kingship, and so had to cover his tracks by always arguing that life in the properly constituted polis was the best life that Greeks could aspire to" (McClelland, 1996, p. 53).

The structure of the text of this work was in disarray, which may have reflected Aristotle's rush to keep abreast with Alexander's lightening fast conquests. "The most poignant image we have of Aristotle is of the old man anxiously waiting in Athens for news of the progress of Alexander's eastern conquests, worrying about the orientalisation of Hellas which is its inevitable result, and hurriedly putting together in the *Politics* everything that was worth saying about those little Greek states before they disappeared into the world empire which was to be the standard political unit for the next two thousand years" (McClelland, 1996, pp. 53-54). Some scholars have suggested that it was so uncharacteristic of Aristotle's other works that Aristotle could not have been its author, while others have suggested that *Politics* was simply a compilation of Aristotle's lecture notes. "Another, equally plausible view is that the order of the *Politics'* eight books has become jumbled during the course of the centuries, and several scholarly careers have been made out of the business of rearranging them" (Ibid., pp. 54-55).

Politics also exposed some important differences in the political thinking between Plato and Aristotle. Aristotle disputed Plato's ideal related to inherited virtue. "Aristotle also specifically refutes the validity of the concept of inherited virtue, noting that although *eugeneia* leads its possessors to act haughtily, in fact most aristocrats are worthless (*euteleis*), and families that were once brilliant tended to breed maniacs and dullards" (Ober, 1989, p. 256). More important still, Aristotle included human experience (history) and reflective opinion within the parameters of his study. Aristotle's investigative methodology separates his approach from the one taken by Plato. Aristotle was especially interested in consulting with those who had wrestled with the issues and problems of societies and states. Even more unlike Plato was Aristotle's use of written texts of other authors, which Aristotle classified as *primary sources*. Aristotle accepted that knowledge could be gleaned from systematic observations about the culture provided that they were written according to a systematic or scientific approach. In addition, knowledge also could be suggested within the laws of society, as he considered a body of *law* to be representative of the collective wisdom and memories of a society.

Like Plato, Aristotle also recognized that not everything that happened in life was natural, and he believed that there were forces in the world and within human culture that worked to frustrate the natural order. According to Aristotle, the role of the philosopher (political scientist) was to identify those things that work, as well as those things that do not work, especially those things that lead to harmful consequences for the society or state. Both Aristotle and Plato were in agreement with the notion that nature would ultimately fulfill its intended purpose (*telos*); consequently the study of politics was a helpful tool to assist societies to develop the best means to work within its natural order.

Another focus in *Politics* was on the interdependence between the ruler and the citizen, as well as the complexities of social and political relationships. "Rulership includes commanding, but it also includes directing, guiding and educating" (McClelland, 1996, p. 60). Through his studies of the city–states, Aristotle hoped to identify natural political relationships, and he formulated his study based on the idea of "natural pairs"; such as between a master and his slave. According to Aristotle, paired relationships often consisted of superior and inferior partners in which one of the parties was superior to the other; but at the same time, both parties were dependent upon each other. The purpose of a paired relationship was to allow each member of a pair to fulfill their separate purpose. In paired relationships the ruling of one by the other allowed both individuals to become self–sufficient and purposeful; therefore, he argued that it was in the interest of the ruler and the one being ruled to maintain this type of relationship. By this time, Aristotle had concluded that in human affairs there are natural patterns, such as pairs and hierarchies, that are associated with "ends", and that these relationships were best maintained within the setting of the good polis. Because of these natural patterns of subordination and domination, members of a community were in relationships that allowed them to achieve their fullest potential.

The study of relationships and pairs also led Aristotle to recognize the importance of *friendship,* which he explored in his *Nicomachean Ethics*. But, there also were some important differences that suggested that Aristotle was in opposition to Platonic *forms*. "He (Aristotle) openly prefers Gorgias's method of enumerating separate virtues to the Socratic demand for general definition of virtue, he calls self–deception, and in the first book of *Ethics*, which contains one of his must sustained and effective attacks on the Platonic theory of Forms, we find a defense of the relativity and multiplicity of good which might almost have been written by Protagoras" (Guthrie, 1971, p. 54). The idea of friendship also became an important topic in Aristotle's treatise on *Politics,* and the importance of friendship also was demonstrated in Aristotle's life, especially in his relationship with Plato, Alexander, and Antipater. According to Aristotle, *friendship* was a relationship that cemented families and communities together. For Aristotle, friendship was the essence of a community based on the principle that "Friends share what they possess." Moreover, the formation and the continuation of friendships involved the notion of human excellence, goodness, and citizenship.

In sum, the good person does the good thing for his own sake and for the sake of his intellect. Wicked persons, on the other hand, oppose themselves because of their appetites. The wicked tend to choose harmful pleasures because they have a wrong or evil mindset; therefore, wicked persons seek company to escape themselves, and their memories and hopes are wretched. The good man will love himself and sacrifice money and honors for the sake of his friend. Therefore, self–love is not vanity, but is based on a life of virtue and good deeds. In his *Politics* and *Ethics*, Aristotle saw *friendship* as the most critical relationship within the polis, as it allowed for the survival of the community as an entity and it was the basis for good citizenship.

Aristotle's intention was to limit political diversity, which he considered an evil, and to apply the golden mean to political systems to check the excessive use of political power. The idea of the golden mean was designed to avoid extremes within social settings in order to escape the evils that brought about class conflict and other sources of social friction. He concluded that the best *form* of government was not a government of men, special interests or social classes, but a government under the rule of the law. "Within this framework, Aristotle makes it a matter of contingent circumstance whether this or that political situation or civic tradition calls for a monarchy, an aristocracy, or a "polity" (*politeia*), that is, a law–governed semi popular regime" (Poulakos and Depew, 2004, p. 13). What constituted the *ideal constitution* was best determined by circumstances and was a point of judgment. Aristotle did not want monarchy to degenerate into a tyranny, or aristocracies to degenerate into oligarchy, or democracy to deteriorate into anarchy.

Aristotle preferred a kingship that served the many, but this kingship was under the *law*, was limited, and could not be inherited. "Law has as its end the good of those who are asked to obey, not the good of those who make it" (McClelland, 1996, p. 65). Without the law, Aristotle reasoned, human beings would be tempted to surrender to their passions or become corrupted. In addition, Aristotle recognized that the rule of law required a compatible education that prepared its youth to live according to the law.

Aristotle's ideal political system also was based on the rule of wise and morally virtuous equals (heads of families, villages or tribes) who, according to their traditional roles, were deemed qualified to rule. These heads of social units would control every aspect of daily living in a society that encompassed every person in the community. Although leadership of the state would be empowered, the elected and rotated kingship was limited to conduct in office by an accountability that judged the ruler according to his justice while in office. The law also prohibited any acts that threatened the good life of the many.

Aristotle rejected the equalization of the classes as an injustice, but on the other hand, he realized that the lower classes had to protect themselves against the power of the wealthy. "Hence he attempted to devise a theoretical constitution based on a mathematical balance between the 'arithmetical' principle of equality (one man–one vote) and the notion that superior individuals deserved superior political powers" (Ober, 1989, pp. 294-295). The only solution open to Aristotle was to retreat into the notion of the *ideal constitution* as one in which elites (aristocrats) were given the power to rule the state as described in books 7 and 8 of his *Politics*.

Aristotle, in his pursuit of an *ideal constitution*, took some interesting political turns, as was indicated by his determination to have a government of equals and rotate an elected kingship. In addition Aristotle attempted to protect his city against powerful individuals. He carried this point to the extreme by claiming that should any man of exceptional ability appear in the polis, he should be exiled so as not to pose a threat to the equality of the many. In other words, while Plato sought after the most capable individuals to rule, Aristotle would dismiss capable individuals because they posed a threat to the community. He had concluded that a rule of equals couldn't tolerate *excellence* of the type recommended by Plato. "There is always the possibility that one man among them would be outstanding, a really kingly man in something like Plato's sense. What should be done about him? Aristotle would say: exile or kill him, because he has no place in the city" (McClelland, 1996, p. 67).

Aristotle's theoretical assertions caused him philosophical problems regarding the authoritarian nature of his elected kingship; therefore, Aristotle now was willing to rest leadership on the ability of citizens to reason together as the essential aspect of good government. The goal of good government, according to Aristotle, was to create leisure that would promote rational and creative activities for its citizens, and to strive for peace so that these activities could be sustained within the culture of the ideal constitution. Aristotle also presented an interesting perspective on war between cities; he viewed war as a natural and just means of establishing the superior state over the dominion of the inferior state. He reasoned that the inferior polis might benefit from being dominated by a superior polis; mainly however, he argued that war should be fought to protect the state and should not be used for aggressive purposes. The tyrannies, or the unlawful states, according to Aristotle, had participated in war for gain; therefore, their virtue was based on the principle that "might makes right." These states were doomed to failure because they were incapable of providing good government, as a good government directed its military toward keeping the peace, while a bad government directed its military power for aggressive and illegal purposes. At this time, Aristotle seemed to support Alexander, who was at the head of the most powerful war machine that the ancient world had ever witnessed.

Self–Perfection and Civism

In his *Ethics,* Aristotle reasoned that each individual contained, within his soul, a conception of a fulfilled human being, and that education could be used in the process to bring about his *self–perfection,* "Thus individuals become good by three means; natural endowment, the habits which they form, and the rational principles within them" (Winn & Jacks, 1967, p. 6). The soul reveals itself in the growth of the individual person and it serves as the guiding mechanism for *self-realization.* In his work, *On The Soul,* Aristotle emphasized the idea that the soul was the vital force that gave the body its *form* and its individual personality. The soul formed the body, as the body was the matter of the soul; accordingly, human growth required three stages that consisted of a period of physical growth, a period of irrational appetites and passions, and a period of reason. An appropriate education, therefore, should address these three *stages* and should include the education of the body, character training, and the training of the intellect.

It is possible that Aristotle might have intended to use the dialectic as a means of training the intellect, but his *Politics* ended in an unfinished condition. Aristotle's analysis suggested that the soul, which he describes as the *psyche,* was the most vital principle of life. The soul, however, had a divided nature, which consisted of two aspects, a "rational" side and an "irrational" side. Because the soul had a divided nature, education could be used to help gain control of passion — that is, to bridle the irrational nature of the soul. Finding a balance between opposites was a means of finding *happiness* based on the standard of the *golden mean,* as it related to polar opposites. Also, through educational means the individual should be provided with an opportunity for rational reflection and to practice, or exercise, self–control. According to Aristotle, virtue was to be developed by a rational process whereby the individual was taught to reason in order to find the middle disposition.

Moral character was the result of virtue, which required the use of practical wisdom. Moral training combined with the development of virtue became the means for controlling passions. Aristotle suggested that virtue came in two forms: a practical form that was acquired through the development of good habits, and a reflective form that belonged to the domain of the philosopher—or the domain of reason. In either case, *virtue* was to serve as a restraint or modifier of passion and emotion. Instruction was required to prepare students to advance in their abilities to acquire a higher level of virtue, which was justified by Aristotle's belief that virtue and reason were connected. Virtue and reason were connected in the form of a two–way path in which the rational side of the soul was enhanced by the acquisition of virtues. Virtues were the product of a greater ability to reason; in other words, reason and virtue were directly paired; therefore it followed that education aimed at the development of virtue also should be directed at the development of the potential to reason. Aristotle followed the dictum that because man is a reasoning animal, *happiness* is associated with his ability to reason. In other words, happiness requires that man restrain his passions through the application of his reasoning powers.

The key to individual happiness also was found in the actions or the functions that best suit the individual. Happiness, in other words, might be attained when a person participated in an activity that was suited to his abilities, such as by playing a musical instrument or by participating in craft–making, as these choices were guided by an individual's striving for self–perfection. Aristotle also dismissed life, nutrition, sensation, and growth from his definition of happiness, as all animals and plants share these traits in common with humankind. The uniqueness of humankind was the ability to reason. *Reason* was the ultimate component of *happiness* for humankind because it was a function of the human *soul* in agreement with virtue and moral character.

The irrational and rational divisions of the soul led to the issue of training both the *body* and the *soul.* According to Aristotle, the body and its nutrition and growth are developed under the irrational side of the soul and reason is developed under the rational side of the soul. The development of the body preceded the development of the reason; therefore it should come first in the educational order. "For Aristotle the educational process begins in infancy with an early habituation to temperance and toughness, and continues till the age of twenty–one, with regular education starting at seven, the division between Primary and Secondary falling at the stage of puberty" (Winn and Jacks, 1967, p. 41). The actual training of the body begins at birth, which includes a proper diet, exercise and the practice of hygiene. As soon as possible, children should participate in simple games. At the same time, children were to be told proper stories with virtuous implications as a part of an early moral training. Slaves, or those without morality, would not be allowed to supervise the nursery, nor would they have any direct contact with children.

Aristotle asserted that *happiness* was the function of the soul in agreement with *reason* and in association with activities that express virtue; therefore, the rational aspects of learning should be reflected in the choices that students make. Choices also were a reflection of a person's moral character and his ability to reason; therefore choices allowed the individual to become oriented toward the good, and the good was expressed in every aspect of the individual's actions, as well as in his relationships.

Because the rational soul was capable of a higher order of thinking, it also could cause problems if it was not channeled for moral purposes. Therefore, the rational nature of the soul should be encouraged to speculate about all aspects of nature, as well as spiritual things. In addition, the rational soul should be educated to deal with polar opposites and the interaction between these opposites, as opposites could be used to educate the rational soul to seek a higher level of moral human conduct.

The above ideas led Aristotle to conclude that virtues were not innate, but were learned. In his *Ethics*, Aristotle wrote that, "The most fortunate of men is he who combines a measure of prosperity with scholarship, research, or contemplation; such a man comes closest to the life of the gods." But even less capable persons were open to moral development. Consequently, the ideal state should educate its citizens to meet the expectations of the state and to their highest potential of development through a process of self–perfection, which is an expression of the citizen's *civism*.

Constitutional Civism

Aristotle feared that a superior and aggressive person would subvert the social and political relationships of the polis by making its general body of citizens inferior. In addition, he feared that the superior person might corrupt all of the institutions of the *polis* and make them subject to his will. In the place of individual excellence (*aretê*), Aristotle substituted the excellence of the constitution of the polis. "His excellence (the citizens) must be an excellence relative to the constitution, and a *Polis* is good in virtue of the goodness of the citizens who share in its government" (Winn and Jacks, 1967, p. 6).

Foremost in Aristotle's mind was a desire to synchronize and harmonize the interests of the individual with the interests of the state's constitution through educational means. Aristotle believed that education (*paideia*) should be subject to legislation, as it was the concern of the entire community. The state, Aristotle reasoned, must be enlightened and flexible enough to allow its citizens to reach and express their potential to *reason* together and to achieve a common sense of fulfillment, or happiness. A Good state, therefore, was one that helped to promote and direct those activities that were naturally proper for human beings as political animals. Therefore, the goal of the good state was to help its citizen become contributors to the development of the state.

Aristotle went so far as to claim that citizens did not belong to themselves, but rather they belonged to the state; therefore, the state, as the parent of the citizen, was required to provide an education to its children. "The polis exists for 'the good life' of its citizens, and the good life depends on nature, habit and a 'reasoned course of life'. Education is concerned with the last two" (McClelland, 1996, pp. 59-60). Therefore, the uniting social bond of the polis was the result of educational means that transformed its citizens into a collective community. Education was to be the guarantor of the survival of the good state. "So if a constitution is to survive, all the elements of the *Polis* must combine to will its maintenance. The best means of ensuring this, therefore, is the education of the citizen in the spirit of their constitution" (Winn and Jacks, 1967, p. 6).

Recalling that Aristotle's analysis of the various political systems had led him to conclude that a state sponsored education was the best means to develop citizens for the polis; his recommendation was for a philosophical education. "He asserts that the theory and practice of education must, without question, be built upon a solid foundation of a philosophical life, especially in the fields of ethics and politics" (Winn and Jacks, 1967, p. 1). In addition, Aristotelian citizenship would be advanced through a series of steps that were designed to lead the youth of his city into the processes and procedures of speculation and intellectual thought. Aristotle's *civism* would assist citizen pupils in confronting the public affairs of the polis, as the goal of the good state was to achieve a life of leisure and peace so that its citizens could develop good relationships (friendships).

These relationships extended to associations within the polis and to individuals residing in other city–states. Within the setting of the state, this meant that education should be used to equip its citizens for the practical duties of living in a community by performing the duties of a good citizen. But at the same time, Aristotle, recognized that the good also resided outside or beyond the boundaries of citizenship and civic duty, and that a philosophical education could not be limited just to the nature of the state. Nevertheless, the first responsibility of every citizen was to the state and to the perfection of the state.

Aristotle did not intend to educate the working classes nor was state education aimed at producing a common school. In addition, he did not intend to educate slaves or women, except in the affairs of the household. Aristotle reserved education in reason, morality, virtue, and happiness for free and capable men. He dismissed slaves and women because he believed them incapable of learning and practicing virtue. He believed that some men, by their nature, were slaves and were incapable of being anything but slaves. Free men born into good families, on the other hand, were destined by their nature to rule in the *good* state as was determined by their capacity for the attainment of virtue; therefore, women and inferior men must be ruled by superior men.

Aristotle viewed women as inferior intellectually and only fit for subjugation since, by nature, they possessed no facility for leadership or self–rule. This belief was in opposition to Plato's view on women. Plato would allow women to become members of the Guardian class, while Aristotle claimed that their proper place, according to their nature, was to obey. "Aristotle thinks that throughout the animal kingdom, though the female has some qualities more strongly developed than the male, she is less complete, less courageous, weaker, more impulsive, and the 'differences is (are) the most obvious in the case of human kind . . . '" (Woody, 1949, p. 451). In addition, although Aristotle admired the Spartans for their dedication to the polis, he did not accept their educational programs because he believed that they were solely aimed at preparing youth for war, and he considered anything in excess to be vulgar and thought that it would lead to an illiberal mind.

According to Aristotle ideology, the ideal citizens is perfected through education to live in harmony with his ideal state: In sum, Aristotle's ideal citizen was expected to live in accordance with the best or highest that was in him and to spend his time in contemplation of what is worthy. Aristotle believed that human beings were partially divine, and therefore should be dedicated to the search for truth to emphasize that part of their divine nature so that during their lifetime they would strive to grasp the universal truths of Godliness.

Nineteen

Xenophonic Civism

Another work of Xenophon's, the Cyropaedia, can claim to be the first historical novel: it is a very long and completely fictitious account of the education and exploits of the founder of the Persian Empire, Cyrus the Great; its usefulness as a mirror for princes and its emphasis on moral leadership made it one of Europe's most popular books until kings went out of fashion.
— Oswyn Murray

Xenophon (c 430 – 355 BCE) was born in Athens during the last years of the Peloponnesian War. He had the same unhappy experiences as Isocrates and Plato in witnessing the final panic and collapse of the Athenian city–state. Xenophon's father, Gryllus, was a member of the *deme* of Erchia, which was located south of Mount Pentelicus and east of Hymettus, or about ten miles to the south of Athens. Gryllus evidently held business interests in the silver mines and may have provided slave labor for the mines at Laurium (Anderson, 1974, p. 10). Although Gryllus was not politically active and did not participate in the class conflicts that characterized the end of the Periclean Age, he was aristocratic and he sympathized with the Athenian oligarchs who opposed the democrats. For safety sake and in light of the Spartan pillage of the countryside, the family had moved to Athens where Xenophon was born.

Xenophon was raised in a modest home where he received a typical Athenian education under the supervision of a pedagogue. His mother, Diodora, mainly was concerned with providing her children an education based on good habits and manners, which contributed to the family's relocation to Athens. "He may also have acquired the useful social grace of accompanying himself on the lyre while singing old–fashioned moral or patriotic songs. But 'music', this side of his education, probably meant less to him than 'gymnastics'" (Anderson, 1974, p. 15).

According to Diogenes Laertius, Xenophon encountered Socrates who barred his way to question him about where things could be purchased. As a part of this encounter, Socrates also asked Xenophon: "How are virtuous men made good?" Xenophon was unable to answer the question and Socrates invited him to follow along and to learn. Socrates influenced Xenophon's intellectual development, which made him aware of philosophical issues related to political and moral issues. As a result, Xenophon increased his dislike of democracy, which led him to become a participant in a movement to repress the democratic resurgence prior to the death of Socrates. This activity made him the enemy of the democrats, but after the defeat of the Thirty Tyrants, Xenophon was covered by the amnesty (reconciliation) accorded by the treaty of 403/2. Xenophon's continued rejection of democracy left him in a political "no man's land".

Soldier of Fortune

In 401 BCE Xenophon departed from Athens to become a soldier of fortune and entered the service of the Spartans. He was hired to serve in the cause of Cyrus II, the son of king Darius II. Cyrus was attempting to gain control of the Persian throne, and was in conflict with his brother, Artaxerxes II. Themistogenes of Syracuse is credited with recording the account of Cyrus' failed campaign against his brother, which also threatened the fate of the 10,000 man strong Greek mercenary army under Spartan leadership. Following a disastrous encounter with Artaxerxes' treachery, the Greek survivors elected Xenophon to lead them through Mesopotamia, Armenia, and northern Anatolia to Byzantium, a trek of over 1500 miles.

This harrowing retreat demonstrated Persian military weaknesses, which allowed the Greeks to escape to Trapezus, located on the shores of the Black Sea. The surviving Greeks were hired to serve as a military force for the king of Thessalia, but they soon abandoned the king to join the Spartan army under Thibron. Thibron was sent by the Spartans to "liberate" the Ionian Greeks in 399 BCE, but after taking charge of the Greek mercenary army, problems arose that led to his dismissal. "For ambitious Greeks who had eyes to see, the military weakness of Persia was nakedly exposed. Politically, however, the expedition was a disaster, for Sparta had helped Cyrus enough to curdle relations with his brother for the next eight years" (Davies, 1993, pp. 142-143).

As a result of his experiences in Persia, Xenophon wrote *Anabasis*, which had the effect of influencing future historical events. Following Thibron's dismissal, Xenophon continued to serve as a Spartan mercenary commander and, as a result of his service, he formed a lasting friendship with the Spartan commander, King Agesilaus II. Xenophon's relationship with the Spartan king was described in *Anabasis*. In addition, this work also served as a posthumous work in praise of Agesilaus' many noble attributes that Xenophon deemed as worthy of imitation.

The Athenian democrats exiled Xenophon from Athens because of his service to the Spartans, but despite his exile, Xenophon did not consider himself to be a traitor to Athens. He justified his service on the grounds that the Athenians were allied with the Spartan's against the Persians following the death of Cyrus. The Athenians may have been attempting to win favor with the Persians by confiscating Xenophon's property in Athens. In response, after the battle at Coronea in 394 BCE, the Spartans awarded Xenophon a large estate at Scillus in Elis, near Olympia. Xenophon was now forced into military retirement and was charged by the Athenians with being a *proxenos* (representative) for the Spartans. He spent the remainder of his life in Corinth, but before he died he was reconciled with the Athenians. His work on *Cavalry Commander* and *Ways and Means* depicted him as possessing a sympathetic attitude toward Athens. In addition, his son, Gryllus, died in the service of the Athenian cavalry, which demonstrated Xenophon's patriotic feelings for Athens.

Antithesis to Plato

Xenophon was a physical man of action who lived the life of a soldier, huntsman, and writer of descriptive prose. His encounter with Socrates seems to have changed the course of his life. "Like many young men of his generation, he was attracted to Socrates; and although he was not strictly a pupil of Socrates, the old man made such a deep impression on him that in later life, after he returned from his Persian expedition, he made more than one lasting memorial to him in his books" (Jaeger, 1944, vol. III, p. 156). As a writer, Xenophon was dwarfed by the achievements of Plato, but his intellectual strength lay in his ability to provide a critical balance between abstract thought and practical knowledge, which allowed him to become somewhat of an antithesis of excessive intellectualism of the fourth century philosophers. In addition, Xenophon attempted to inject a dose of Spartan discipline into Athenian affairs in order to offset the extreme reactions generated by free–thinking. Xenophon's love of the practical side of wisdom led him to dislike the various forms of Athenian (sophist) education, which had been colored by his many years of military service under Spartan leadership. As an adventurer and soldier of fortune, Xenophon could relate and translate Spartan education and discipline as a model for living the good life, good government, and good citizenship.

Xenophon's real life experiences led him to conclude that knowledge of goodness was not enough, and could not make men Good. For Xenophon, the great Socratic defect was Socrates' blind faith in the belief that knowledge could cure what was ailing Athens. "Before the citizens could be brought back to their loyalty by getting a rational basis for their lives, the city might come to an untimely end because of their disloyalty" (Boyd and King, 1995, p. 32). Although accepting the Socratic view that man must be made intelligent to be made *Good*, Xenophon maintained that *goodness* came from a particular type of work, activity, or occupation. He also viewed intelligence as the individual's ability to perform his duties properly and to do *excellent* work.

Because of his disapproval of the sophist self–centered form of career training, Xenophon attempted to offer a more practical approach to work. In describing women's work in his *Economics,* Xenophon presented the capacity of women to do excellent household management and to master all aspects of their domestic duties. "His education of her consists in making her understand the meaning of duties.

That is to say, she is made good, as Xenophon understands the term, by getting an intelligent insight into her own special work" (Ibid., p. 30).

Xenophon's emphasis on practical wisdom made him popular with ancient readers. In his biography of Socrates, *The Memorabilia of Socrates,* Xenophon also presented the practical side of Socrates thought, and he pictured him as holding various conversations with ordinary people that covered a variety of topics including religion, moderation, friendship, virtue, and duty, based on his standard of *areté*.

Written Works

Xenophon's written works were based upon his personal experiences, which also contained his thinking on moral issues, which expressed a "blood and guts" philosophy of life. Xenophon also expressed an interest in human behavior and in the importance of omens and rituals and a seeking after divine intervention. In addition, Xenophon struggled with ideal models associated with the human need to attain a higher level of excellence (*areté*) related to courage and valor. His focus on courage reflected an attempt to promote a revitalized morality aimed at the perfection of humankind through educational means that contained strong moral components. In addition, Xenophon's fascination with military matters led him to write several training manuals aimed at perfecting the art of warfare, which was almost always related to the education of the leader. Xenophon believed that these principles could make a difference between the success and the failure of the state.

Scholars have classified Xenophon's written works according to three categories, which include historical works, Socratic works, and technical works. The range of his writing included a historical prose, Platonic dialogues, descriptive technical writing, and a novel. In several of these works, Xenophon presented Socrates as a man of exceptional moral integrity and goodwill by reflecting on what the master might have said about an issue. "Xenophon's dialogues in the *Memorabilia* are for the most part short discussions between Socrates and one other person, aimed at establishing a single point" (Anderson, 1974, p. 21). Socratic themes related to religion and public life, as well as relationships related to friendship and family, were aimed at demonstrating Socrates' good will toward the community. As a teacher, he was striving to educate youth in *temperance* and *justice*. In addition, these works contained short vignettes that depicted Socrates' ability to deal with various practical problems. In these works, Socrates was depicted as a person who seemed to get a great deal of enjoyment from discussing with individuals, as well as delighting in stripping away the false façades of the sophists. In addition to *courage*, the virtues that Xenophon stressed throughout his written works include piety, justice, prudence, patriotism, wisdom, and continence.

Cyropædia

Cyropædia became Xenophon's greatest contribution to an ideology related to *civism*. In this work he addressed the rearing and schooling of Cyrus the Great (Cyrus the

Elder and founder of the Persian Empire). This work was written in novel form some time around 362 BCE or after Xenophon had written his history of the Greeks. Various commentators have claimed that this work expressed Xenophon's Spartan outlook and his ideal of education, only in a more moderate form. "Under the guise of describing the training of a Persian prince, he practically presented the old Greek plan of education, partly as it was in vogue at Athens, but mostly as in Sparta" (Graves, 1929, p. 179). Xenophon's ideal leader was Agesilaus who represented a tough–minded commander who was not seduced by a desire for personal gain, but promoted a common soldiers simple lifestyle. "Xenophon gives an imaginary picture of how Cyrus the Great and his 'Persian peers' made their commoners into an army, which may be drawn from the training that Agesilaus gave his recruits" (Anderson, 1974, pp. 152-153). According to Xenophon, a good education should be based on military discipline and training as an alternative to the type of education advanced by Plato's *Republic*. Xenophon's ideal state was a military state under the control of outstanding military leaders who were capable of training excellent soldiers. *Cyropædia* also revealed something of Xenophon's thinking about education in the Ideal State and the role of the leader in advancing a submissive type of citizenship in which Xenophon portrayed his hero Cyrus, as a leader who possessed the skills to manipulate a large population made up of diverse cultures.

The Persian Empire attracted the attention of thoughtful men, including Socrates, who saw Persian leadership as a possible solution to the disintegration of the Greek *polis*. Socrates, for example, recognized the nobility of Persian leaders who seemed to possess the political skills needed to hold a large and diverse empire together. These Persian qualities appealed to Greek scholars in light of the growing weaknesses of the Athenian culture. "The *Cyropaedia* is not about the Persia that Xenophon or any of his putative sources knew at first or second hand, but rather the 'Persia' that Greece could and would once again become with the destruction of the political way of life embodied by the polis" (Nadon, 2001, p. 32). In other words, Xenophon's novel may have been an attempt to provide an argument for the transformation of the Greek polis into something more viable. For Xenophon, the key to unlocking the success of this transformation was a state system of education that would help to equip its leaders with the complex skills needed to build and maintain a more powerful state. "To grasp the character and aims of that education, one must understand the regime of which it forms a part" (Ibid., p. 29). Cyrus represented Xenophon's ideal ruler because he possessed the qualities needed to win the devotion and loyalty of his subjects. "The key to Cyrus' success lies in his natural endowments (handsome, generous nature, ambitious, courageous, with devotion to learning) and in his training 'in conformity with the laws of the Persians'" (Woody, 1949, p. 459). Xenophon believed that the Athenian democracy had only produced disunity and social antagonism among its social classes by undermining the virtues that were needed for the continuation of the state. To save the Greeks, Xenophon looked to the virtues that could be used to re–invigorate new forms of leadership, and these were Spartan forms.

Xenophon was among the individuals who contributed to the attitudes of the Greeks prior to the arrival of Philip and Alexander, and his intellectual production also had an influence on the three–hundred year Hellenistic era that was swiftly approaching. "His mind is that of a self–sufficient, religious country squire, ambitious adventurer, boastful soldier, who, in retirement on his estate, devoted himself to writing prolifically and often skillfully, particularly when dealing with subjects of which he was a master" (Woody, 1949, p. 458). Although Xenophon admired many of the virtues and the orderly rule found among Near East societies, he stayed true to the belief that Greek culture was superior to their cultures, as was illustrated in his *Anabasis*. But at the same time, he could not help but admire the Persians as empire builders and held on to the hope that their example might become a source of political power for the revitalization of Greece. By the time that Xenophon had written *Cyropaedia*, he had long concluded that Athenians had become corrupted by their democratic indulgences, which he believed also had become a source of instability.

His remedy for the woes of Greece was to re–establish the principles of the old oligarchy and the old education that still survived in Sparta. "He would have the Athenians go back to the old education and adopt the Spartan régime, the herd organization under officers of State, the hard physical and dietetic discipline, the hunting and swimming and drilling, the constant supervision and exhortation by men of practical experience" (Boyd and King, 1995, p. 30). According to Xenophon's *civism*, a stricter form of education could serve as the means to focus the attention of the Greeks on those virtues and the development of good habits. Xenophon also placed much of the blame for this destruction of the moral fiber of Greece on the philosophers' search for the secrets of nature, life, and the universe. He was convinced that the inquiry into nature had led to an extended investigation that dismissed fixed social conventions and religious beliefs. He also believed that once the laws of social convention were questioned, it opened the way for all sorts of new ideas regarding personal codes of conduct. Xenophon was especially concerned with the disintegration of the traditions of Greek religion that were being destroyed by self–interest, greed, and self–pleasures.

Cyropædia as Civism

In *Cyropaedia* Xenophon presented Cyrus as a skillful politician who used education as his means to establish a new state based on new virtues and a new *civism*. In this process, the citizens were stripped of their understandings and their values, in order to adopt new social and political virtues. To accomplish this goal, Cyrus used seductive rational methods of *persuasion* to disarm his subjects of their pre–set values, their individualism, and their traditional education. Xenophon, in other words, demonstrated that re–education could be used as a means of state building, especially when the state was in decline and had lost its cultural safeguards. Applied to Greece, *Cyropaedia* could be viewed as a tale of the impending disintegration of Greek civilization and Xenophon's warning to the Greeks to return to the old virtues that had been embedded in the old Homeric education. For Xenophon, traditional Spartan education was a better solution to the problems of the disintegration of Greece. He believed that the key element in a revitalized education was hunting, as it hardened the individual and encouraged the development of discipline.

The Spartan decline, which Xenophon also witnessed, was described as a decline in cultural values caused by a senseless pursuit of wealth and empire. These factors eventually ruined Spartan education, which then contributed to the decline of its society. The Spartan decline, however, did not weaken Xenophon's admiration for the Spartan educational system. However, in *Oeconomicus* Xenophon seems to have modified his views about society, as he appeared to have found a more viable state based on the relationship between agriculture, new cultural ways of living, and checks on the excessive power of the aristocracy. Agriculture now provided Xenophon with a new framework for his educational ideas, as it appeared to provide the basis for a healthier lifestyle. This new society would replace the one that had been organized around the polis, for one organized around a territorial state under the rule of a wise monarch. This was Xenophon's answer to Plato's *Republic*; however, like Plato he rejected democracy and hoped to replace it with a more disciplined system of political rule.

Conclusion

The freedom the Athenians wanted was not just a release from bondage; they wanted political freedom, the right to help decide their own destiny through active participation in government.
— Paul Woodruff

The origins of western *civism* began in ancient Greece prior to the formation of the *polis,* when citizenship qualifications were determined by basic tribal or kinship relationships. "It (kinship) was reinforced both by the tribal nature of the segments which comprised every Greek polity we know of, and by the way in which citizenship was purely hereditary status" (Davies, 1993, p. 14). For centuries the Ionian aristocracy formed important social and religious relationships with oligarch families from other city–states that comprised the Panhellenic aristocracy. These families formed alliances that included military, social, religious, political, and economic ties, which also were solidified in a *symposia* where politically active men pooled their wealth and power to advance shared interests. Also, for centuries the unity of the Greek world depended on the ability of aristocrats to serve as leaders of culture; therefore, the unifying virtues of the aristocracy required the skills of public speaking, religious piety, reverence for traditional customs, and military virtues related to courage and physical endurance. The power of the archons was so great that they could select and influence the magistrates and their courts, which then ruled in favor of the aristocrats, to the disadvantage of the smaller landowners and the commercial classes. The absolute power of the aristocracy may have led to a "hoplite revolution", and by the sixth century, the smaller farmers and the emerging urban commercial interests were demanding political rights. These growing demands led to class conflicts that eventually produced a series of political reforms that resulted in the establishment of the "first democracy".

The transformation of Athens from a traditional tribal aristocracy to a democracy and empire contributed to the development of new political conditions that gave rise to *civism*. *Civism* in Athens touched on issues related to moral questions pertaining to the role of the state in shaping citizenship understandings aimed at promoting a democratic *ideology*. In addition, democratic *civism* also became associated with the operations of democratic institutions and *law* codes that governed *polis* institutions. "Lacking a formal state–run system of formal education, the demos itself, through the Assembly and courts took on a larger part of the task of instilling social values in the citizens" (Ober, 1989, p.162). Athenian citizenship was seldom granted to individuals from outside Attica, as the basis of citizenship was primarily the kinship descent group. Ionians of the Aegean Islands and Asia Minor were not considered citizens, even though they had a special tribal relationship with the Athenians.

The defeat of Athens in the Peloponnesian War at the end of the fifth century BCE brought on new concerns regarding the viability of democracy as an effective political system. During the fourth century, important scholarly written works were produced that addressed issues pertaining to Athenian *civism*. The works of Plato, Aristotle, Isocrates, and Xenophon especially addressed these issues and provided some original principles related to ideology, political perceptions, the techniques of persuasion, and the state's responsibilities related to the education of youth for citizenship.

* * * *

During the Mycenaean Age a form of *knightly civism* emerged in connection with the family and the practice of tribal religion. Families and tribes identified with specific deities that were used to strengthen the bonds of kinship. Powerful elite families met annually to celebrate religious ceremonies and to participate in athletic contests that helped to build the bonds of a common identity that could be used to form mutual support alliances. Aspects of an *elite civism* were infused into a code of knightly honor that were shared by members of the Panhellenic Greek aristocracy.

During the eighth through the sixth centuries, the centuries that Star calls "The Great Intellectual Upheaval I and II", a new age emerged based on new cultural foundations that produced the Hellenic outlook. This outlook centered on the formation of the Greek polis, which would begin to appear from 750 to 650 BCE. The polis was organized around a local central public temple; but in addition, a concentration of a greater population density created the need for government and the services that only a government could provide. At first, the polis consisted of an intimate face to face community that operated according to the rules of long standing social relationships that determined the nature of local politics. Aristotle believed that the strength of the polis and its *residential civism* relied on the development of close male friendships. This type of citizenship only was available in small or intimate communities, and the polis eventually gave rise to new social classes and to a greater social stratification that soon formed into a social pyramid that was controlled by aristocratic wealth and power.

In the seventh century Lycurgus provided Sparta with a distinct military constitution due to Dorian concern about the surrounding helot serfs that greatly outnumbered their citizenship class. As a consequence, the Spartan constitution and its laws resulted in a very disciplined form of citizenship. Education as provided by the Spartans, represented a state-sponsored curriculum. Consequently, education became the single most important community activity, and was directed toward the development of martial skills needed by its powerful land army. The Spartan army became the most important institutional agency of the state and the cities means of controlling its allies. The values associated with the military culture dominated all social relationships, as well as city–state politics, and therefore its *civism*.

Meanwhile, a growing egalitarian outlook gave rise to a form of *democratic civism*, and this new outlook began to shift the Athenian culture away from its traditional cultural understandings. The democratic system in Athens gave rise to a self-centered *individualism* that appeared to be more suitable for a growing and diverse sophisticated urban population. Pericles, at the height of Athenian wealth and power, used the Ionian league treasury to help bring about a greater political unity by shaping the citizen perception related to *democratic citizenship*, which also expressed the mission of the Athenian Empire. He used publicly supported works that incorporated the use of the visual arts to teach this new form of *democratic civism*. For a time, it appeared that Athenian political success would spread democracy throughout Greece, but the oligarchic Spartans took exception to the growing influence of the Athenians.

The Peloponnesian War had the effect of blunting the growing enthusiasm for democracy, and in the fourth century, the consequences of Greek state conflicts led to the rise of powerful new states under authoritarian or military leadership. In addition, the new politicians that succeeded Pericles often were demagogues who used their persuasive talents to arouse citizens attending the Assembly into making rash decisions that were fatal to the survival of Athens. Beginning in the fifth century, public speaking was taught by traveling professors called sophists, who tended to embrace a relativistic outlook. These sophists gained notoriety with the claim that "man was the measure of all things," thereby dismissing the gods as the source of influence in human affairs. This humanist form of *civism* already was present in the fifth century writings and teachings of Protagoras.

Protagoras also may have advanced the idea that citizens should act in accordance with local political values, as a practical means of advancing their own self-interests. Ironically, Protagoras also advanced moral training by advocating that children should be taught what was just and honorable and what was unjust and shameful. He also insisted that his form of *humanist civism* should be taught as a craft, or a political art, and he believed that virtue could be taught. Sent by Pericles to Thurii, Italy, he developed the laws (constitution) for the state. He also advocated the possibility of a state-supported education that would prepare orphan children for their civic responsibilities in the service of the state.

Oratory, based on rhetorical techniques became an important political means of *civism* with the rise and the spread of assemblies and courts throughout Greece. The ancient Greeks recognized the power of the spoken and written word as a means of conveying ideas, values, and purposes from one person to another. The sophists worked to advance the science of the spoken and the written word as an instrument of public persuasion. Words, they believed, were so powerful that they could be used to create meanings, change perceptions, settle disputes, and cause changes in political attitudes and behaviors; therefore, words could be used to persuade citizens to follow a leader or to support a political cause. The power of words could serve as an instrument to create and support ideas that promised desired outcomes, as words could be used to create powerful mental images that shaped values that led to perceptions about reality, especially when factual evidence was not obtainable. The sophists often taught logos as a craft to aid in winning a political debate or a court case, but a few exceptional sophists also combined logos with moral instruction as a means of developing a vigorous political art form espoused by Isocrates.

Isocratic *civism* led Demosthenes, Athens' greatest fourth century orator, to formulate an alternative *logolatry* argument in opposition to the military designs of Philip II. This opposition led Demosthenes to write a series of speeches that were aimed at awakening the Greeks to the idea that if they did not stand together they were doomed and they would soon lose their independence. He attempted to unify all of the Greek city–states into a new Greek–only alliance that would be militarily strong enough to resist the Macedonian threat. This seemingly impossible task was accomplished by appealing to Greek patriotism in the cause of being willing to forego their self–interest and in order to work for the survival of Greece.

In the fourth century the students of Socrates developed schools of philosophy, which advocated forms of *civism* that related to fixed values in a metaphysical sense. These values provided the foundation for a philosophic education for students of philosophy who were taught to examine questions, problems, and issues from a critical perspective based upon logic and the processes that came to be associated with scientific investigation. Socrates searched endlessly for a "good man" and never found what he was seeking, but in general it can be surmised that a good man was a person who filtered his thoughts and actions through the processes of reason and virtues of goodness. His *civism* was based on self–reflection and the denial of material wealth in search of human perfection.

During the fourth century, the students of philosophy tended to explore their awareness of the role of the state in a great many written works that were aimed at creating new forms of citizenship based on their higher ideals of citizenship and civilization in accordance with well-thought out constitutions. Plato's *civism* was in association with his philosophical views regarding the leadership of the Ideal State. He based his *civism* on his assumption that values were fixed and unchanging and therefore could serve as his standard for moral excellence. Elements of *civism* are contained within his many dialogues, but his greatest consideration for leadership and citizenship was presented in *The Republic* and *The Laws*. In the *Republic*, Plato warned that democracy contained fatal flaws that would cause the state to descend into license, and the resulting chaos would eventually destroy the liberty that democracy claimed to embrace. In addition, Plato described a fatal cycle that would befall Greece and Rome. According to the sequential phases of this cycle, monarchy led to aristocracy, aristocracy led to oligarchy, oligarchy led to democracy, democracy led to revolutionary chaos, revolution led to dictatorship, and dictatorship led to the decline of the state. Each stage of this cycle, according to this author's thesis, would be accompanied by its own unique form of *civism* in support of the nature of each type of constitution and regime.

Aristotle, like Plato, came to realize that the state must play a role in the education of its citizens by providing instruction aimed at their moral development according to the virtues of goodness. Aristotle and his students directed their political studies at various forms of government to determine which constitutions were the best forms of rule. As a result of these studies, Aristotle was able to evaluate the various political systems. Consequently, he recommended a mixed constitution that had monarchial elements based on moderation according to a "golden mean" as a normative standard. Aristotle's *civism* was based on his desire to help citizens develop those rational skills needed to analyze and understand the affairs of the state. Aristotle advanced *civism* through his emphasis on the idea that the state could advance an education that allowed citizens to achieve a higher level of *self-perfection*. More important still, was Aristotle's development of a type of *civism* that promoted those values and virtues contained within the states constitution. *Constitutional civism* was a means, or an attempt, to protect the state against the encroachment of aggressive or politically corrupt individuals and groups.

Xenophon, also a student of Socrates, railed against the corruptive influences of the Athenian democracy and came to believe that Cyrus The Great had devised a system of rule that had succeeded in creating a greater and more stable society. According to Xenophon's *Cyropaedia*, the best form of *civism* came from the Spartan constitution and its state-supported system of education. *Civism*, for Xenophon, was a matter of political control that could be used to consolidate and regulated a diverse cultural population spread over a large geographic area.

* * * *

Civism in the ancient Athenian polis became an important means to develop and to control the citizens' perceptions regarding the nature of the state and the values that should be embraced as a means to maintain the state. As a result of the reforms of Solon, Cleisthenes, Ephialtes, and Pericles, the Athenians produced a unique system of rule that was based on a democratic ideology. This ideology evolved over time as a means to curb and to reform an excessive aristocratic oligarchy that allowed a minority of the population to exploit their social, economic and political advantages over a larger citizenship body. Over the course of two hundred years of the Athenian democratic experiment, a new *civism* emerged based on the ideology that the common citizens could be trusted to direct and to lead the state. This *civism* first emerged during the Periclean enlightenment and Pericles used public works and oratory as a means of influencing the political perceptions of the citizenship body. At the same time, thoughtful individuals began to suggest that the state should consider educational means as positive sources of influence to shape the perceptions of the citizenship body, although no serious effort was made to implement this idea.

The implementation of democratic reforms in fifth century BCE Athens had the effect of shifting political power from the aristocrats to the proletarian masses, and as a result, new urban political leaders were able to gain control of the decision–making processes associated with the political institution of the polis. During and following the Peloponnesian War, the leadership of the state fell to "new men" who would use the power of the state to advance various agendas, which also led to the corruption of the state and to a bitter social chaos that created new conditions for class conflict, revolution, and civil war.

During the fourth century BCE, some attempts were made to reform the perceived weaknesses of the democracy, but these reforms were accompanied by a new wave of self–gratifying individualism that weakened the Athenian polis and led to the eventual political and military collapse of the Athenian state. At the same time, the collapsing democratic Athenian experiment led some thoughtful individuals to re–examine the Athenian democratic system to reveal the nature of its weaknesses, and they prescribed various political remedies related to the development of an Ideal State. A growing body of political thought began to reveal more and more about the relationship between *civism* and *citizenship*, according to the nature of the state. Mainly, there was a new awareness that the mindset of the citizen body was an important means for controlling the state; therefore, the power over the citizens' value perceptions was an important non–coercive means that could be used to determine the nature and the operation of the state, in compliance with the accepted ideology of the state and its operational constitution.

Appendix

Maps

200 • *Appendix*

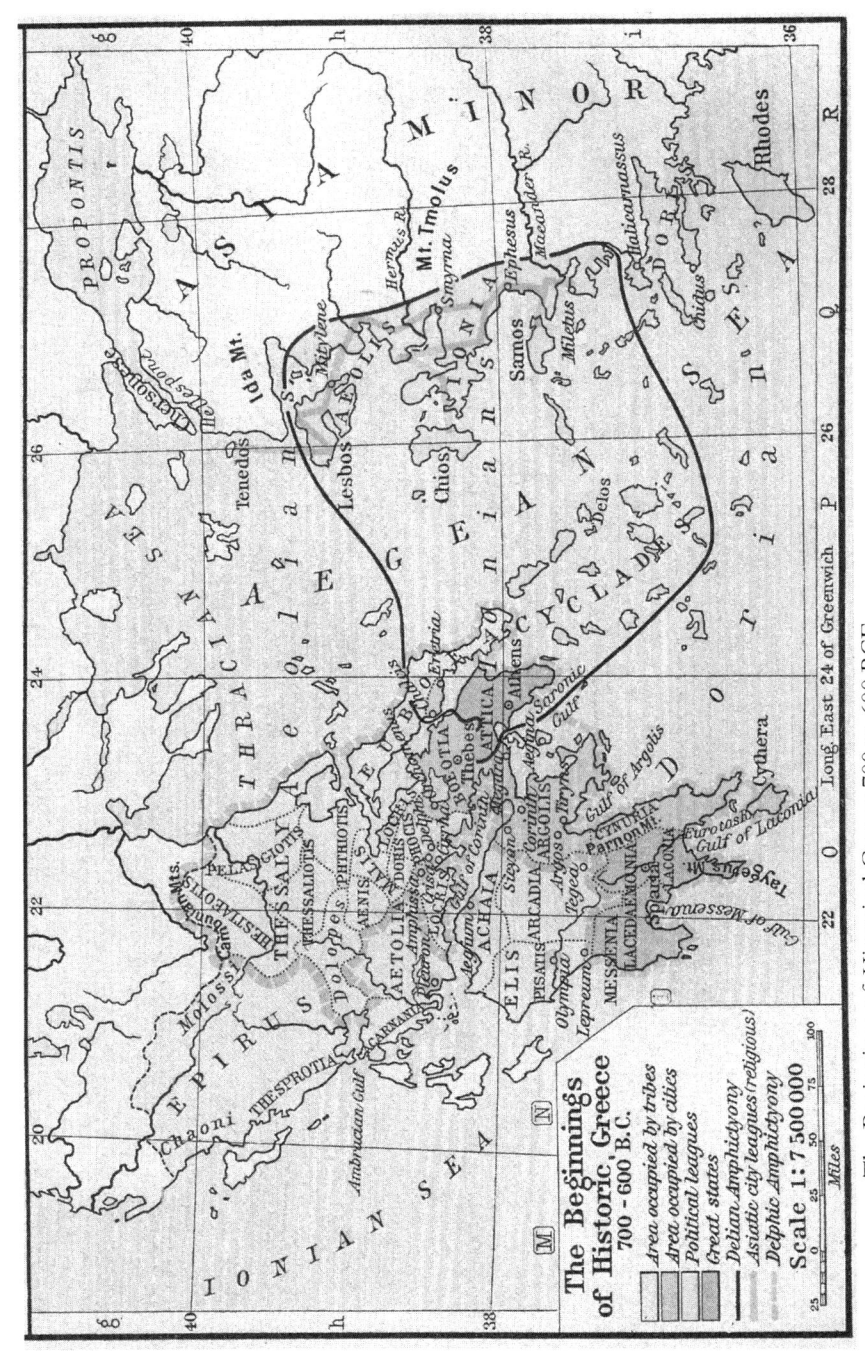

The Beginnings of Historical Greece 700 to 600 BCE

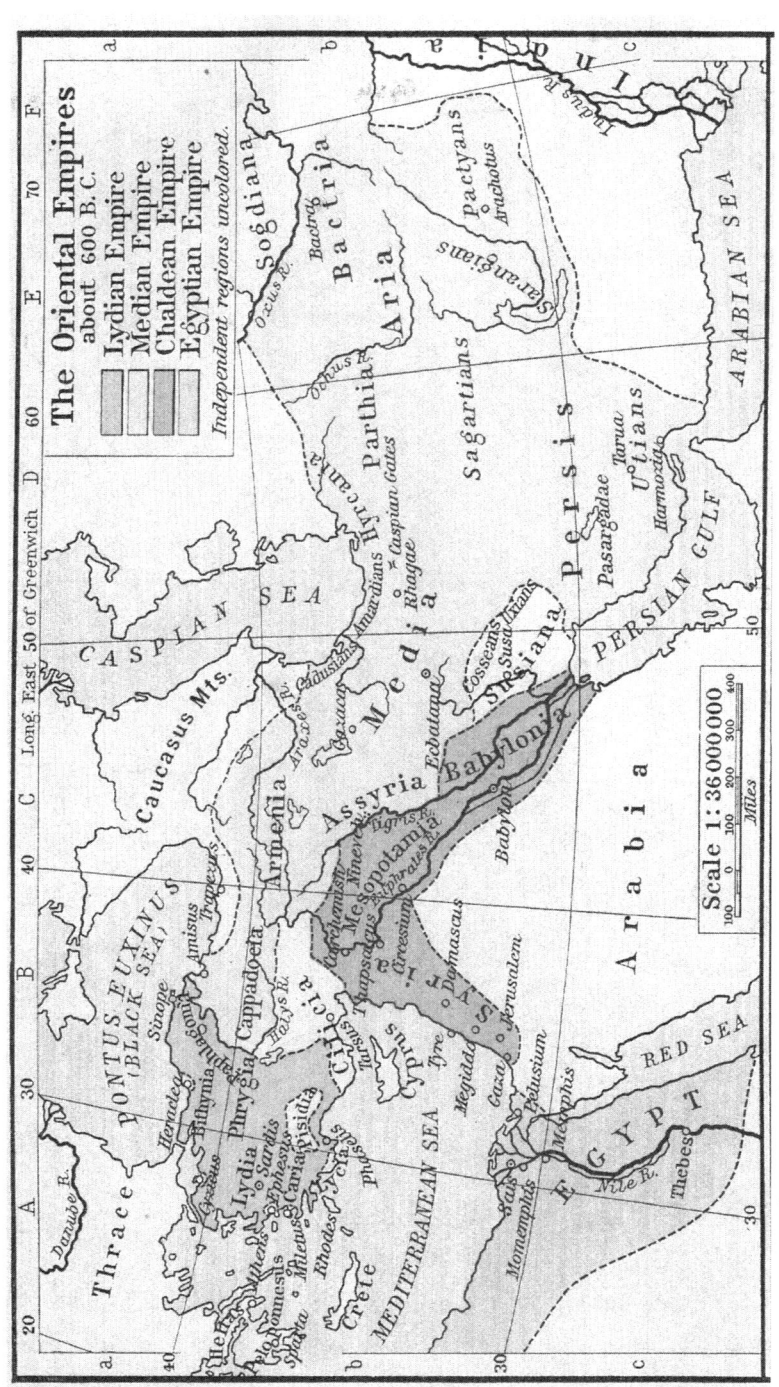

The Oriental Empires

202 • *Appendix*

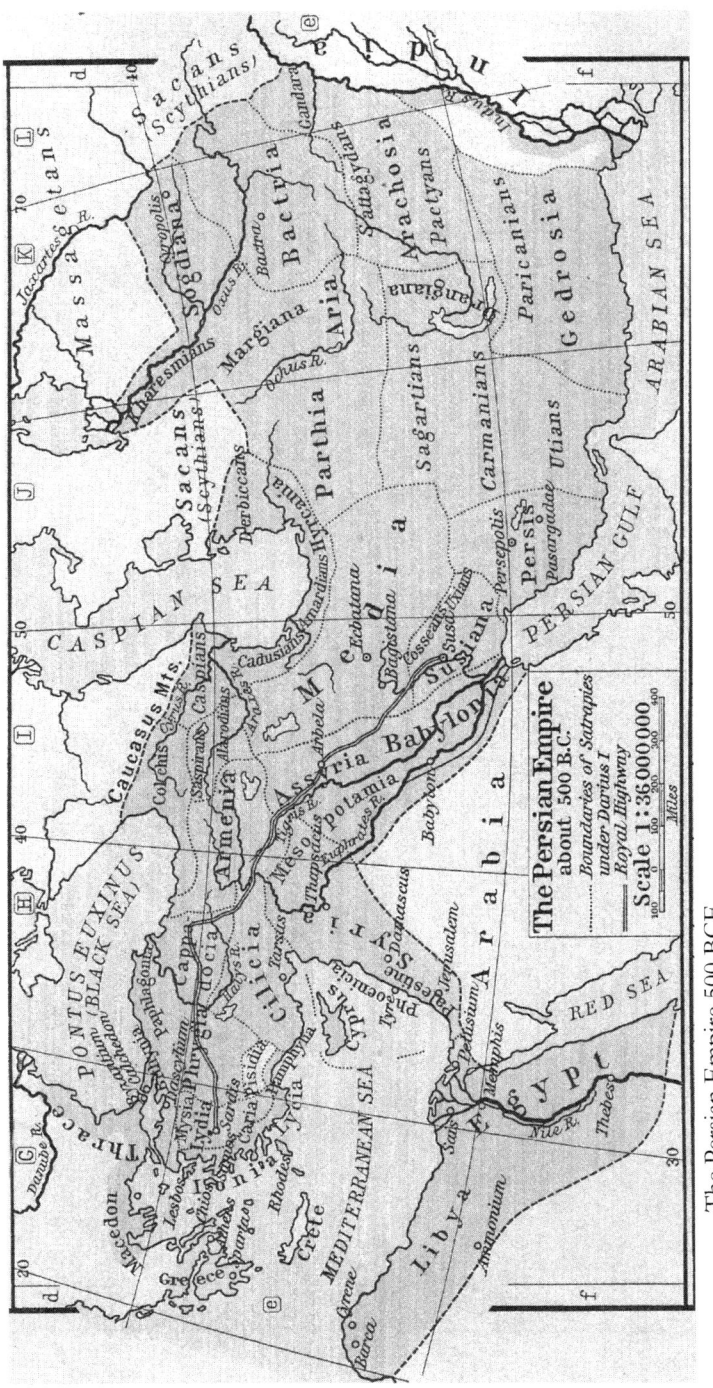

The Persian Empire 500 BCE

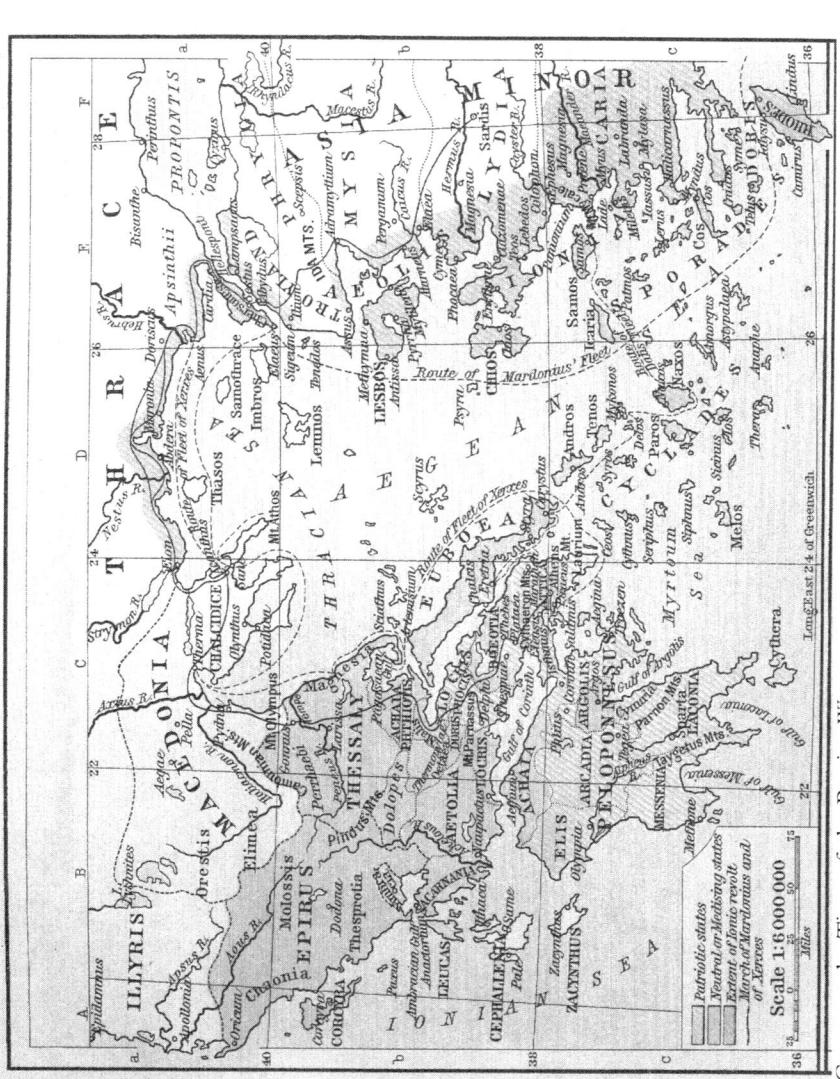

Greece at the Time of the Persian War

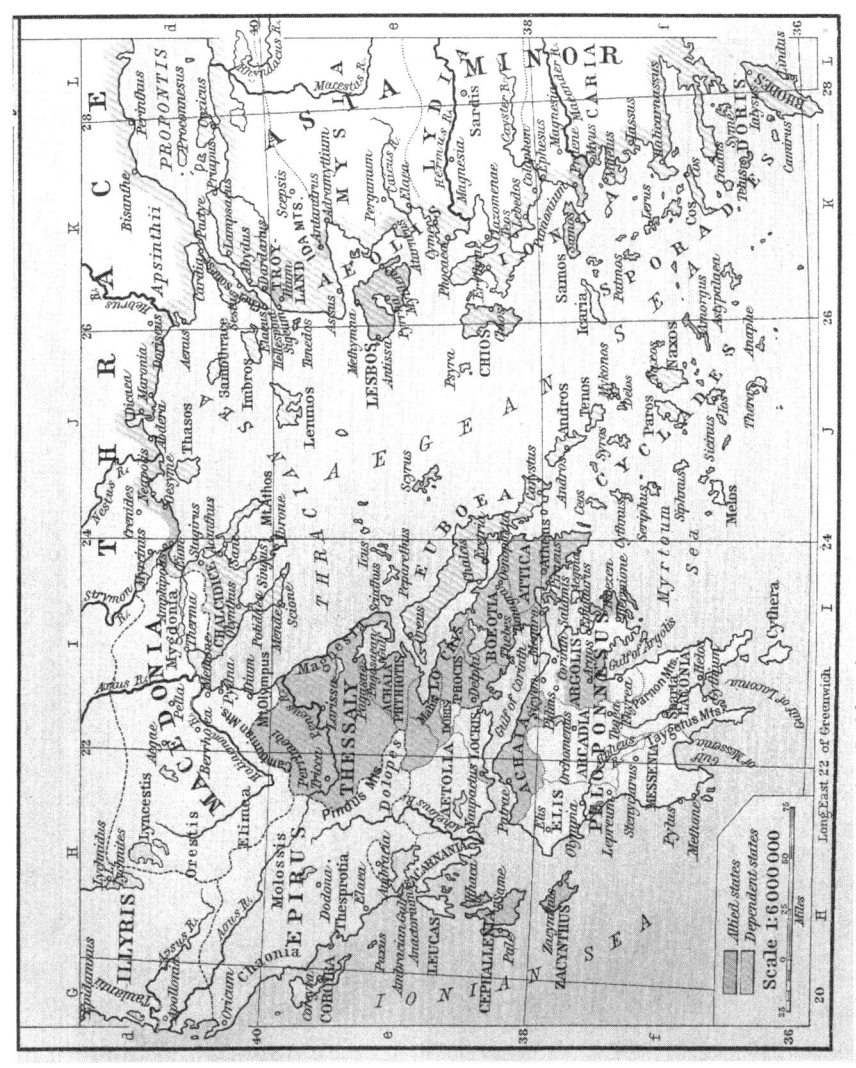

The Athenian Empire in the Golden Age

BIBLIOGRAPHY

Anderson, J.K. *Xenophon*. NY: Charles Scribner's Sons, 1974.
Annas, J. 'Classical Greek Philosophy'. In *The Oxford history of the Classical World*, edited by J. Broadman, J. Griffin, & O. Murray. New York, NY: Oxford University Press, 1986.
Aristotle. *The soul and its facilities*. Translated by P. Wheelwright. Riverside, CA: The Odyssey Press, 1935.
_____. *Politics and poetics*. Translated by B. Jowell and S.H. Butcher. NY: Heritage Press, 1964.
_____. *The politics*. Translated by T.E.A. Sinclair and revised and re-presented by T. J. Saunders. London: Penguin Books, 1988.
_____. *Aristotle: The politics and constitution of Athens*. Translated by S. Everson. Cambridge: Cambridge University Press, 2002.
_____. *The Athenian Constitution*. London: Penguin Classics, 2002.
Barnes, J. 'Hellenistic Philosophy and Science'. In *The Oxford history of the Classical World*, edited by J. Broadman, J. Griffin, & O. Murray. New York, NY: Oxford University Press, 1986.
Blackburn, S. *The Oxford dictionary of philosophy*. New York, NY: Oxford University Press, 1996.
Boyd, W. & E. J. King. *The history of Western Education*. Lanham, MD: Barnes & Noble Books, 1995.
Brunschwig J., & G. E. R. Lloyd, with P. Pellegrin, editors. "Protagoras." In *Greek Thought: A guide to classical knowledge*. Cambridge, Mass.: Belknap Press, 2000.
Burrow, J. *A History of Histories: Epics, Chronicles, Romances and Inquiries from Herodotus and Thucydides to the Twentieth Century*. New York: Alfred A. Knopf, 2008.
Cartledge, P. *The Greeks: Crucible of civilization*. NY: Atlantic Productions Ltd., 2000.
Casson, L. *Libraries in the Ancient World*. New Haven, CT: Yale University Press, 2001.
Cole, L. *A history of education*. NY: Holt, Rinehart, and Winston, 1950.
Cole, T. *The origins of rhetoric in Ancient Greece*. Baltimore, MD: The Johns Hopkins University Press, 1991.

Cribiore, R. *Gymnastics of the mind: Greek Education in Hellenistic and Roman Egypt.* Princeton, NJ: Princeton University Press, 2001.
Cubberley, E.P. *The History of Education.* NY: Houghton Mifflin, 1920.
_____. "Editor's Introduction". In *Education for Citizenship,* by John C. Almack. NY: Houghton Mifflin Company, 1924.
Davies, J.K. *Democracy and Classical Greece.* Cambridge, MA: Harvard University Press, 1993.
Durant, W. *The Life of Greece.* NY: Simon and Schuster, 1939.
Dynneson, T. L. *Civism: Cultivating citizenship in European History.* NY: Peter Lang Publishing, 2001.
Euben, J. P. *Corrupting youth: Political education, democratic culture, and political theory.* Princeton, NJ: Princeton University Press, 1997.
Finley, M. I. *Democracy Ancient and Modern.* New Brunswick, NJ: Rutgers University Press, 1973.
Fornara, C.W. *Archaic times to the end of the Peloponnesian War: Translated documents of Greece and Rome.* Translated and edited by C. W. Fornara. Cambridge: University of Cambridge Press, 1983.
Freeman, C. *Egypt, Greece and Rome: Civilization of the Ancient Mediterranean.* Oxford: Oxford University Press, 1996.
Gordon, S. *Controlling the state: Constitutionalism from Ancient Athens to today.* Cambridge, MA.: Harvard University Press, 1999.
Grant, M. *The founders of the Western World: A History of Greece and Rome.* New York, NY: Charles Scribner's Sons, 1991.
Graves, F. P. *A History of Education: Before the Middle Ages.* New York, NY: The Macmillan Company, 1929.
Guthrie, W.K.C. *A History of Greek Philosophy:* Vol. 3, *The Sophists.* Cambridge, England: Cambridge University Press, 1971.
_____. *A History of Greek Philosophy:* Vol. 4, *Plato: The Man and his Dialogues: Early Period.* Cambridge, England: Cambridge University Press, 1975.
_____. *A History of Greek Philosophy:* Vol. 6, *Aristotle: An Encounter.* Cambridge, England: Cambridge University Press, 1981.
Gutek, G.L. *A History of the Western Educational Experience.* Prospect Heights, IL: Waveland Press, 1971.
Hansen, M.H. *Polis: Introduction to the Ancient City-state.* London: Oxford University Press, 2006.
Heater, D. *Citizenship: The civic ideal in World History, politics and education.* London: Longman, 1990.
Hooker, J. T. *Mycenaean Greece.* London: Routledge and Kegan, 1976.
Huffman, C. "Pythagoras", In *The Stanford Encyclopedia of Philosophy.* Edited by Edward N. Zalta, Spring 2005. URL = http://plato.stanford.edu/archives/spr2005/entries/pythagoras/.
Jaeger, W. *Paideia: the ideals of Greek culture,* Vol. 1. (Archaic Greece the mind of Athens). Translated by Gilbert Highet. New York, NY: Oxford University Press, 1945.
_____. *Paideia: The ideals of Greek culture,* Vol. 2. (In search of the divine centre).Translated by Gilbert Highet. New York, NY: Oxford University Press, 1943.
_____. *Paideia: The ideals of Greek culture,* Vol. 3 (In The conflict of cultural ideas in the age of Plato). Translated by Gilbert Highet. New York, NY: Oxford University Press, 1944.
Jones, A.H.M. *The later Roman empire: A social economic and administrative survey,* Vol. II. Norman, OK: University of Oklahoma Press, 1964.
Jones, N. F. *Politics and society in Ancient Greece.* Westport, CT.: Praeger. 2008.
Kagan, D. *Pericles of Athens and the birth of democracy.* New York, NY: The Free Press, 1991.
Kagan, D. *The Peloponnesian War.* New York, NY: Viking, 2003.
Klosko, G. *The development of Plato's political theory.* New York, NY: Methuen, 1986.

Kroeber, A. *Anthropology: Race, language, culture, psychology, prehistory.* New York, NY: Harcourt, Brace, and World, 1948.
Lanni, A. *Law and Justice in the courts of Classical Athens.* Cambridge: Cambridge University Press, 2006.
Marrou, H. I. *A history of education in antiquity.* Translated by George Lamb. Madison, WI: The University of Wisconsin Press, 1956.
Martin, T.R. *Ancient Greece: From prehistoric to Hellenistic Times.* New Haven, CT: Yale Nota Bene, 2000.
McClelland, J.S. *A history of western political thought.* London: Routledge, 1996.
McIlwain, C.H. *Constitutionalism: Ancient and modern.* Ithaca, NY: Cornell University Press, 1947.
Murray, O. 'Greek Historians'. In *the Oxford History of the Classical World*, edited by J. Broadman, J. Griffin, & O. Murray. New York, NY: Oxford University Press, 1986.
_____. 'Life and Society in Classical Greece'. In *The Oxford History of the Classical World*, edited by J. Broadman, J. Griffin, & O. Murray. New York, NY: Oxford University Press, 1986.
Nadon, C. *Xenophon's prince: Republic and empire in the Cyropaedia.* Berkley, CA: University of California Press, 2001.
Nussbaum, M. C. 'Aristotle'. In S. Hornblower and T. Spawforth, *Who's who in the Classical World*. New York, NY: Oxford University Press, 2000.
Ober, J. *Mass and elite in democratic Athens: Rhetoric, ideology, and the power of the people.* Princeton, NJ: Princeton University Press, 1989.
_____. 'Civic Ideology and Counterhegemonic Discourse: Thucydides on the Sicilian Debate'. In *Athenian identity and civic ideology*, edited by A. L. Beogehold and A. C. Scafuro. Baltimore, MD: The John Hopkins University Press, 1994.
_____. *Political Dissent in Democratic Athens.* Princeton: Princeton University Press, 1998.
_____. 'Quasi–Rights: Participatory Citizenship and Negative Liberties in Democratic Athens'. *Social Philosophy and Policy* 17 (2000): 27–61.
_____. 'The Athenian Debate over Civic Identity'. In *Athenian Legacies: Essays on the politics of going on together*, edited by J. Ober. Princeton: Princeton University Press, 2005.
Ostwald, M. *From popular sovereignty to the sovereignty of law: Law, society, and politics in fifth-century Athens.* Berkeley, CA: University of California Press, 1986.
Plutarch. *On Sparta.* Translated by Richard J.A. Talbert and edited by Christopher Pelling. London: Penguin Classics, 2005.
Pomeroy, S.B., S. M. Burstein, W. Donlan, & J. T. Roberts. *A brief history of Ancient Greece: Politics, society, and culture.* London: Oxford University Press, 2004.
Poulakos, T. & D. Depew. *Isocrates and civic education.* Austin, TX: The University of Texas Press, 2004.
Polybius, *The rise of the Roman Empire.* Translated by Ian Scott–Kilvert. New York, NY: Penguin Books, 1979.
Reese, W. L. *Dictionary of philosophy and religion.* Amherst, NY: Humanities Press, 1996.
Riesenberg, P. *Citizenship in the Western Tradition.* Chapel Hill, NC: The University of North Carolina Press, 1992.
Rodgers, G. M. *Alexander: The ambiguity of greatness.* New York, NY: Random House, 2004.
Samaras, T. *Plato on democracy.* New York, NY: Peter Lang Publishing, 2002.
Schiappa, E. *The beginning of rhetoric theory in Classical Greece.* New Haven, CT: Yale University Press, 1999.
_____. *Protagoras and logos.* Columbia, SC: The University of South Carolina Press, 2003.
Smith, L. G. & J. K. Smith. *Lives in education: A narrative of people and ideas.* New York, NY.: St. Martins Press, 1994.
Starr, C. *The Origins of Greek Civilization 1100-650 B.C.* New York, NY: Alfred A. Knopf, 1961.

Thucydides. *The history of the Peloponnesian War.* (revised edition). Translated by R. Warner and edited by M. I. Finley. London: Penguin Classics, 1954.
Too, Y. L. *The rhetoric of identity in Isocrates: text, power, pedagogy.* Cambridge: University of Cambridge Press, 1995.
———. (ed.). *Education in Greek and Roman Antiquity.* Leiden: E. J. Brill, 2001.
Vernon, R. *Citizenship and order: Studies in French political thought.* Toronto, Canada: University of Toronto Press, 1987.
Villa, D. *Socratic citizenship.* Princeton, NJ: Princeton University Press, 2001.
Walbank, F.W. *The Hellenistic World.* Cambridge, MA: Harvard University Press, 1982.
Winn. C. & M. Jacks. *Aristotle: His thought and its relevance today.* London: Methuen and Company, 1967.
Woodruff, P. *First democracy: The challenge of an ancient ideal,* New York, NY: Oxford University Press, 2005.
Woody, T. *Life and education in early societies.* New York, NY: The Macmillan Co., 1949.

Some Recent and Related Periodic Literature

Bartlett, R. C. 'Political Philosophy and Sophistry: An Introduction to Plato's Protagoras'. *American Journal of Political Science*, 47 (Oct., 2003): 612–624.
Bosworth, A. B. 'The Historical Context of Hellenic Studies'. *The Journal of Hellenic Studies*, 120 (2001): 1–16.
Charbit, Y. & A. Virmani, 'The Platonic City: History and Utopia. *Population' (English Edition)*, 57 (March–April, 2002): 207–235.
Collins, S.D. 'Moral Virtue and the Limits of the Political Community in Aristotle's Nicomachean Ethics'. *American Journal of Political Science,* 48 (January, 2004): 47–61.
Cory, D. D. 'Socratic Citizenship: Delphic Oracle and Divine Sign', *The Review of Politics*, 67 (Spring, 2005): 202–228.
Frank, J. 'Democracy and Distribution: Aristotle on Just Desert'. *Political Theory*, 26 (December, 1998): 784–802.
Howland, J. 'Xenophon's Philosophic Odyssey: On the Anabasis and Plato's *Republic*'. *The American Political Science Review*, 94 (December, 2000): 875–889.
Lutz, M. J. 'Civic Virtue and Socratic Virtue'. *Polity*, 29 (Summer, 1997): 565–592.
Mara, G. M. 'Thucydides and Plato on Democracy and Trust.' *The Journal of Politics*, 63 (August, 2001): 820-845.
———. 'Interrogating the Identities of Excellence: Liberal Education and Democratic Culture in Aristotle's Nicomachean Ethics'. *Polity*, 30 (Winter, 1998): 301-329.
Miller, T. P. 'A Rhetorical Stance on the Archives of Civic Action'. *College English*, (May, 1999): 591–598.
Monoson, S. S. 'Remembering Pericles: The Political and Theoretical Import of Plato's Menexenus'. *Political Theory*, 26 (August, 1998): 489–513.
Montiglio, S. 'Wandering Philosophers in Classical Greece'. *The Journal of Hellenic Studies*, 120 (2002): 86–105.
Papillon, T. L. 'Review: Recent Writings in Greek Rhetoric and Oratory'. *The Classical Journal*, 93 (February–March, 1998): 331–344.
Rosano, M. J. 'Citizenship and Socrates in Plato's Crito'. *The Review of Politics*, 62 (Summer, 2002): 451–477.
Schemeil, Y. 'Democracy before Democracy'. *International Political Science Review*, 21 (April, 2000): 99–120.
White, P. 'Political Education in the Early Years: The Place of Civic Virtues'. *Political Education*, (March–June, 1999):59–70.

Index

A

Academy, 152, 170
Achaean Age, 13
acroatic instruction, 172
Acropolis, 29, 68
Aeschylus, 58
Against Aristocrates (Demosthenes), 132
Against the Sophists (Isocrates), 104, 121
Age of Pericles, 37
Agesilaus, 88
agnosticism of Protagoras, 110–111
agricultural village, 18
Alcibiades, 76–77, 79–80
Alcmaeonids, 52
Alexander, 90–92, 135, 170
alphabet, 16
Anabasis (Xenophon), 186
anakrisis, 45
Anaxagoras, 49–50, 57
Ancient Greek civism, origins of
    Athenian constitution, 29–35
    city-states, 15–19
    introduction, 7–8
    Mycenaean Greeks, 9–14
    Spartan constitution, 21–28
Anderson, J.K., 185, 188, 189

Annas, J., 141, 173
anti-democratic coup, 79–81
Antidosis (Isocrates), 86, 125
antithesis, 103
apella, 23
Apollo, 27
archaic age, 7, 16
Archidamian War, 71
Archidamus, 73
architecture of city-state, 18
archon court, 30–31
archons
    in Cleisthenes' constitution, 44
    defined, 10
    in oligarchic constitution, 30–31
Areopagitcus (Isocrates), 124, 127
Areopagus
    Athenian constitution and, 37
    defined, 31
    vs. Ephialtes, 53
    Isocrates on, 127
areté
    civism and virtue, 115
    defined, 3
    in Homeric civism and citizenship, 13
    of Isocrates, 125
    of logos and rhetoric, 102

Periclean civism, 60
  in polis citizenship, 21
  of Protagoras, 113
  of Socrates, 142
  in Socratic civism, 149
Arginusae, 80–81
Aristides, 52
aristocracy. *see also* class systems
  Athenian civism, 33–35
  of Athens, 29–31
  citizenship and social stratification, 31–32
  Cleisthenes' constitutional revolution, 45
  vs. Ephialtes, 53
  foundation of Greek polis, 17–18
  in Spartan constitution, 23
ariston, 169
Aristophanes, 69
  criticism of Sophists, 104–105
  on Socrates, 141
Aristotelian civism
  constitutional, 182–184
  Lyceum, 172–173
  overview, 169–172
  politics, ethics and, 175–180
  science of, 173–175
  self-perfection and, 180–182
Aristotle
  Athenian constitution and, 37
  civism of, 197
  on Cleisthenes, 43
  fourth century civism and, 93–94
  as origin of Athenian civism, 5
  philosophy, civism and, 137–138
  on political nature of man, 21
  on Spartan military, 28
army. *see* military
art, political. *see* political art
Artemis Orthia, 28
arts, 85–86. *see also* music
Assembly
  birth of Probouloi, 76–78
  Cleisthenes' constitutional revolution, 44
  demagogues in, 65
  Demosthenes as leader of, 135
  role in Athenian civism, 63–64
  sacrilege and the lost peace, 81
  Solonian reforms and, 41
  start of Peloponnesian War, 71–72
asty, 18
Athena, 35, 61–63
Athenian constitution, 29–35

Athenian democracy
  anti-democratic coup, 79–81
  Athenian Empire, 67–70
  Athens in decline, 85–94
  civil war and democratic resurrection, 83–84
  constitution, 37–38
  decline of, 65–66
  defeat in Peloponnesian War, 82–83
  development of civism, 2–5
  Golden Age of, 49–50
  new politicians, 74–76
  Pericles, 57–64
  Persians and Peloponnesian War, 78–79
  plague, 73–74
  prelude to age of Pericles, 51–56
  reforms, 197–198
  reforms of Cleisthenes, 43–47
  reforms of Solon, 39–42
  sacrilege and the lost peace, 81–82
  Syracusans, 76–78
  tragedy of Peloponnesian War, 71–73
Athenian Empire
  creation of, 67–70
  decline of, 85–94
atrocities by Athenians, 75–76

B
balance of clause, 103
basileit, 17
basileus, 11, 30
battle of Leucimne, 71
battle of Marathon, 51–52
battle of Syota, 72
battle of Thermopylae, 25
body
  in Aristotelian thought, 175
  in Athenian aristocratic civism, 33
  Plato vs. Isocrates, 120
  self-perfection and, 181–182
  training in Platonic civism, 153
Bolingbroke, Lord, 21
boulé, 30–31, 41
Boyd, W.
  on Aristophanes, 105
  on Ideal State, 154
  on Isocrates, 122
  on Plato, 162
  Socratic civism, 139, 141
  Socratic knowledge, 147–148
  on Sophists, 98

on Spartan civism, 25
on Xenophon, 187–188
bravery
    in *Republic*, 158
    of Spartan civism, 24
    in Xenophonic civism, 188
Brunschwig, J., 111
Burrow, J., 49
Busiris (Isocrates), 126

C

Callicratidas, 80–81
Canon, 80–81
censorship, 160, 166
character development, 7–8, 164
checks and balances, in civism, 46–47, 55
children, 25
Cimon
    Athenian democracy and, 49–50
    factional politics in Greece and, 52–53
    Pericles and, 58
citizenship
    Aristotle's constitutional civism, 182–184
    Athenian, 31–32, 194
    city-states, 18–19
    in civism of Cleisthenes, 45–46
    in civism of might, 69
    defined, 2
    democratic Athenian, 37–38
    democratic roots in Athenian civism, 4
    Demosthenes on, 131
    fourth century civism, 92–94
    in Golden Age of Athens, 63
    Homeric, 13–14
    in Periclean civism, 59–61
    Protagoras on, 112
    Spartan school of, 26–28
city-states
    Athenian constitution and, 29–35
    dawn of, 15–19
    inequality leading to Peloponnesian War, 67–70
    Panhellenism as political ideology, 123–124
    Spartan constitution and, 21–28
civic culture of Sparta, 22–24
civil war, 83–84
civism
    Aristotle and. *see* Aristotelian civism
    defined, xi–xiii
    origins of Ancient Greek. *see* origins of

Ancient Greek civism
    overview of, 1–5
    Socratic, 139–150
    Solon's, 41–42
    Xenophonic, 185–191
Civism: Cultivating Citizenship in European History (Dynneson), xii
clans, 10
class systems
    in Athenian social stratification, 31–32
    conflicts in Athenian society, 32–33
    in constitutional civism of Aristotle, 183
    in Ideal State of Plato, 154
    in *The Laws*, 163–167
    reforms of Ephialtes and, 53–54
    in *Republic*, 158–159
    Solonian reforms and, 40–41
Cleisthenes, 43–47
Cleon, 74–76
Cleophon, 81–83
cleruchies, 69
Clouds (Aristophanes), 104–105
Cole, L.
    on Plato, 155
    on Socrates, 146
    on Socratic knowledge, 148–149
Cole, T.
    on Isocrates, 125
    on logos and rhetoric, 102
    on persuasion, 99
collective constitution, 22, 24
colonists, 16–17
Commander of the Greeks, 134
commanders, mercenary, 89–90
communication, 38
community, 4
Companions, 91
complete man, 120
Concerning the Chariot-team (Isocrates), 126–127
Conon, 87
constitutional civism, 197
constitutions
    Aristotelian civism, 182–184
    Athenian, 29–35
    democratic Athenian, 37–38
    ideal of Aristotle, 179
    in origins of Ancient Greek civism, 8
    Sophism and, 106
    Spartan, 21–28
Corcyra, 71–72
Corinthians, 71–72, 76

corruption
    political, 156–157
    Socrates on trial, 144–146
Council of 400
    anti-democratic coup, 79
    defined, 37
    formation of Probouloi, 77–78
    Solonian reforms and, 41
Council of 500, 44
courage, 188
courts
    of Athens, 30–31
    reforms of Ephialtes and, 53
    Solonian reforms and, 41
    sources of democratic civism, 55
    sycophants and, 86
creativity, 16–17
Crete, 10
cultural influences
    civism, 2–5
    constitutions, 21
    Mycenaean Age, 12–13
    new literacy of Greece, 16–17
    Sparta as military state, 25
cultural revolution
    emergence of aristocratic civism, 33–35
    origins of Ancient Greek civism, 8
Cyropædia (Xenophon), 188–191, 197
Cyrus, 80, 81–82
Cyrus II, 51–52

D

daimonion, 143
Damon, 57–58
Darius I, 51–52
Darius II, 79–80
Davies, J. K.
    anti-democratic coup, 80
    on Athenian Empire, 69
    on Conon, 87
    fourth century civism, 92, 93
    on kinship, 193
    on Peloponnesian War, 71
    political art, 95
    on political education, 97
    on social change, 85
    on Xenophon, 186
dawn of city-states, 15–19
Days and Works (Hesiod), 35
debate. *see also* rhetoric
    logoi of Protagoras, 109
    in Plato's *Protagoras*, 114–115
    Plato vs. Isocrates, 120
decarchies, 82
declamation, 102
deductive reasoning, 173
definist fallacy, 2
Delian League
    new politicians of Athens, 74–76
    role in Peloponnesian war, 68
    Spartans and, 54
demagogues
    of Athenian Assembly, 65
    new politicians of Athens, 74
    sacrilege and the lost peace, 81
demes, 30, 44
Demetrius, 172
demiurgoi, 32, 40
democracy
    Aristotle's criticism of, 171
    Athenian. *see* Athenian democracy
    Polybius on, 22
    Protagoras justifies, 110–111
    reforms of Cleisthenes, 43–47
    reforms of Solon, 39–42
    in *Republic*, 158–159
    in Spartan constitution, 23
democratic civism, 4, 195
dêmokratia, 64
demos, 37, 53–54
Demosthenes
    civism of, 129–136, 196
    Syracusans and, 76–77
dêmotikos, 94
Depew, D.
    on Aristotle, 179
    on Isocrates, 120, 124–125, 126
design of city-states, 18
development, character, 7–8, 164
dialogues of Plato, 155
dikastêria, 41, 53
dike, 19
Dionysius II, 152
Dionysius of Syracuse, 89–90
dokimasiai, 53, 55
domimasia, 31
Dorian Invasion, 12
Dorians, 76
Draco's Code
    Athenian constitution and, 37
    defined, 31
    social class conflict in Athens, 33
dualism, 152

dual monarchy, 23
Durant, Will, 9
    on Demosthenes, 130
    on Isocrates, 124
    on Pericles, 57
    on Socrates, 142

E

Early Hellenic period, 8
ecclesia, 30, 41
economics
    in *The Laws*, 163
    social class conflict in Athens, 32–33
    Solonian reforms, 40
Economics (Xenophon), 187, 191
education
    Aristotle's constitutional civism, 182–184
    Aristotle's Lyceum, 172–173
    Athenian, 4, 33–35
    civism as public works, 62
    civism of Cleisthenes, 47
    communication as part of, 38
    in *Cyropædia*, 190–191
    democracy and, 59–60
    fourth century, 92–94
    Homeric civism and citizenship, 13–14
    Isocrates' rhetoric, philosophy and civism, 124–125
    Isocratic, 118–120, 127
    in *The Laws*, 164–167
    in Mycenaean civilization, 10–13
    origins of Ancient Greek civism, 7–8
    of Pericles, 57–58
    philosophy and, 137–138
    of Plato, 151–152
    Plato's reconstruction of Greek society, 153–154
    political art as civism, 95–96
    Protagoras' civism, 112–115
    in *Republic*, 158–163
    Socratic civism, 147–150
    Sophism, 97–106
    Spartan school of citizenship, 26–28
Egypt, 126–127
ekklesia, 37
elite civism, 194
empire
    Athenian, 67–70
    building with mercenaries, 89–90
entelecheia, 93
Ephialtes, 53–54

ephors, 23–24, 72–73
Epidmnus, 71
epistatês, 44
eponymous archon, 30
equality
    in civism of Cleisthenes, 45
    ideal constitution of Aristotle, 179
    lead-up to Peloponnesian War, 68
    in Periclean civism, 60
    sources of democratic civism, 55
eristics, 118
esprit de corp, 27
Ethics (Aristotle), 5
    civism in, 175–180
    self-perfection in, 182
eunomia, 19
eupatrid aristocrats, 29, 32, 40
euthynai
    defined, 31
    reforms of Ephialtes and, 53
    sources of democratic civism, 55
excellence. *see* areté
exoteric instruction, 172

F

factional politics
    in Greece, 52–53
    new politicians of Athens, 75
    unity as result of Persian war, 54–55
farmers, 33
final assonance, 103
Finley, M.I., 145
First Phillipic (Demosthenes), 132–133
form and function, 173–175
For the Liberty of the Rhodians (Demosthenes), 131
fourth century civism, 92–94
Fourth Philippic (Demosthenes), 134
freedom, 4
Freeman, Charles
    on Alexander, 91
    on Aristotelian thought, 174–175
    on Aristotle, 169, 171
    on Isocrates, 124
friendship, 178
function and form, 173–175
Funeral Oration, 60

G

gentes, 10
georgoi, 32, 40

214 • *Index*

Golden Age of Athenian democracy
   overview, 49–50
   Pericles, 57–64
   prelude to Pericles, 51–56
golden mean
   in Aristotelian civism, 176, 179
   self-perfection and, 181
   in Socratic civism, 147
Good
   in Aristotelian civism, 176
   in Platonic civism, 156–157
   in Socratic civism, 144
   in Socratic knowledge, 148–149
   in Xenophonic civism, 187
Gorgias
   Isocrates and, 119–120
   Socratic civism and, 142
   Sophism of, 102–103
Gorgias (Plato), 122
governments
   Athenian constitution, 29–35
   Spartan constitution, 23–24
grammar, 108–109
grammatikê, 108
Graves, F.P.
   on Aristotle, 173
   on Socrates, 146
   on Socratic knowledge, 149
   on Xenophon, 189
Greeks
   Athenian democracy. *see* Athenian democracy
   development of civism, 2–5
   factional politics, 52–53
   origins of Ancient Greek civism. *see* origins of Ancient Greek civism
   reconstruction of Greek society, 153–154
group setting, 2
Guardians, 158–163
Gutek, G.L.
   on excellence, 142
   on Isocrates, 123
   on philosophers, 137
Guthrie, W.K.C.
   on Aristotle, 170, 172
   civism and virtue, 115–116
   on *Ethics*, 176
   on *Ethics*, 178
   on Hermias, 169
   on Isocrates, 126
   on logoi, 142–143
   on Protagoras, 108, 110
   on rhetoric, 97, 102
   on Socrates, 142
   on Sophists, 100
gymnastics, 160

H

Hansen, Mogens Herman
   on city-states, 17
   on democratic civism, 55
   Golden Age of Athenian democracy, 51
happiness
   in Aristotelian civism, 175–176
   in Platonic civism, 156
   self-perfection and, 181–182
   in Socratic civism, 144
Heater, D., 99
hegemony, 54–55, 88–89
hêliaia, 41
Hellenic outlook, 15
heritage of Mycenaean civilization, 12–13
Hermias, 169–170
Herms, 102
heroism, 24, 62
Hesoid, 35
hippes, 32, 40
history, written, 94
History of the Peloponnesian War (Thucydides), 77
Homer, 10, 13–14
humanist civism
   defined, 195
   Isocrates as father of, 123
   of Protagoras, 110

I

ideal constitution of Aristotle, 179
Ideal Reality, 1–2
Ideal State, 154–155, 182
identity
   development of civism, 3–4
   Panhellenism as political ideology, 123–124
ideology, 137–138
Iliad (Homer), 10
individualism
   in civism of Cleisthenes, 47
   decline of Athens, 85–86
   importance in culture, 22
   role in Athenian civism, 35
   Socratic rejection of, 141–142
   Sophism and, 100–101

injustice, 42
inner life, 149
instructions, 7
international aristocracy, 33–34
invention, 103
Ionian Greeks, 7–8, 68
Ionian War, 71, 78
Isocrates, 1, 86, 196
   civism and, 117–127
   criticism of Sophists, 104
   vs. Demosthenes, 136
   fourth century civism, 92–93
   influence on Aristotle, 176
Isonomia, 45

J

Jacks, M.
   on Aristotelian thought, 174
   constitutional civism, 182–183
   on self-perfection, 180–181
Jaeger, Werner, xi
   areté, 3
   on Athenian community, 4
   on Demosthenes, 129
   on Ideal State, 154
   on Plato, 153
   on Socrates, 139
   on Xenophon, 187
Jouvenel, Bertrand de, 49
judiciary systems. *see also* courts
   of Athens, 30–31
   in city-states, 19
juntas
   under Lysander, 82
   Socrates on trial, 144
juries
   in civism of Cleisthenes, 47
   fourth century civism, 94
   reforms of Ephialtes and, 53
   Socrates on trial, 145
   sources of democratic civism, 55
justice
   in Platonic civism, 156–157
   in Plato's *Protagoras*, 114–115
   Protagoras on, 112
   in *Republic*, 158
   in Xenophonic civism, 188

K

Kagan, Donald
   on Athenian Empire, 67

   on birth of Pericles, 57
   on civism of might, 69–70
   on democracy, 39
   on freedom, 4
   on Greek factionalism, 75
   on Ionian War, 78
   on Parthenon, 62
King, E. J., 25
   on Aristophanes, 105
   on Ideal State, 154
   on Isocrates, 122
   on Plato, 162
   Socratic civism, 139, 141
   Socratic knowledge, 147–148
   on Sophists, 98
   on Xenophon, 187–188
kingships
   Aristotle's defense of, 179–180
   in Spartan constitution, 23
King's Peace, 88–89
knightly civism, 194
knowledge
   methodology of, 148–150
   in Platonic civism, 153–154
   Socratic, 146–147
   Xenophonic civism and, 187
Konon, 87
Kuhrt, A., 7

L

landowners, 32–33, 163
laws. *see* legal systems
The Laws (Plato), 196, xi
   Platonic civism, 163–167
   reconstruction of Greek society, 153–155
layout of city-states, 18
legal systems
   Athenian constitution, 29–35
   in city-states, 19
   dawn of city-states, 15
   fourth century civism, 94
   in *The Laws*, 163–167
   Spartan constitution, 21–28
legislature
   Solonian reforms of, 41
   Spartan constitution, 23–24
leiturgia, 58
Leonidas, 25
Lesbos, 75
Leucimne, battle of, 71

library of Lyceum, 172
literacy. *see also* education
    dawn of city-states, 16–17
    in democratic Athens, 37–38
    Spartan civism, 26–28
logic
    Aristotelian science, 173–175
    formation of proofs, 93–94
    of Protagoras, 108–109
    of Socrates, 141
logographos, 117, 129
logoi, 108–109, 142–143
logolatry, 196
logos
    defined, 95
    education and civism, 113
    of Isocrates, 118
    Platonic civism, 156
    Socrates and, 142–143
    Sophism and, 102–104
lot, selection by, 46–47
Lyceum, 172–173
Lycurgus, 22–24, 195
Lysander, 81–83

M

Macedonian monarchy, 90–92
Marathon, battle of, 51–52
marriage in Spartan civism, 25
Marrou, H.I.
    on education, 112–113
    on Isocrates, 119
    on oratory, 105
    on philosophers, 137
    on Plato, 160–161
    political art, 96
    on Protagoras, 109, 110
    on rhetoric, 99
    on Socrates, 147
Martin, T.R., 35
    on Aristotelian thought, 174
    on Aristotle, 171
    on Athenian education, 33
    on Demosthenes, 132
    education and civism, 113
    on Isocrates, 119, 123
    on *The Laws*, 164
    on legal rights in city-states, 19
    on Plato, 151–152, 157
    on Protagoras, 109, 110
    on Socrates, 140, 142

    Socrates on trial, 145
    on Spartan civism, 26
martyrdom of Socrates, 146
mass killing by Cleon, 75
mathematics, 160–161
McClelland, J.S.
    on Aristotelian civism, 176–178, 179–180
    Aristotelian education, 183
    on Aristotle, 170
    on Aristotle's Lyceum, 173
    on cities, 19
    on happiness, 156
    on law, 54
    origins of civism, 8
    on Plato, 161
    on Sophists, 97, 102
Megara, 72
The Memorabilia of Socrates (Xenophon), 188
men, Spartan, 24–28
mercenaries, 89–90
Metaphysics (Aristotle), 174
metaphysics of Plato, 159
middle class, 32–33. *see also* class systems
migration
    creation of city-states, 16–17
    spreading democracy, 59
military
    Athenian class systems, 32
    in Athens, 30
    civism of might, 69–70
    Cleisthenes' constitutional revolution, 44
    Delian League, 54
    juntas under Lysander, 82
    mercenary commanders, 89–90
    Peloponnesian War. *see* Peloponnesian War
    in Pericles' democracy, 59–60
    role in Pericles' education, 58
    training in Athenian society, 35
military state, Sparta, 24–28
Minoan civilization, 10
misthos, 107
moderation, 147
modern democratic civism, 4
monarchy
    Macedonian, 90–92
    in Spartan constitution, 23
morals
    changing in Greece, 85
    in Homeric poetry, 13
    in *The Laws*, 164–165
    in orations of Isocrates, 122–123
    in Plato's *Protagoras*, 114–115

self-perfection and civism, 180–182
  of Socratic civism, 140–141
  of Sophism, 101
  of Sparta, 24
  in Xenophonic civism, 188
mothax, 76
Murray, Oswyn
  on Aristotle, 176
  on Isocrates, 122–123
  on Sophists, 104
  on Xenophon, 185
music
  importance to Sophism, 98
  in Platonic civism, 160
  role in Athenian civism, 33
  role in Pericles' education, 57–58
Mycenaean Age, 194
Mycenaean civilization, 7–8
Mycenaean Greeks, 9–14
Mytilene, 75

N

Nadon, C., 189
national identity, 123–124
natural pairs, 178
Neolithic Age, 9
new politicians, 74–76
Nicias, 74–77
Nicomachean Ethics (Aristotle), 21, 170, 175–180
nomoi, 94, 115
Nussbaum, M.C., 174

O

oath at Plataea, 61
Ober, Josiah, 3, 194
  on Aristotelian civism, 179
  on Aristotle, 171, 177
  on collective wisdom, 59
  on demagogues, 65
  on Demosthenes, 131
  on Isocrates, 119
  on law, 94
  on sycophants, 86
Odeum, 62
Odyssey (Homer), 13
oligarchs
  anti-democratic coup, 79–81
  vs. new politicians of Athens, 75
oligarchy
  defined, 30–31
  imposed by Spartans, 83–84
  vs. reforms of Ephialtes, 53–54
  Xenophon on, 190
Olympicus (Gorgias), 119
On Armanents (Demosthenes), 132
On the Crown (Demosthenes), 136
On the False Legation (Demosthenes), 133
On the Gods (Protagoras), 110–111
On the Peace (Demosthenes), 133
On the Peace (Isocrates), 130
On the Sophists (Isocrates), 118
On the Soul (Aristotle), 180
oral tradition
  decline of Athens, 86
  Homeric civism and citizenship, 13–14
  of Isocrates, 122–123
  of Mycenaean civilization, 11–13
  persuasion, 96
  vs. written, 101
oratory
  civism and, 196
  decline of Athens, 86
  of Demosthenes, 129–131
  of Isocrates, 117–118
  logos and rhetoric, 102–103
  perception and persuasion in *Philippic* speeches, 132–136
  political art as civism, 96
  Sicilian school of, 99–100
Organon (Aristotle), 173
origins of Ancient Greek civism, Ancient Greeks, origins of civism
Otswald, M., 31, 86

P

pædonomus, 27
paidagogos, 42
paideia
  of civism, 127
  defined, 4, 7, xi
  of Isocrates, 119
paired relationships, 178
palaestra, 98
pancratium, 27
Panegyricus (Isocrates), 119, 123
Panhellenic Congress, 61
Panhellenism
  defined, 34
  of Demosthenes, 133–134
  of Isocrates, 120
  as political ideology, 123–124

218 • *Index*

Papyrus Decree, 61–62
Parthenon, 61–62, 68
parts of speech, 108
patriotism
   in city-states, 19
   as result of Persian war, 55
   in Sparta, 25
   of Spartan women, 26
Peace of Antalcidas, 88
pedagogues
   political art as civism, 106
   Socrates argument against, 147
   of Sophism, 100
Peloponnesian War
   anti-democratic coup, 79–81
   Athenian defeat, 82–83
   Athenian Empire and, 67–70
   civil war and democratic resurrection, 83–84
   defined, 65–66
   Demosthenes' criticism of, 132
   influence on democracy, 194–195
   influence on Plato, 151
   new politicians, 74–76
   Persians, 78–79
   plague, 73–74
   sacrilege and the lost peace, 81–82
   Syracusans, 76–78
   tragedy of, 71–73
Pentacosiomedimni, 40
Pentecontaetia, 67
perception
   in *Philippic* speeches, 132–136
   Socratic knowledge and, 148
perfection
   in political systems, 1–2
   of self, 180–182
Periclean civism, 58–61
Pericles, 37, 65
   Golden Age of, 57–64
   Golden Age of Athenian democracy, 49–50
   lead-up to Peloponnesian War, 68
   plague of Athens, 73
   Plato on, 151
   prelude to age of, 51–56
   Protagoras and, 110
   on war, 71
Peripaetic School, 172
Persians
   in Peloponnesian War, 78–79. *see also* Peloponnesian War

   Periclean civism and, 61
   role in decline of Athenian democracy, 78–79
   Xenophon's relationship with, 186–187
Persians (Aeschylus), 58
Persian War, 51–55
persuasion
   in Athenian constitution, 37–38
   in *Cyropædia*, 190
   Isocrates and, 121
   logoi of Protagoras, 108–109
   in *Philippic* speeches, 132–136
   political art as civism, 96
   in political systems, 1–2
   power of Demosthenes, 130
   rhetoric as civism, 131
   Sicilian school of, 99
   used by Pericles, 63
   used to teach morals, 115
   used to teach virtue, 115–116
Philip II, 90–91, 132
Philippic speeches, 132–136
Philippos (Isocrates), 118
Philippus (Isocrates), 125
philosopher-kings
   Aristotle's ideal of, 169–170
   Plato's ideal of, 157–158
philosophers, 92–94
philosophy
   Aristotelian civism. *see* Aristotelian civism
   civism and, 124–125
   criticism of Sophists, 104–105
   ideology, civism and, 137–138
   of Isocrates, 121–123
   Platonic civism. *see* Platonic civism
   Plato vs. Isocrates, 120
   Socratic civism, 139–150
   vs. sophism, 100–101
   Xenophonic civism, 185–191
physical strength, 23
Physics (Aristotle), 174
physis, 115
plague, 73–74
Plataea, 72, 75
Plato, 22, xi
   civism of, 196–197
   criticism of Sophists, 104–105
   on Damon, 57–58
   fourth century civism, 92–94
   influence on Aristotle, 176–177
   vs. Isocrates, 120
   origins of Athenian civism, 5

philosophy, civism and, 137–138
  on Protagoras, 108
  Protagoras, 114–115
  on rhetoric, 121–122
  on Sophists, 101
  women's education, 26
  Xenophon vs., 187–188
Platonic civism
  dialogues, 155
  good in civism, 156–157
  Ideal State, 154–155
  The Laws, 163–167
  overview, 151–152
  political corruption, 157
  reconstruction of Greek society, 153–154
  Republic and civism, 157–163
  rhetoric and philosophy, 156
Plutarch
  on Demosthenes, 130, 135
  Spartan civism, 25–26
Pnyx, 41
poetry
  censorship in *The Laws*, 166
  Homeric civism and citizenship, 13
  Plato and, 160
  vs. prose, 109–110
  Solon as poet, 39
polemarch, 30, 44
polis
  constitutions, 21–22
  dawn of city-states, 15–19
  of Mycenaean civilization, 11
political art
  Aristotelian civism, 175–180
  in Aristotelian civism, 176
  as civism, 95–96
  Demosthenes and civism, 129–136
  Isocrates and civism, 117–127
  Protagoras and civism, 107–116
  Sophism and, 97–106
politics
  corruption, 157
  development of civism, 1–5
  Socrates on, 143–146
  unity as result of Persian war, 55
  virtue, 63–64
Politics (Aristotle), 5, 175–180
Polybius, 22, 24
Pomeroy, S.B., 34
positivist thinking, 108
Potidaeans' rebellion, 72–73

Poulakos, T., 120, 124–126, 179
primary sources, 177
private education, 34–35
Prouboloi, 77–78
prose, 109–110
prostates, 81
Protagoras, 5, 92–93, xi
  civism and, 107–116
  civism as public works, 62
  humanist civism, 195
Protagoras (Plato), 92, 114–115
prytaneis
  defined, 44
  new politicians of Athens, 74
  sacrilege and the lost peace, 81
Prytany, 144
psyché, 121–122
public arts, 57–58
public speaking. *see* oratory
public works, 61–64

R

reading, 26
reason, 181–182
rebellion
  Athenian civil war, 83–84
  lead-up to Peloponnesian War, 68–69
  Potidaeans', 72–73
reforms
  of Cleisthenes, 43–47
  of Ephialtes, 53–54
  of Isocrates, 120
  of Solon, 39–42
relativism
  civism as, 111–112
  justice and, 114–115
  Sophism and, 100–101
religion
  Athenian aristocratic civism, 33–34
  Athenian constitution, 30–31
  in civism, 8
  civism as public works, 62
  civism as relativism, 111
  in Mycenaean civilization, 11
Republic (Plato), 157–163
  conclusion, 196–197
  reconstruction of Greek society, 153–155
  women's education, 26
residential civism, 194
reverence, 114–115

revolution
    anti-democratic coup, 79–81
    civil war and democratic resurrection, 83–84
    Cleisthenes' constitutional, 43–45
    cultural, 8, 33–35
    heritage of Mycenaean Age, 12
    Solonian, 39–41
    urban, 15, 17–18
rhetoric
    in Aristotle's Lyceum, 172
    civism as, 131–132
    of Isocrates, 124–125
    Platonic civism, 156
    Plato vs. Isocrates, 121
    political art as civism, 96
    Sicilian school of, 99–100
    Sophism and, 102–104
    of Sophists, 97
rhetôrikê, 103
Rhodians, 131
Riesenberg, P., 145
right mindedness, 146
rights
    in civism of Cleisthenes, 45
    in dawn of city-states, 19
The Rise of the Roman Empire (Polybius), 22
rules, 2

S

sacrilege, 81–82
Samaras, Thanassis
    on free will, 167
    on *The Laws*, 165
    on philosophers, 137
    on Plato, 158–159
Satyrus, 130
Schiappa, Edward
    on fourth century civism, 93
    on Isocrates, 120–121
    on logos, 95, 98
    on prose, 110
    on Protagoras, 107, 108, 110, 113
    on rhetoric, 100, 103
    on Sophists, 101
schools. *see also* education
    Aristotle's Lyceum, 172–173
    Isocratic, 118–120
    of logos, 96
    philosophy, 92
    Sicilian school of Sophism, 99–100

Spartan school of citizenship, 26–28
science, Aristotelian, 173–175
scribe culture, 12
Second Philippic (Demosthenes), 133
selection by lot, 44, 46–47
self-knowledge, 140–141
self-perfection, 180–182
self-realization, 180
Senate of Sparta, 23
Seven Sages, 98
shared identity, 3–4
Sicilian school of Sophism, 99–100
Sicily, Athenian defeat at, 77
siege of Syracuse, 76
skepticism
    of Socratic civism, 141
    Sophism and, 100–101
slavery
    civism of might, 69
    foundation of Greek polis, 17–18
    Plato on, 163
Smith, J.K., 107, 141, 144
Smith, L.G., 107, 141, 144
Smith, S., 145
social classes
    in Aristotle's constitutional civism, 183
    conflicts in Athenian society, 32–33
    in Ideal State of Plato, 154
    in *The Laws*, 163–167
    Panhellenism as political ideology, 123–124
    reforms of Ephialtes and, 53–54
    in *Republic*, 158–159
    Solonian reforms and, 40–41
    stratification in Athenian society, 31–32
Socrates, 81, 196
    criticism of Sophists, 104–105
    fourth century civism, 92–93
    relationship with Thirty Tyrants, 84
    Sophism of, 98–99
    Xenophon and, 185–186
Socratic civism, 139–150
Solon, 37, 39–42
Solon's Constitution, 40
sophia, 98
Sophism
    orations of Isocrates, 122–123
    Plato vs. Isocrates, 120
    political art and, 97–106
Sophistai, 98
sophistês, 98
Sophists, 95

sophos, 98
Sorel, G., 145
sortition, 44
soul
    in Aristotelian thought, 175
    Athenian aristocratic civism, 33
    of Platonic civism, 153
    Plato vs. Isocrates, 120
    self-perfection and civism, 180–182
    of Socratic civism, 140
Spartans
    civism of, 4
    constitution, 21–28
    Delian League and, 54
    factional politics in Greece, 53
    hegemony, 88–89
    influence on Xenophon, 190–191
    in Peloponnesian War. *see* Peloponnesian War
    Xenophon's relationship with, 186–187
speeches. *see* oratory
Starr, Chester
    on city-states, 15, 18
    on Hellenic outlook, 194
    on legal rights in city-states, 19
states
    Aristotle's constitutional civism, 182–183
    city-states. *see* city-states
    Ideal State of Plato, 154–155
    Isocrates vision of, 123
    Sparta as military, 24–26
    sponsored education, 26–28, 113
statesmen, 165
stoa, 18
strategoi, 44
sycophants, 86
syllabic writing, 12
syllogism, 173
Syota, battle of, 72
Syracusans, 76–78

T

technai, 100, 102–103
technê, 108, 115
teleology, 174
telos, 169, 177
temperance, 158, 188
temples, 18, 61–62
terrorism, 75–76
Thasos rebellion, 68
Thebes, 72
Themisocles, 52

Theseus, 29
thesmothetai, 30
thetes
    anti-democratic coup, 79
    Athenian social stratification, 32
    reforms of Ephialtes and, 53
    Solonian reforms and, 40
Third Philippic (Demosthenes), 133–134
Thirty Tyrants, 83–84, 144
tholos tombs, 11
Thrasyllus, 79–80
three Gorgiac figures, 103
Three Olythiacs (Demosthenes), 133
Thucydides
    civism of might, 69
    on Peloponnesian War, 77
    on Pericles, 57
timocracy, 40
Too, Yun Lee
    on Aristotle, 175
    on fourth century civism, 92
    on Ideal State, 154
    on Isocrates, 117, 125
    on *The Laws*, 167
    on orations of Isocrates, 123
    origins of civism, 126–127
topoi, 3
trial of Socrates, 144–146
The Trial of Socrates (Sorel), 145
tribal customs, 8–10
tribute, 69–70
triremes, 80
two–logoi
    civism as relativism, 111–112
    debate in Plato's *Protagoras*, 114–115
    defined, 108–109
tyranny
    civism of might, 69–70
    imposed by Spartans, 83–84
    in Spartan constitution, 23–24

U

unity of Panhellenism, 123–124
upper city, 29
upper classes, 31–33. *see also* aristocracy
urban revolution, 15, 17–18

V

values. *see also* virtue
    dawn of city-states, 15
    need for, 2

verbs, 108
Vernon, R., 145
Villa, Dana, 140
Vinogradoff, Sir Paul, 29
virtue
 civism as, 147–148
 of philosopher-kings, 158
 philosophy of Isocrates, 121
 of Platonic civism, 153
 self-perfection and civism, 180–182
 of Socratic civism, 141–142
virtue, political
 defined by Pericles, 63–64
 fourth century civism, 92–93
 in Plato's *Protagoras*, 114–115
 Protagoras and, 115–116

W

war, Peloponnesian. *see* Peloponnesian War
war, Persian. *see* Persian war
warriors, Spartan, 24–28
wars, Spartan, 25
Wasp (Aristophanes), 69
Winn, C., 174, 180–181, 182–183
wisdom, 158
women
 Aristotle's view of, 184
 role in *Republic*, 162–163
 role in Spartan city-state, 26
 Xenophon's view of, 187–188
Woodruff, P., 114, 143, 146, 193
Woody, T.
 Aristotle's view of women, 184
 on Plato, 156–157
 on Platonic censorship, 160
 on slavery, 163
 on women in *Republic*, 162
 on Xenophon, 190

writings
 of Isocrates, 117–118
 prose of Protagoras, 109–110
 rhetoric and, 104
 of Xenophon, 188–190
writing systems
 dawn of city-states and, 16–17
 fourth century civism, 94
 in Mycenaean civilization, 10–13
 role in democracy, 86
written law, 94

X

Xenophon
 conclusion, 197
 fourth century civism, 94
 Spartan constitution and, 22
Xenophonic civism, 185–191

Z

zeugitai
 defined, 32
 reforms of Ephialtes and, 53
 Solonian reforms and, 40